ROCK CLIMBING
WYOMING

The Best Routes in the Cowboy State

Sam Lightner Jr.

FALCON GUIDES

GUILFORD, CONNECTICUT
HELENA, MONTANA

FALCONGUIDES®

An imprint of Rowman & Littlefield
Falcon, FalconGuides, and Chockstone are registered trademarks and Make Adventure Your
Story is a trademark of Rowman & Littlefield.

Distributed by NATIONAL BOOK NETWORK

Photos by Sam Lightner Jr. unless otherwise noted.
The Bucking Horse & Rider image is a federal trademark of the State of Wyoming and is
used with permission.
Maps and topos by Melissa Baker and Sue Murray © Rowman & Littlefield

British Library Cataloguing in Publication Information available

Library of Congress Cataloging-in-Publication Data
Names: Lightner, Sam, 1967- author.
Title: Rock climbing Wyoming : the best routes in the Cowboy State / Sam Lightner Jr.
Description: Guilford, Connecticut : FalconGuides, [2016] | "Distributed by
    NATIONAL BOOK NETWORK"—T.p. verso. | Includes bibliographical references
    and index.
Identifiers: LCCN 2015043616 (print) | LCCN 2015046096 (ebook) | ISBN
    9781493016129 (paperback) | ISBN 9781493016136 (e-book)
Subjects: LCSH: Rock climbing—Wyoming—Guidebooks. | Wyoming—Guidebooks.
Classification: LCC GV199.42.W82 L54 2016 (print) | LCC GV199.42.W82 (ebook)
    | DDC 796.522/309787—dc23
LC record available at http://lccn.loc.gov/2015043616

∞™ The paper used in this publication meets the minimum requirements of American
National Standard for Information Sciences—Permanence of Paper for Printed Library
Materials, ANSI/NISO Z39.48-1992.

WARNING:

Climbing is a sport where you may be seriously injured or die. Read this before you use this book.

This guidebook is a compilation of unverified information gathered from many different sources. The author cannot assure the accuracy of any of the information in this book, including the topos and route descriptions, the difficulty ratings, and the protection ratings. These may be incorrect or misleading and it is impossible for any one author to climb all the routes to confirm the information about each route. Also, ratings of climbing difficulty and danger are always subjective and depend on the physical characteristics (for example, height), experience, technical ability, confidence, and physical fitness of the climber who supplied the rating. Additionally, climbers who achieve first ascents sometimes underrate the difficulty or danger of the climbing route out of fear of being ridiculed if a climb is later down-rated by subsequent ascents. Therefore, be warned that you must exercise your own judgment on where a climbing route goes, its difficulty, and your ability to safely protect yourself from the risks of rock climbing. Examples of some of these risks are: falling due to technical difficulty or due to natural hazards such as holds breaking, falling rock, climbing equipment dropped by other climbers, hazards of weather and lightning, your own equipment failure, and failure or absence of fixed protection.

You should not depend on any information gleaned from this book for your personal safety; your safety depends on your own good judgment, based on experience and a realistic assessment of your climbing ability. If you have any doubt as to your ability to safely climb a route described in this book, do not attempt it.

The following are some ways to make your use of this book safer:

1. Consultation: You should consult with other climbers about the difficulty and danger of a particular climb prior to attempting it. Most local climbers are glad to give advice on routes in their area, and we suggest that you contact locals to confirm ratings and safety of particular routes and to obtain firsthand information about a route chosen from this book.

2. Instruction: Most climbing areas have local climbing instructors and guides available. We recommend that you engage an instructor or guide to learn safety techniques and to become familiar with the routes and hazards of the areas described in this book. Even after you are proficient in climbing safely, occasional use of a guide is a safe way to raise your climbing standard and learn advanced techniques.

3. Fixed Protection: Because of variances in the manner of placement, and weathering of fixed protection, all fixed protection should be considered suspect and should always be backed up by equipment that you place yourself. Never depend on a single piece of fixed protection for your safety because you never can tell whether it will hold weight, and in some cases, fixed protection may have been removed or is now absent.

Be aware of the following specific potential hazards that could arise in using this book:

1. Misdescriptions of Routes: If you climb a route and you have a doubt as to where the route may go, you should not go on unless you are sure that you can go that way safely. Route descriptions and topos in this book may be inaccurate or misleading.

2. Incorrect Difficulty Rating: A route may, in fact, be more difficult than the rating indicates. Do not be lulled into a false sense of security by the difficulty rating.

3. Incorrect Protection Rating: If you climb a route and you are unable to arrange adequate protection from the risk of falling through the use of fixed pitons or bolts and by placing your own protection devices, do not assume that there is adequate protection available higher just because the route protection rating indicates the route is not an "X" or an "R" rating. Every route is potentially an "X" (a fall may be deadly) due to the inherent hazards of climbing—including, for example, failure or absence of fixed protection, your own equipment's failure, or improper use of climbing equipment.

There are no warranties, whether express or implied, that this guidebook is accurate or that the information contained in it is reliable. There are no warranties of fitness for a particular purpose or that this guide is merchantable. Your use of this book indicates your assumption of the risk that it may contain errors and is an acknowledgment of your own sole responsibility for your climbing safety.

CONTENTS

Overview

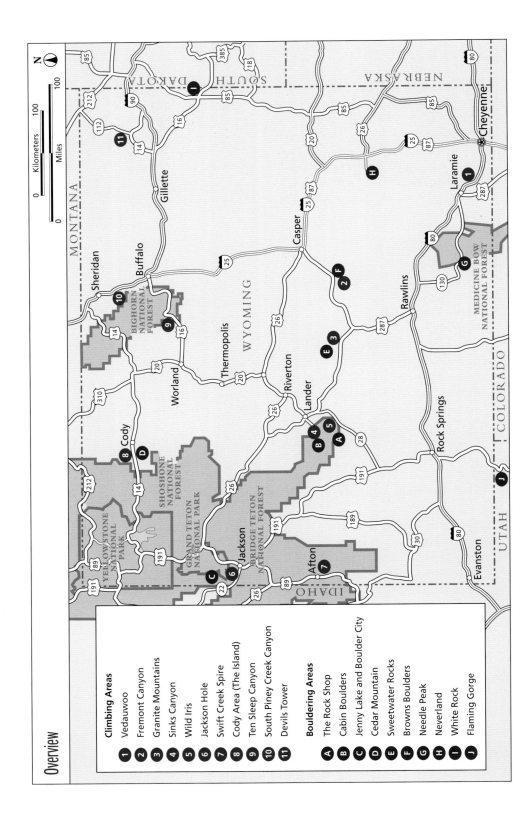

Climbing Areas
1. Vedauwoo
2. Fremont Canyon
3. Granite Mountains
4. Sinks Canyon
5. Wild Iris
6. Jackson Hole
7. Swift Creek Spire
8. Cody Area (The Island)
9. Ten Sleep Canyon
10. South Piney Creek Canyon
11. Devils Tower

Bouldering Areas
A. The Rock Shop
B. Cabin Boulders
C. Jenny Lake and Boulder City
D. Cedar Mountain
E. Sweetwater Rocks
F. Browns Boulders
G. Needle Peak
H. Neverland
I. White Rock
J. Flaming Gorge

ACKNOWLEDGMENTS

The first people who should be thanked for their efforts and contributions are the folks who wrote the guidebooks I have used over the years. This includes Steve Bechtel, Layne Kopischka, Micah Rush, Greg Collins, Vance White, Wesley Gooch, Aaron Huey, Steve Petro, Forest Dramis, Trevor Bowman, Steve Gardiner, Zach Orenczak, and Rachael Lynn. We usually think of their effort as something written to assist our entertainment, but they are also historians. Also of note here are all the people who submitted information or even just comments on climbs on Mountain Project. Your input was factored into opinions on grade, quality, etc., for the climbs in this book. Thank you all for noting the climbs.

I had particular people who assisted me in each climbing area. Some helped with belays, some gave information, some gave opinions, and many volunteered their time to help with photography. I am deeply thankful for their time and effort. If I left your name out, please know it was by accident and accept my apology. The people who assisted in the various areas include:

Vedauwoo: Todd Skinner, Amy Skinner, Jacob Valdez, Paul Piana, Bill Walker so many years ago, Simeon Caskey, Leon Pennington Burris III, Mandy Fabel, and Brian Fabel

Fremont Canyon: Micah Rush, Karl Rigrish, Steve Bechtel, and Mandy Fabel

Granite Mountains: Elyse Guarino, Steve Bechtel, Tom Rangitsch, Vance White, Greg Collins, Mike Lilygren, and Brian Fabel

Devils Tower: Becca Skinner, Mike Lilygren, Bill Walker, Gabriel Skiera, Julius Brewczyck, Meera Usha Andersen, Curtis Allred, and Frank Sanders

Piney Creek: Brian and Mandy Fabel, Terry Twomey, and Braden Herbst

Cody: Zayne Hebbler, Mike Snyder, Mike Lilygren, and Christian Baumeister

Ten Sleep Canyon: Mike Snyder, Terry Twomey, Elizabeth Tai, Eric Wynn, Becca Roseberry, Liz Lightner, and Cory Lamblin

Lander: Liz Lightner, Steve Bechtel, Andy Skiba, Jill Hunter, Kyle Vassilopoulos, Mandy Fabel, Jaimie O'Donnel, Todd and Amy Skinner, Paul Piana, and Jacob Valdez so many years ago

Jackson: Anthony Menolascino, Jenny Karns, Hans and Nancy Johnstone, Forest Dramis, Mark Newcomb, Rod Newcomb, Liz Lightner, and Armando Menocal

Swift Creek: Kyle and Kim Mills and Sandy Boling

I want to thank Clyde Soles for getting this ball rolling, and Katie Benoit for continuing it. My wife, Liz, has been very supportive, as have Moki, Zoe, and Lexi. John Burbidge at Falcon helped to make this book better than it otherwise would have been.

INTRODUCTION

It could easily be argued that Wyoming is the most beautiful and naturally diverse state in the union. It is home to the world's first national park, Yellowstone in 1872, and an active caldera that created the largest geothermal geyser region of the world. The state has more than fifty peaks that rise above 13,000 feet and thirty-eight glaciers, including the largest glacier in the lower 48 states (Gannet). The headwaters of the Mississippi, Colorado, and Columbia Rivers are all in Wyoming, as are the Killpecker Sand Dunes of the Red Desert, one of the largest dune fields in North America. This geographic diversity is habitat to the largest herds of big-horn sheep and pronghorn in the nation, the latter of which usually outnumbers the human population. Bison, elk, mule deer, grizzly bears, wolves, beavers, otters . . . the list of wildlife adds up to over 600 species, making Wyoming one of the most naturally diverse regions of its size in the world.

The abundance of wildlife has not been lost on humanity, and thus the region has been coveted by people for thousands of years. Just in the last 500 years, sections of the state were fought for by the Arapaho, Cheyenne, Crow, Ute, and Blackfeet. More recently, the Sioux migrated into the northeast corner of the state from their traditional land in Minnesota and the eastern Dakotas, and through military horsemanship made themselves the dominant force in the region. Quickly following the Sioux were the Europeans. On maps in Washington, DC, Paris, Madrid, and London, the land that is now Wyoming lay at the intersection of the British Oregon Territory, Spanish Nuevo Mexico, and the French Louisiana Territory. Through purchase, war, and treaty, the United States came to be the dominant power in western North America, and the fate of the area fell into the hands of Washington, DC.

The geology of Wyoming is so diverse that it simply cannot be covered in a single chapter, much less a paragraph. From the 2.5-billion-year-old Precambrian granite of the Granite Mountains to the 9-million-year-old gneiss infants, otherwise known as the Tetons, climbers in Wyoming recreate on the entirety of the earth's geologic history. The state has been under oceans many times, had peaks that jutted well above anything in the Rockies now, done a complete barrel roll with the overthrust belt, and had various bits of magma poke through and form iconic spires like Devils Tower. Rather than try and explain it all, I invite every visitor to the state to read one of the best books ever written on geology and the American West, *Rising from the Plains* by John McPhee. The story is set in the center of the state and gives a great history of the Lander area; when you finish this book, you'll realize you read about Wyoming and accidentally learned the science of geology.

The source of the name "Wyoming" has almost nothing to do with the state. The Munsee Indians of Delaware, New Jersey, and Pennsylvania used the name "Wyoming" for a "large, flat, open" valley in Pennsylvania. Ohio's Congressman James M. Ashley first coined the name in his efforts to create the territory. It appears that the fact that Wyoming Valley was his birthplace had more to do with the name choice than the "large, flat, open" attributes. The names "Cheyenne," "Arapaho," and "Sioux" were also considered, but for obvious reasons (like the state of war), none of these people held enough sway in Congress to be taken seriously. For the most part, actual Wyoming Territory residents cared little for what the territory was called, though one poll showed if given a choice they would have preferred the name "Lincoln." Of course they

Wild horses west of the Wind River Range.

had little say in Washington, DC, when Wyoming Territory was created in 1868. Wyoming was upgraded from a territory to a state in 1890 as the forty-fourth state in the union.

With 48 percent of the state's 97,818 square miles owned by the federal government, Wyoming's 564,000 residents are known for their distrust of the whims and rules of Washington, DC. Historically, the "Cowboy State's" frontier lifestyle often put men out on the range and thus gave women far more authority on fiscal and social issues. Wyoming Territory gave women the right to vote in 1869, a full fifty-one years before the 19th Amendment was ratified for the United States. Wyoming was the first state to elect a female governor, Nellie Ross in 1924, and the Petticoat Rulers of Jackson (1920) represented the first all-female town government in the United States. Most of the state's residents don't know this, but for this reason the state motto is "The Equality State" and not "The Cowboy State."

Wyoming's dominant industry is mineral extraction, with coal, natural gas, uranium, and trona being the largest shares of that pie. This industry has to be balanced with the second-largest, tourism, which brings in over $2 billion a year in revenue. Demographically, Wyoming is a slice of Wonder Bread, with nearly 95 percent of the population being Caucasian. The next largest ethnic group is Native American, at 2.5 percent. No matter what ethnicity, there aren't very many Wyomingites compared to the size of the state. Wyoming is the least populous state in the union and falls behind only Alaska in population density at six people per square mile. The largest city, if you can call it that, is Cheyenne with just over 60,000 residents. Take a 2-hour drive anywhere in the state and you will see multiple municipalities with an official population in the single digits. The creation of these small towns dates back to the 1880s when township was required to receive a federal post office. A general store amid hundreds of miles of ranchland, like Crowheart or Sweetwater Station, would incorporate to receive the nearby

Cowboy State Trivia

Here are a few Wyoming facts to mull over around the campfire.

- As noted, Yellowstone was the first national park (1872), but Devils Tower was the first national monument (1906) and the Shoshone National Forest was the first national forest (1891).
- The JC Penney Company was founded in Kemmerer, Wyoming, in 1902.
- Wyoming is a "fence out," or "open range," state. That means cattle have the right to wander about as they wish, and if you don't want them on your lawn, it is your job to build a fence and keep them out.
- The Wyoming license plate depicts the bronco Steamboat trying to buck Stub Farrow of Lander in a rodeo. To the left is a number that represents one of the twenty-three counties in the state. The number was determined based on the value of land in that county in 1930, with "1" being the most spendy, and "23" quite affordable.
- The Great Divide Basin, seen south of Wild Iris and the Wind River Range, is a split in the Continental Divide known as an endorheic drainage basin. Geologists define this as a valley or basin with no draining stream.
- Wyoming has three major mountain ranges: the Tetons, Bighorns, and Wind Rivers. The high point of the state is Gannet Peak at 13,804 feet in elevation. The lowest point is on the South Dakota border at 3,101 feet.
- With a statewide average altitude of 6,700 feet above sea level, only Colorado is higher than Wyoming.
- Wyoming is the tenth-largest state in the country by geographic size. However, it is not a square. Wyoming is actually an isosceles trapezoid laid out by latitude and longitude. The south border is 23 miles longer than the north border.
- Author Owen Wister wrote his famous book *The Virginian* about a cowboy working near Medicine Bow, Wyoming (near Vedauwoo). It was the first western novel, and much of it is thought to have been written while Wister was visiting a dude ranch in Jackson.
- The largest surface coal mine in the world, the Black Thunder Mine, is in northeast Wyoming.
- The state flower is the Indian paintbrush, a plant with red petals that grows in such abundance in the grasslands that it used to be called "Prairie Fire."
- Eleven of the fifteen famous Mountain Man Rendezvous were held in Wyoming between 1825 and 1840.
- Southwestern Wyoming produces 90 percent of the nation's trona, a necessary component in the manufacturing of glass. There is a little bit of Wyoming in most of the world's glass.
- The state dinosaur, as if we knew any state had such a thing, is *Triceratops*. This is because the first identified triceratops was found near Lusk, Wyoming, in 1888. Many other dinosaurs have been found in Wyoming, including *Tyrannosaurus rex* and *Archaeopteryx*.
- By the way, when on back roads in Wyoming, you will notice everyone waves. You don't need to know someone to say "hi." Give it a try.

ranchers' mail. The "town" may have had a population of five, all having the same last name and working in the general store.

Wyoming is the epitome of "rural," and virtually all the residents of the state would like to keep it so. With the majority of land owned by the federal and state governments, and the harshness of the climate for much of the year, it will likely be a long time before the Equality State sees a population of 1 million. Enjoy the open spaces.

WYOMING CLIMBING AREAS

What follows is a short description of each of the major areas in this book.

Vedauwoo

A bastion of crack climbing on the windswept domes of Wyoming's high plains, this area is famous for its flares and offwidths. However, there are also perfect finger and hand cracks, plus a few bolted faces, if placing gear is not your thing.

Fremont Canyon

A picturesque granite canyon with splitter hand and finger cracks and bolted lines of steep face climbing. These climbs have one of the shortest approaches in the world.

Granite Mountains

Remote yet reachable, these granite domes at the very center of the state have multi-pitch bolted slabs and steep crack and face climbs.

Sinks Canyon

Sport climbing with edges, pockets, and even cracks on gently overhanging brown dolomite. Just minutes from Lander, these walls face due south, which makes this area ideal for, but not limited to, fall and winter climbing.

Wild Iris

Sport climbing at the foot of the Wind River Range on ivory-white, pocket-riddled dolomite. This area is famous for its bouldery, finger-isolating climbs at a cool 9,000 feet above sea level.

Jackson Hole

Sport routes on limestone and dolomite, or mixed-gear multi-pitch routes on Teton gneiss, make this beautiful valley something you should not miss. The easy access to the Tetons and Yellowstone doesn't hurt either.

Swift Creek Spire

A roadside pinnacle of steep Madison limestone—in a canyon you will likely have to yourself—makes this little crag worth a stop if you are in the area.

Cody Area (The Island)

This amazing granite amphitheater, nestled between tunnels on the road to Yellowstone National Park, is loaded with fun sport climbs and a few gear lines of all grades.

Ten Sleep Canyon

Hundreds of endurance-focused sport climbs on walls of steep dolomite make this one of America's greatest sport climbing destinations.

South Piney Creek Canyon

A small sport climbing area with a big future, this easily accessible canyon of Bighorn dolomite is a great place to get away from crowds.

Devils Tower

Unique in the world, this crack climbing area is one of the icons of American climbing. Bring a big rack and good footwork for the long stemming corners.

WYOMING BOULDERING AREAS

This is not a bouldering guide, but here are some short descriptions of the most notable bouldering areas in the state, with a mention of where you might find more information.

Neverland

Hard to reach and set in a maze of public land and private land, you will likely need to find a Laramie local to visit these boulders. Considered one of the best areas in the state, this climbing is characterized by featured gneiss with roofs and steep overhangs.

Needle Peak

This is referred to as Baggot Rock in Tim Toula's tome *Rock and Road*. It is found off WY 230 near Encampment and Saratoga. These odd granitic formations are featured with edges and broken crack systems at all angles. A book is said to be in the works from the Laramie boys, but nothing yet is in print.

Browns Boulders

Located south of Casper where the North Platte River flows from Fremont Canyon and becomes the Alcova Reservoir, this is a sandstone area with plenty of horizontals, slopers, and the odd pocket. Though it is only a stone's throw from the Fremont Canyon crags covered here, you reach the area by driving down the west side of Alcova Reservoir past the Lakeside Marina to a parking area near the mouth of the canyon. Walk southwest a few hundred yards and you can't miss it. At this time there is no guidebook.

Sweetwater Rocks

At the very center of the state, along Agate Flats Road and the approach to Lankin Dome, is one of the better bouldering areas in the state. This is 2.5-billion-year-old granite, the oldest rock you will ever climb on, and it is featured with cracks, knobs, and square-cut edges. David Lloyd and Ben Sears's *Bouldering in the Wind River Range* has the details on how find the boulders.

Cabin Boulders

Just a few hundred yards from Bruce's Parking Lot in Sinks Canyon, this granite field of erratics has great landings and is an easy outing from Lander. David Lloyd and Ben Sears's *Bouldering in the Wind River Range*, available at Wild Iris Mountain Sports in Lander, has all the info you need for this area.

The Rock Shop

Another great bouldering area, this place is made up of Wind River granite that has eroded differently than other areas of a similar base geology. Lots of square-cut edges on steep, clean stone characterize this, the most popular of Lander's bouldering areas. It's located southwest of Wild Iris, about 33 miles from Lander. David Lloyd and Ben Sears's guidebook gives clear directions to the Rock Shop.

Flaming Gorge

OK, it's not in Wyoming, but only barely, and most people get there by driving from Wyoming. This Uinta quartzite area, known for square-cut edges and good landings, can be found 5 minutes north of the bridge just west of Flaming Gorge Dam. There was a copied guide floating around Wyoming and Salt Lake bouldering crowds, but it's hard to find.

Jenny Lake and Boulder City

Made famous by John Gill's Red Cross boulder problem, perhaps the world's first V7 (and V9 the way he did it), there are actually only a couple of boulders here. However, Boulder City, about 3 miles to the north along the String Lake Road, has far more problems on Teton

Steve Bechtel enjoying a post-storm, warm January day on Drug Enemy (5.12a), Sinks Canyon.

gneiss. John Sherman's *Stone Crusade* talks of Jenny Lake, and Mountain Project has some information and directions.

Cedar Mountain

A beautiful area overlooking Cody and Shoshone Canyon, these sandstone boulders are reminiscent of Joes Valley. One of the great features of this area is that you can find stuff to climb all year. It's thought there are nearly 1,000 problems in this area, but sadly the only guidebook is out of print. The folks at Sunlight Sports can give you some information, and Mountain Project has good directions and a few of the problems listed. Some would say it is the best bouldering area in the state.

White Rock

Just a couple miles east of Newcastle off US 16, this little Dakota Sandstone area has a rich history. It is similar in style and quality to Horsetooth Reservoir near Fort Collins, Colorado. Tim Toula wrote a guidebook way back in 1988 that you might be able to find at Chessler Books in Evergreen, Colorado. Mountain Project has some limited information, and Sherman visits it in *Stone Crusade*.

HOW TO USE THIS BOOK

This book is intended to give you a healthy overview of the Cowboy State's climbing resources. In the author's mind, the ideal readers are a group of climbers taking a road trip through Wyoming with the intention of climbing and seeing the most beautiful state in the union. They hit a climbing area, do the classics over a few days or weeks, and move on to the next area. The book is not intended to be a comprehensive guide to any of the areas covered. Some of these areas have hundreds, and possibly even thousands, of rock climbs. With that in mind, you can see that a comprehensive guide to the entire state would likely be a 10,000-plus-page book.

The book is broken into an initial chapter of general information on Wyoming, followed by chapters for each of the eleven areas covered. Before reading the pertinent information on the areas you plan to visit, I recommend you read the introductory chapter. The history of Wyoming is interesting, and it is important to familiarize yourself with the various land agencies in the state and the particular dangers and annoyances associated with Wyoming climbing.

The chapters on the various climbing areas traverse the state from the southeast to Jackson in the west, then turning back east and ending in the northeast corner with Devils Tower. There is an introduction, usually with some climbing-related history, followed by key points of information you might need to plan a trip. Of particular importance is the "Restrictions and access issues" information. We are all ambassadors of our sport, and you don't want to be the person that gets a particular crag closed to climbing.

The details on how to reach each crag, generally with a map of the area, are included for each area. Keep in mind this information sometimes changes as land managers close and open trails, move parking areas, etc. You can also find what kind of rock climbing and what special equipment a crag requires in this section. It is assumed you know intimately how all this gear is used, and if you don't, then you need to get a professional guide to teach you.

The routes are laid out in an order that corresponds to a topo. A star rating comes with each route. Three stars means the route is an excellent example of the style of climbing found at that crag; zero stars means the route may be of lesser quality, but is still included because 1) it is right next to star-worthy routes, and 2) sometimes less "worthy" routes also tend to be less crowded and a good option for those seeking solitude. In general, though, this book strives to point climbers in the direction of the best routes each area has to offer.

The grade is given using the Yosemite Decimal System. For multi-pitch routes, like at Devils Tower, you will see a grade with the acronym "obl." This stands for "obligatory" and tells you the grade you must be able to climb to get up the route (hanging to rest), not the overall difficulty. In other words, it gives you the grade of the hardest move that you cannot pull through on gear. Some routes might have a letter grade after this, as in PG, R, or X. PG implies the route is a little runout and long falls are possible, an R means very big falls with the possibility of injury are part of the climb, and X means you could die if you fall in the wrong place. This all assumes you get in the best possible equipment. Obviously, any rock climb can have an X rating if you do not place proper gear.

The length of the route is usually given, but this number needs to be taken with hesitation. Over time, anchors are often moved, thus changing the length of a rappel or lowering point. All climbers should have knots in both ends of their ropes when rappelling, and in the end of the rope when lowering. This is especially true on multi-pitch climbs.

Simeon Caskey enjoying a warm fall day on Deception (5.9), Vedauwoo.

Mike Lilygren belaying Becca Skinner on the second pitch of Soler (5.9), Devils Tower.

Next you will find a brief description of the route. This description assumes you have the skills to look at a climb and see what it will basically entail. The exact gear for each climb differs from person to person, as a 5.13 climber may not need more than a few hand-size pieces on a 50-meter hand crack, while a 5.10 climber might need a dozen. For this reason the book gives a generalized description of the necessary gear, such as "extra hand-size pieces are useful." It is up to you to determine what you need based on the grade of the route, its assumed length, and the difficulty. If a number is given for the cam sizes, it represents the size in inches (e.g., Friends) and not another manufacturer's arbitrary number for a given cam.

For sport climbs the exact number of quickdraws is rarely given and should always be seen as a minimum. Many of Wyoming's sport climbing areas are going through a retro-bolting phase, and the exact number of bolts, as well as the placement of the anchor, often changes in the process. This means that giving the number of quickdraws needed might leave you short one or two, so use your discretion as a climber to determine how many a given line requires. Also, if you are leaving draws at the anchor, as you should if you intend to toprope it, you'll need a couple more than stated. Keep a knot in the end of your rope when lowering off the long routes, and remember that rarely in this state does lowering on a sport climb exceed the parameters of a 70-meter rope.

Finally, historical information on who first free climbed the route is given with the letters "FA" for "first ascent." If there is no mention of the first ascensionists, it means that information is perhaps lost in time. Feel free to get in touch with me if you have that info, and I will try to incorporate it in the next edition.

I should say something on the grading of the routes. Wyoming climbing areas have a huge disparity in how they are graded. Devils Tower, for instance, with its long pitches of technical footwork that require large amounts of gear, has a tradition of very stiff grades. Meanwhile, the sport climbs of Ten Sleep Canyon have a reputation of being "soft" relative to other sport climbing areas. The grades of Wild Iris feel hard to an endurance-oriented sport climber, but a boulderer might find them easy. Since this book is for visiting climbers more than anyone else, it attempts to even out the grades, and to some locals that may be bothersome. Deal with it. Grades were established so we could determine how hard a thing is and then attempt something at that grade, or avoid it if it is beyond our abilities. Grades are for information, not ego. I have done my best to give the grades according to the North American Yosemite Decimal System, which has become an average of areas like the New River Gorge, Red River Gorge, Smith Rock, Rifle, the crags of Wyoming, and of course Yosemite.

All that said, here is a list of the routes that I and my peers feel are the very best climbs of the Cowboy State. These have been picked using an extremely accurate discipline of science that takes in quality of rock, enjoyment of movement, unique intrinsic traits, and the sensations gathered from the location, collectively known as the "Gut Feeling Algorithm." Using these as the focus of travel will make for a great road trip.

Edwards Crack (5.7), Main Wall, Vedauwoo

Feelin' All Right (5.8), Cody Area (The Island)

Soler (5.9), Devils Tower

Walt Bailey Memorial (5.10a), Devils Tower

Dillingham Blues (5.10b), Fremont Canyon

Claim Jumper (5.10c), Wild Iris

El Matador (5.10d), Devils Tower

The Devil Wears Spurs (5.11a), Wild Iris

Friday the 13th (through roof, 5.11b), Vedauwoo

Max Factor (5.11c), Vedauwoo

The Joy of Heresy (5.11d), Ten Sleep Canyon

Wind and Rattlesnakes (5.12a), Wild Iris

Happiness in Slavery (5.12b), Ten Sleep Canyon

Exo-atmospheric Kill Vehicle "EKV" (5.12c), Ten Sleep Canyon

Addiction (5.12d), Sinks Canyon

Cranner Roof Crack (5.13a), Granite Mountains

Samsara (5.13b), Sinks Canyon

Endeavor to Persevere (5.13c), Sinks Canyon

Gold Member (5.13d), Ten Sleep Canyon

Bus Load of Faith (5.14a), Sinks Canyon

Genetic Drifter (5.14c), Wild Iris

Eric Wynn feeling the pump of EKV (5.12c), Ten Sleep Canyon.

BE A GOOD AMBASSADOR: DEALING WITH LANDOWNERS AND LAND MANAGERS

Once upon a time, when the first routes were being established in Wyoming, climbers had almost no impact on the world. We were a free-ranging group of "thrill-seekers" who rarely walked the same ground, and when we did it was months, if not years, apart. That era of do-as-you-want is no more. With millions of self-proclaimed "climbers" living all over the world, we are a large user group, and as such we have an impact on the environment. Climbers are recognized as a user group by the people who own the land we play on. Like hunters, hikers, boaters, and four-wheelers, if we want to maintain access to that land, we all need to be good ambassadors of the sport.

There are six principal owners of the land in Wyoming. Four of them represent the people of the United States in the form of the federal government, as over 48 percent of Wyoming is federally owned. The Bureau of Land Management (BLM) has the largest share with nearly 30,000 square miles. Just behind the BLM is the USDA Forest Service, which not only governs most of Wyoming's forests, but also a huge amount of the prairie with its national grasslands. The Forest Service controls six different forests and grasslands, all adding up to something larger than most states in New England. The third federal agency is the National Park Service, which obviously makes the rules in the major national parks, but also governs our national monuments. A fourth agency, the US Bureau of Reclamation, is generally only something boaters need to be concerned with, but they do control a small strip of land in Wyoming that climbers enjoy.

Just 6 percent of the state is owned by the State of Wyoming, but they are a significant player in the lives of Wyoming climbers with a couple of state parks. Finally, there is the private landowner, the person people east of the Mississippi have to work with the most. There are at least a couple of climbing areas in Wyoming that straddle public and private land, and access is always dependent on how we behave when visiting those places.

Land Managers

Each land manager has particular rules for a given area. These are mentioned in the individual chapters. Here is a breakdown of the primary land managers in Wyoming.

Bureau of Land Management (BLM): For the most part, the BLM in Wyoming, where mineral extraction and ranching are the biggest industries, has far bigger concerns than the generally "green" climbers. Currently there are no access issues in Wyoming's BLM climbing areas. Continue to use Leave No Trace ethics and there likely won't be any. Areas in this book that are managed by the BLM are Fremont Canyon and the Granite Mountains.

USDA Forest Service (USFS): When combining the crags in the Shoshone, Bridger-Teton, Medicine Bow–Routt, and Bighorn National Forests, the Forest Service governs more climbing areas in Wyoming than all the other organizations combined. For most USFS areas, the rules are similar to those of the BLM, and the Leave No Trace ethic is the norm. Vedauwoo, Ten Sleep Canyon, South Piney Creek, The Island, Jackson Hole Mountain Resort, and both Sinks Canyon and Wild Iris are all on US Forest Service land.

National Park Service (NPS): The Park Service manages the climbing areas a bit more like wilderness areas. There are a lot of rules you are expected to follow at these crags, including no dogs on trails (essentially they have to stay in your car), no camping except in designated sites, no fires except in designated sites, and no power drills or mountain bikes. Each park may also have laws for its particular area, like seasonal bird nesting closures. It's best to check with the Park Service when you enter these areas and make sure you know the rules. Blacktail Butte lies within Grand Teton National Park, and Devils Tower is a national monument and thus managed like a national park.

Wyoming state land: For the most part, the State of Wyoming is very supportive of climbing. Sinks Canyon State Park is the only state park covered in this guide. The one rule that they try to get climbers to follow is that all dogs must be on a leash. They also embrace Leave No Trace and expect climbers to do the same.

Bureau of Reclamation (USBR): This division of the federal government generally oversees the distribution of water, so both Fremont Canyon and the Riverside Granite near Cody are under the control of the USBR. There are currently no special requirements for the use of this land other than you have to stay off dams, out of tunnels, and away from areas they deem sensitive. Fortunately, none of those places are of any interest to climbers.

Private land: Private land is just that, private. You may be allowed on it if the landowner agrees, but otherwise it is unlawful to trespass on private land. Much of the Granite Mountains, including a section of the road to Lankin Dome, is privately owned. If you see a No Trespassing sign, obey it. They will call the sheriff. The Jackson Hole Mountain Resort does not own the land it uses, but it does lease that land and thus has rights to deny climbers access to certain areas. Rock Springs Buttress is not one of those areas, but Corbet's Couloir is. Obey their rules and be a good ambassador of the sport when at the ski area.

Many climbers want to establish new routes, and Wyoming is a great place for it. But before you do so, we recommend you get in touch with locals about the particular rules a given area has for bolting. There may be an obvious line that isn't bolted because of cultural relics near its base or simply for reasons that land managers have. You may also not realize you are bolting on private land. Simply ask around or check with the land manager of an area.

Leave No Trace

The Access Fund estimates that one in five climbing areas in America is at risk of being closed to climbing or has already been closed to climbing. Most of the access issues at those crags could have been avoided if climbers had been good ambassadors from the start. To be a good ambassador to any climbing area, we simply need to follow the Leave No Trace ethic. For the purposes of this book, Leave No Trace is summed up as follows:

Plan ahead and prepare: Poorly prepared people, when presented with unexpected situations, often resort to high-impact solutions that degrade the outdoors or put themselves at risk. Proper planning leads to less impact. A typical example of this would be bringing a waste disposal bag to the crag, rather than leaving human waste along the base of the cliff. Forgetting your jacket and creating a fire is another, and still another is forgetting your map and thus not using the trails.

Travel durable surfaces: Damage to land occurs when surface vegetation is trampled beyond repair. The resulting barren area leads to unusable trails and dusty campsites. In other words, stick to trails that already exist. Don't make a new one.

Dispose of waste properly: Pick up all your garbage, including micro trash like bits of tape and the ends of energy bar wrappers. As for human waste, if there is a toilet within reasonable walking distance, walk to it. Burn or carry out your toilet paper.

Leave it as you found it: Leave No Trace asks people to minimize site alterations, such as digging tent trenches, hammering nails into trees, permanently clearing an area of rocks or twigs, and removing items.

Minimize campfire impacts: In general, bring a coat. Land managers hate campfires at the base of a wall, and honestly, so do I. Keep in mind that Wyoming is almost a desert and can be very arid. If your campfire gets out of hand, you may be held liable for it.

Respect wildlife: Minimize your impact on wildlife and ecosystems. The most common way climbers break this rule is by letting our four-legged friends off the leash when there are deer nearby. Wildlife-chasing dogs can legally be shot in Wyoming. You are responsible for your pet's impact, as well as its safety.

Be considerate of other visitors: Following hiking etiquette and maintaining quiet allows visitors to go through the wilderness with minimal impact on other users. Remember that some visitors are not climbers. They may want to look at Devils Tower without hearing Jay-Z and Korn. Try not to yell swear words in any tantrums, and just generally be aware that there are many people in this area and your actions may have a negative impact on their enjoyment.

CLIMBING DANGERS AND SAFETY

This book is not a "how to" for climbers. This is a guide to established rock climbing areas that require experience and a solid understanding of rock climbing skills. If you have any doubts at all in your knowledge or abilities, you need to hire a guide and hand this book to him. There is a reason for this: Climbing is dangerous.

Aging hardware, lightning strikes, blizzards, and user error all combine to make climbing an activity that is dangerous enough to preclude us from many life and health insurance plans. Our sport is not a safe activity, no matter how proficient each of us may be. Keep in mind that climbing in Wyoming has its own characteristics that may be different from what you have to contend with at home.

For instance, Wyoming has the lowest population density of any state except Alaska. This means that when you need search and rescue, it is likely to come from a volunteer organization that is not on standby. It might take hours to get help, and that is if you can get in touch with the county dispatch to let them know you're in trouble. Half the climbing areas in this book have spotty cell service, and a couple have absolutely no service. It might be impossible to get help without sending someone to a town some 60 miles away.

Then there are the approaches to the climbs. They are probably no more exposed or loose than those in your home area, but they have residents your state may not have. For instance, Wyoming has bears, and not the cute ones you see in Yosemite and Colorado. Some of ours weigh 750 pounds or more. Wolves and mountain lions get some press, but we also have moose and bison, each of which contributes to more deadly attacks on humans than bears do. But honestly, you are likely to never see any of these creatures because you need to keep watching where you step to avoid the rattlesnakes. Multiple climbers have been bitten in the few years leading up to the publication of this book, and while none died, it was a life-changing event for all of them. You don't want to get a $100,000 emergency room bill and then have to watch your hand or foot rot off.

And then there is the weather. All of the areas in this book are frequently hit by severe thunderstorms in the summer. Lightning has killed a few friends of mine over the years, and a few more, including me, have been hit. I know one Lander climber who has been hit twice, and although he lived to tell about it, it made him a bit quirky. Of course lightning doesn't kill as many as exposure, otherwise known as freezing to death. Winter temperatures can dip into the minus 50°F range in Wyoming, but few climbers are killed by those cold snaps because we are prepared for cold in the winter. It's the spring, summer, and fall storms that kill Wyoming climbers, where rain changes to snow in a matter of minutes as the temperature falls and freezes the rope into an undescendible, icy cable. Every area in this book has been hit by a summer snowstorm that surprised meteorologists. And again, you can't call search and rescue for help . . . just ride it out, cowboy.

This all sounds melodramatic, but it's also true. Almost all the areas covered in this book do not have a qualified, high-angle search-and-rescue department nearby. An accident will likely put you at the whims of your fellow climbers, so be nice. Bears, lions, and bison are not your biggest worry, but it is wise to carry bear spray with you to the crags in the northern and western part of the state. Pay attention to where you place your hands and feet because rattlesnakes love cracks, even cracks 50 feet off the ground, and they do not always "rattle." And finally, there are maybe three days a year I don't carry a puffy coat with me to the crag, and none that I don't carry a good rain shell. You need to be prepared for any kind of weather, because you are the only one who can get yourself out of a bad weather problem.

If this all sounds like fun, then you are in for a treat, because climbing in Wyoming is wonderful. It is often secluded with spectacular weather and amazing wildlife . . . all of the same things that make it dangerous.

PLANNING FOR THE WEATHER

To call Wyoming's weather a collision of extremes is to not paint it as gnarly as it can actually be. Cold winter storms from Alaska and Canada flow down along the Continental Divide, and monsoonal moisture creeps up from the desert Southwest every summer. It has been as hot as 114°F, in Basin near Ten Sleep Canyon, and as cold as -68°F, in Moran near Jackson. This isn't wind chill; if you want wind chill, add a digit.

The most consistent meteorological phenomenon is the wind, with speeds in excess of 75 mph (Category 1 hurricane) common. Most Wyoming towns have average wind speeds above 10 mph, with Casper averaging 16 mph in January. Homes and barns have been buried in blizzarding drifts of snow, and snow fences line the highways in an attempt to keep the roads open. The wind, scouring across the plains and rocks with granules of ice and sand, is actually the largest single component of geologic erosion in places like Wild Iris and Vedauwoo.

Thunderstorms, often the result of warm monsoonal moisture from the south, are so common in summer months that one region of the state is officially named Thunder Basin. Like a supernatural lightning rod, Devils Tower rises straight out of Thunder Basin so it can properly catch the electrical brunt of all those storms. Climbers have been hit and killed by lightning in all the major mountain ranges, and deadly strikes happen every summer. Keeping an eye on the western horizon in the summer months is always a good idea.

I tell you this to let you know that Wyoming's weather is not to be taken lightly. There is no day of the year that you cannot possibly get snow; conversely, midwinter Chinook winds can drive the temperatures high enough to force you into shorts and a T-shirt. This means that when planning for a climbing trip to Wyoming, you should pack a lot of layers. Any trip to Wyoming should include a down jacket, no matter the month, as well as a rain shell. Sunscreen is just as necessary, as the thinner atmosphere of high altitude blocks far less UV radiation from the sun. The home page most Wyoming climbers use is a weather source, as it dictates every aspect of climbing life. Pay attention to the weather and be prepared for anything.

That said, there are seasonal expectations. Technically, you can climb in Wyoming all year. Steve Bechtel, the author of *Lander Sport Climbs*, likes to point out

Brian Fabel in a sea of pockets on Take the Ride (5.11b), South Piney Creek Canyon.

that Lander has over 300 climbing days a year. However, it's better known for its severe winters. Wyoming generally rolls out of winter in April, with all of the areas in this book having climbable days in that month. April tends to be one of the wetter months of the year, and snowstorms are more common than rain. At higher elevations like Jackson and Cody, March, April, and May are often referred to as "mud months." The atmosphere warms into summer by the end of May, when precipitation is sparse and usually falls as afternoon thundershowers. Summer can be quite hot at all of these crags, and even at the higher elevations, climbers are often looking for shade. Fall, beginning in September, is often the driest time with the best climbing temperatures. This is tempered by the threat of a blizzard descending out of the north at any time, turning a Wyoming climbing trip into a jaunt to Vegas instead. Winter months, November through March, have climbable days at areas like Sinks Canyon and Cranner Rock, but it is hard to book a long-term climbing trip around those days knowing snow and below-zero conditions are just as likely.

The Cliff's Notes on planning for the weather are really simple: Bring layers for all kinds of weather. No matter the month, bring a down jacket, a rain shell, and a pair of shorts. Do that, and bring a healthy respect for thunderstorms and lightning, and you will have a good time in Wyoming.

Map Legend

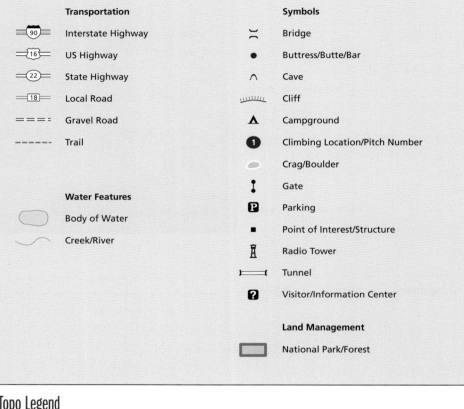

Transportation

Interstate Highway	
US Highway	
State Highway	
Local Road	
Gravel Road	
Trail	

Water Features

Body of Water

Creek/River

Symbols

Bridge

Buttress/Butte/Bar

Cave

Cliff

Campground

Climbing Location/Pitch Number

Crag/Boulder

Gate

Parking

Point of Interest/Structure

Radio Tower

Tunnel

Visitor/Information Center

Land Management

National Park/Forest

Topo Legend

○   Natural gear belay stance

×   Single piece of fixed protection (bolt or piton)

××   Fixed belay or rappel station

VEDAUWOO

■ OVERVIEW

The Arapaho called it bit-oh-woo, or "place of the earth spirits," and are thought to have given a wide berth to the ghostly landscape. Pioneer diaries lamented the constant dry wind howling in their faces as they plodded west, and early settlers found the high ground between Laramie and Cheyenne too cold and blustery to farm. Knowing its isolation, outlaws used the rock outcroppings to hide, though some were never seen again after disappearing into the landscape. The Transcontinental Railroad braved the area, tagging their highest elevation at 8,800 feet above sea level, but then later moved the tracks to a lower and less forbidding location. Even the highway department contemplated skirting the region when building I-80 to avoid the treacherous, seemingly never-ending winter. Desolate but beautiful, easily accessed but wild, and certainly haunted by ferocious weather if not earthly spirits, Vedauwoo (Vee-dow-woo), as we now refer to it, has become a popular climbing area.

Vedauwoo really is a cold, windy place for much of the year, but it also has a lot to offer climbers. The rock, Precambrian Sherman granite, is at least 1.4 billion years old, and may be much older than that. The granite formed as part of the earth's crust but was lifted to just below the surface roughly 70 million years ago. The sediment around the rocky hills slowly wore away in the scouring wind, leaving the wildly shaped granite domes we see today. Those domes are part of a much larger mountain range known as the Laramie Mountains, which extend north almost to the town of Casper.

Rock climbing as a sport came to Vedauwoo at the end of World War II with returning members of the US Army's 10th Mountain Division. The various formations and many of the most obvious 5.4 to 5.8 lines were first climbed in the 1950s. In the 1960s students from the University of Wyoming, like Rick and John Horn, Rex Hoff, and Chuck Schapp, established the 5.10 grade at Vedauwoo before it was nationally recognized. Pitons were dropped for nuts and cams in the 1970s, and local swim coach Layne Kopischka led the charge with troops of his high school swim team. Amazingly they almost never lost a swim meet despite the number of hours spent belaying Coach Kopischka. In the 1980s local Bob Scarpeli, a true offwidth master if there ever was one, established some of the hardest wide crack lines in the world at Vedauwoo. Students putting in a four-year (OK, four- to seven-year) stint at the university have been the backbone of climbing here over the years, as the likes of Paul Piana, Todd Skinner, Steve Bechtel, and Mike Lilygren have all called Vedauwoo home at one time or another. The 5.14 grade was finally established in 2009 with Justin Edle's Home on the Range.

Mike Lilygren gets an early ascent of Air Travel With Report (5.12c) at The Nautilus, Vedauwoo. JACOB VALDEZ/COWBOYOGRAPHY. SAM LIGHTNER JR. COLLECTION

Vedauwoo has an infamous reputation as a difficult, wide crack climbing area. In fact, there may be more 5.11 to 5.13 off-width cracks here than at any other single area in the world. But don't let that scare you, as it's not all wide cracks. There are also flared cracks! No, seriously, Vedauwoo has a whole array of crack climbing options, and all of them are a short walk from the car. If cracks aren't your thing, there are friction slabs and a few crimpy, steep sport climbs as well.

The Climbing and Gear

Vedauwoo climbing is very physical. The cruxes may not be any harder for a given grade, but even moves way below your grade can take the wind out of your sails. It is tradition here that the ratings be sand-bagged . . . hard. The history of this grade deflation may be tied to Jim Halfpenny's first guidebook to the area published in the mid-1960s. Many in that era saw the Yosemite Decimal System as closed at 5.9, meaning 5.9 was the hardest any climb could be rated. This led to numerous routes being graded 5.9 when they were actually what we now call 5.10d or harder. I find that history interesting, but then so is arsenic for treating syphilis. In an effort to make things level, so to speak, throughout the state I have put grades in place that I think are more reflec-tive of the rest of the country.

The rock at Vedauwoo has managed to erode so that a diverse rack is often required for each pitch, and an offwidth-size piece almost always comes in handy. Generally speaking, throwing a double to triple set of cams into your pack, with extras of your favorite sizes, plus nuts and slings, will get you by for a day. A cordelette can also be useful for anchoring at the top of walk-off climbs. As you read the descriptions, remember that the gear mentioned for each route assumes you have at least one set of the full range of cams and nuts as a base to build on.

The Arapaho might have named it Vedauwoo, but many a climber has renamed it Craque-eetsmy-phlesh. The large quartz crystals that make up the stone, combined with the need to reach deep into the cracks, can really serve you up as hamburger, and for this reason tape should be an integral part of your rack. For extra protection, most Vedauwoo locals wear long sleeves and pants no matter what the temperature.

And again, one cannot overstate the wind here—come prepared for all types of weather.

Trip Planning Information

General description: Mostly traditional granite crack climbing with a tendency toward flares and offwidths

Location: Southeast Wyoming, 15 miles east of Laramie

Land manager: Medicine Bow–Routt National Forest

Fees: Vehicle entrance fee charged in part of the area, with other crags being free

Climbing seasons: Late spring, summer, early fall

Camping and hotels: Laramie is 15 miles west of Vedauwoo and has a host of hotels. However, it's a college town, and if you happen to be coming on a weekend when the Pokes are playing football, you will need a reservation.

For camping we recommend the inex-pensive Forest Service campground in the heart of the climbing area. It is somewhat sheltered from the wind, has toilets, fire rings, water, and is 5 minutes walking distance from the crags. On weekends you might want to get there early, as the campsites are first-come, first-served. Follow Vedauwoo Road from I-80 for 1.2 miles, turn left, and look for the campground on the right.

If you want free camping, you are on Medicine Bow–Routt National Forest land, so technically you can camp anywhere that is at least 0.25 mile away from the Forest Service campground and not along a stream. There are plenty of pullouts that fit this description.

Food: Grocery stores and restaurants abound in Laramie, but there are no food services at Vedauwoo.

Guidebooks and other resources:
Vedauwoo is a fairly large area, so if you want to explore the hinterlands, get the local guidebook, *Heel and Toe: The Climbs of Greater Vedauwoo*. There is also *The Voo: Rock Climbing in Vedauwoo* by Zach Orenczak and Rachael Lynn, and *Vedauwoo Bouldering*. All are available in Laramie. Mountain Project has a long catalog of routes, and there is a lot of information to be found on www.vedauwoo.org.

Nearby shops and guide services: Cross
Country Connection at 222 S. Second in Laramie has been the go-to climbing shop for decades. All Terrain Sports, though primarily a Laramie bike shop, also sells climbing gear. In Cheyenne there is a meager selection of gear at the Sierra Trading Post.

If you need a guide to the area, a really good option is Exum Mountain Guides' Micah Rush of Casper. Micah can be reached at (307) 267-4815 or wyoboulder@ hotmail.com. He also has a Facebook page he checks daily.

Emergency services: The Albany County Sheriff's office in Laramie can be reached at (307) 721-2526. If that doesn't get you to the dispatch, try (307) 755-3520. There is the Albany County Search and Rescue, if you need it, and the Sheriff's Department can connect you to them. Ivinson Memorial Hospital in Laramie is at 255 N. 30th St., just off Grand Avenue after you enter town at exit 316. For what it's worth, the higher elevations have decent cell coverage, but down in the hollows, like below Main Wall, can be pretty iffy.

Restrictions and access issues: Vedauwoo is in the Medicine Bow–Routt National Forest and has no restrictions on climbing. There is a fee to drive and park near the Main Wall, though a Golden Eagle Pass covers it, and you can always just walk in rather than drive. This adds about 8 minutes to the approach time.

Getting there: There are flights to Laramie and Cheyenne, but if you are coming from across the country, you might as well fly into Denver and drive up. It only takes a couple hours. Vedauwoo is on the north side of I-80 between Cheyenne and Laramie. Use exit 329, which is about 15 miles east of Laramie, and follow Vedauwoo Road for 1.2 miles. You can't miss it.

The Classics

Edwards Crack, 5.7 (hands)

Finally, 5.10a (offwidth and lieback)

Curry's Diagonal, 5.10d (fingers and face)

Horns Mother, 5.11a (fists to offwidth)

Friday the 13th, 5.10a/5.11b (fingers to wide hands)

Right Torpedo Tube, 5.11c (offwidth)

Max Factor, 5.11c (fingers)

Fourth of July Crack, 5.12a (fingers and stemming)

Vedauwoo Overview

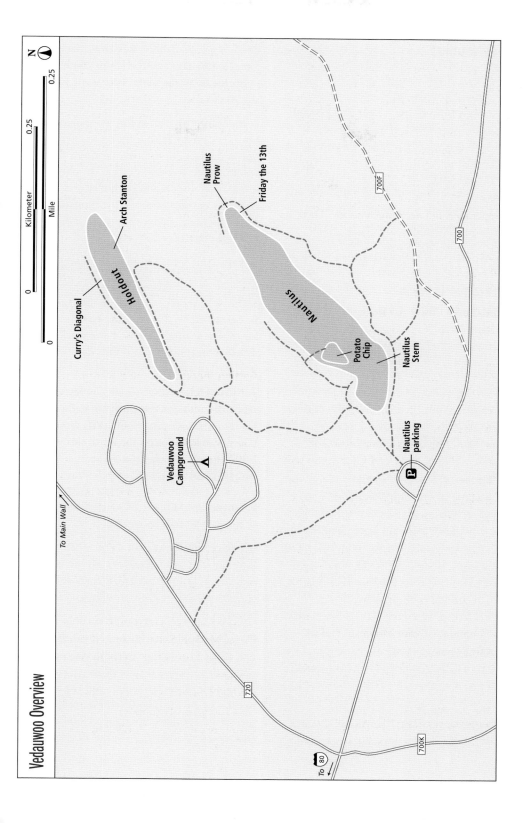

Curry's Diagonal

Arch Stanton

Holdout

Nautilus Prow

Friday the 13th

Nautilus

Potato Chip

Nautilus Stern

Vedauwoo Campground

Nautilus parking

To Main Wall

To 80

720

700K

700

700F

N

Kilometer

0   0.25

Mile

0   0.25

The Nautilus

The stern of the Nautilus is obvious, just past the turnoff into the main Vedauwoo area, as you come in from I-80. The main parking area can be found by driving straight (don't turn left toward the campground) and following the dirt road another 0.25 mile to a lot with a toilet on your left. If this lot is full, continue down the road a bit more and look for pullouts for parking. A network of trails all but circle the Nautilus. To reach the routes on its west side, follow the trail toward the Nautilus and trend left.

Piton's Perch (aka Potato Chip)

Piton's Perch, more commonly referred to as the Potato Chip, is perhaps the most recognizable feature of Vedauwoo, and certainly its most sought after summit. Off its northwest side, about 100 feet left of the Finally area, are three lines that get you to the summit. Go just past the chip and look for a trail going left to the base of the routes.

1. Mother #1★★★ (5.8) 100 feet. If you want to become an offwidth climber but don't know a thing, this is where you start. Take some hand-size gear and larger, like #5s. The Potato Chip slab is not protected but is easy. Rappel off the back side of the Chip (a single 60-meter rope reaches the ledge you can then traverse for a downclimb) or off Father #1's anchor with two ropes to the base. **FA:** Rex Hoff and Bob Frisby.

2. Father #1★ (5.11a R) 100 feet. Hand crack to seam to thin face. **FA:** Paul Piana and Lisa Schassberger.

3. The Postman★ (5.10c) Climb the first bit of Father #1 and then traverse out onto the face on bolts. There is a bolted anchor, but it

does not get you all the way to the base with a single rope. Take two ropes or continue on to the lip of the Chip. **FA:** Wade Griffith and Matt Filcek.

4. Hair Lip★★ (5.10a) 45 feet. A strange combination of styles makes this route interesting. A full rack, from finger gear to a #4, will find their use. Lower from the chockstone, or do the second pitch that goes up and right traversing around the formation (take thin gear). **FA:** Unknown, but perhaps the Horn Brothers.

5. Easy Jam★★ (5.5) 40 feet. Another good option for your first offwidth. Take a few #4 cams. Rappel anchors are to the right.

6. Cornelius★★★ (5.6) 40 feet. This is a short but excellent finger- to hand-size crack, trending up and right with thin feet. There is an anchor atop the crack.

7. Nitrogen Narcosis★ (5.11b) 50 feet. Difficult hands and fingers in a leaning corner. Don't break your elbow. **FA:** Doug Cairns and Bob Scarpeli.

Nautilus Stern

8. Lower Slot Left (5.7) 45 feet. Takes lots of finger- to hand-size gear.

9. Lower Slot Right (5.8) 45 feet. Not the most fun you will have today. Up on the right crack, transfer to the left crack and cheer at the ledge. Plan for wide, and tape up an extra layer.

To approach the next routes, either climb one of the Lower Slots or climb the 3rd-class slabs and corners right of them. From the summit of the formation, you can rappel to the east next to The Central Scrutinizer, then walk around to the right and 3rd-class back down.

Potato Chip and Nautilus Stern

10. Upper Slot Left (5.10a) 50 feet. An odd shape to this climb makes you wonder if you could fall in or out of it. Take hand gear and, as always, some wide stuff. Belay at the summit.

11. Upper Slot Right★★★ (5.8) 50 feet. This is the standard for wide hands and fists. Belay in the hueco with some wide hand-size pieces or on the summit with two old bolts.

12. Finally★★★ (5.10a) 50 feet. A fun lieback and offwidth crack with great exposure. Take a couple of #4s and #5s; hand pieces are handy topping out, and a couple of finger pieces help midway. Use wide hand pieces in the giant hueco or summit bolts for the belay. **FA:** Pete Hollis, John Garson, and Scott Heywood.

13. Drunken Redneck Rappelers★ (5.12a) 50 feet. Up the obvious colorful face right of Finally. A bouldery start to thin, consistent tweaking. It's a bit runout, though a small nut behind the flake helps. **FA:** Scott Blunk, Steve Millard, and Sam Lightner Jr.

14. The Central Scrutinizer★ (5.12a) 50 feet. If you like hard Tuolumne Meadows–style knob climbing, this might be your thing. Around the corner and facing east, find a thin hands and finger crack that leads to four bolts on a thin, knobby face. This route has its own anchor. **FA:** Sam Lightner Jr., Bill Walker, and Leon Pennington Burris III.

15. Harder than Your Husband★ (5.12c) 35 feet. On the large boulder below and right of the approach to the upper routes is a flaring, desperate finger crack. Use lots of small gear—conservatively graded. **FA:** Paul Piana.

Nautilus Prow

Trend right from the parking area and traverse the breadth of the Nautilus, eventually going uphill to the alcove at the base of Friday the 13th. Continuing on 100 feet puts you under the Torpedo Tubes, and another 100 feet to below Max Factor.

Getting down from this end of the feature can be done by a couple of rappels. Above Middle Parallel Space you can do one big, double-rope rap or a couple small raps that a single 60-meter rope can handle. The other option is rappelling War Zone with a 70-meter rope, or breaking it in two with a 60. As always, tie knots in your ends.

Friday the 13th Area

16. War Zone★★ (5.8/5.11b R) 60/80 feet. An interesting face climb on flakes and edges with good gear for the first pitch. Pitch 2 is mostly bolts and a bit of small stuff, and is fairly runout. **FA:** Sean Bradley.

17. Deception (5.9) 70/100 feet. A mix of fingers to large hands in the corner. Above the first anchor at 70 feet, continue up the corner. A large cam (#4 to #4.5) helps here. You can also venture out onto the slab finish of War Zone.

18. H+H Grunt (5.5) 100 feet. More of a spelunking operation than a climb. Climb up the cracks just inside the chimney, then tunnel inward. Split it into two pitches. There are a couple of ledges to belay from with your own anchor. It is runout in here, and cold even on the warmest days. **FA:** Rex Hoff and John Horn.

19. Friday the 13th★★★ (5.10a/5.11b/5.11d) Fingers to hands, so an assortment from 0.5 to 3.5 protects the climb well. Most people climb to the first anchor at 5.10a and come down. Through the first roof is 5.11b; a large hex placed at the lip helps to keep the rope from biting into cam lobes. There is an anchor above the first roof. The second roof is 5.11d. **FA:** No telling on the first pitch, but Todd Skinner and Paul Piana on the highest roof.

20. Hesitation Blues★★ (5.11b) A fingery lieback to easy ground starts this off. Thin hands pieces to tight fingers and small nuts protect the crux, while a few large hand pieces protect above. Originally you climbed this and belayed at the base of the steep corner as the route went up and then back across to the Friday the 13th anchor. A new anchor allows you to climb the upper part on big hands and fists in one big, 110-foot pitch. You need a 70-meter rope to lower from here. **FA:** Steve Matous and Doug Cairns.

21. Middle Parallel Space★★★ (5.9/5.8) Two pitches of fun. First do a bit of offwidth to a wide hand crack, rest on the ledge, then stem, jam, and chimney to the top of the pillar and a bolt anchor via the chimney and its hidden hand crack. Pitch 2 continues on the crack up and to the right to the rappel anchor. A couple #4 cams help at the start, and then lots of hand- and fist-size gear. **FA:** Dan McClure and Doug Snively, or Royal Robbins and gang.

22. Air Travel With Report★★ (5.12c PG) Thin, pumpy face climbing to the anchor used by Middle Parallel Space. Craig liked doing things runout, and this route was typical of that style with only five bolts in 80 feet. The lead bolts are aging, so we recommend you toprope it instead of lead it. **FA:** Craig Reason.

Friday the 13th Area

Torpedo Tubes (The Prow)

Follow the trail around and left to the following routes. All descents are done via rappel from the Middle Parallel Space anchors.

23. Right Parallel Space* (5.6 R/X) With a #4 cam protecting the start, climb up and left into the chimney. You eventually get one old bolt in the chimney. The climbing is not difficult but extremely committing, as falling is really not an option. **FA:** Dan McClure and Doug Snively.

24. Vulture (5.8) Climb up and right on big gear to a chockstone belay. Traverse right and then go up to reach the summit. A direct version, starting on the right crack, can be done at 5.10.

25. Left Torpedo Tube (5.10d) As a chimney to bombay offwidth, this route has been called everything from 5.9 to 5.13. Wear clothing as you will have to get

among it, and take #5 and #6 cams plus large Big Bros.

26. Right Torpedo Tube★★ (5.11c) The classic fist and offwidth crack at Vedawuoo. Dress appropriately; a few #4 cams should be on your rack. **FA:** Ray Jardine and Bill Forest.

27. Gravity's Rainbow (5.11c) Do the unprotected 5.10a start, then place mid- to small-size gear in the corner and out the undercling. Take a few fist-size pieces as you finish on Right Torpedo Tube. **FA:** Chace and Steve Levine.

28. Bolted Project It seems like this thing has been here a really long time.

Continuing around the bow to the starboard side of the Nautilus you reach the Max Factor area. Most of these routes have their own anchor and do not require you to climb to the summit.

Torpedo Tubes (The Prow)

Max Factor Area

29. Grand Traverse★★ (5.10b) 90 feet. A steady dose of finger- and hand-size pieces on easy 5.10 terrain will get you to an anchor under the roof. Judiciously use slings to limit drag and traverse right with fingery to tight hands placements to the anchor above Max Factor. The seldom-done second pitch (5.10c), straight up from here, requires fist-size gear. **FA:** Phil Fowler and Dan McClure.

30. Max Factor★★★ (5.11c) Thin feet and fingerlocks, with the occasional jam, make this a classic. Small and midsize Stoppers and a few smaller cams will be your best friends. **FA:** Kim Carrigan and Steve Levin.

31. Bug Squad★ (5.11d R) A rounded lieback protected by manky pins add headiness to this one. It may be possible to get a small cam in to back up the pins, but like I said, "a rounded lieback." The protection is bigger and better as you get higher.

32. Baalbek★ (5.9) A chimney with chockstones that is more fun than you would guess. You get jams around the stones, and the chimney part is not bad. Small to midsize stuff, plus a couple of quickdraws, will protect to the anchor.

33. Maxilash★ (5.11a) If you like the physical nature of offwidth, where 3 minutes of climbing yields 3 feet of elevation, you will love this. Take a #5 and a #4 cam for protection, plus a number of hand and wider hand pieces for above. **FA:** Bob Scarpeli and Layne Kopischka.

Max Factor Area

Holdout

The Holdout sees fewer visitors than the other central areas, and its northwest face is a great place to hide from the summer sun. The best parking, if you are a day visitor and not staying in the campground, is at the Nautilus lot. Follow the trail toward the north side of the Nautilus, then hang a hard left and cross through the campground. The split in the trails to the northwest and southeast faces is pretty obvious. If you are staying in the campground, offer your neighbor some beer later as you cross his site to the crag.

The approach to the far climbs on the northwest face involves some scrambling on large boulders. It is not a good place for toddlers.

Holdout—South East Face

1. Flaming Blue Jesus★ (5.10b R) Climb up and left into a dihedral with a shallow crack.

Gear is there, but technical, except in the first 30 feet where boldness is required. Take small and midsize nuts and small cams, plus a few hand pieces and a quickdraw for the ancient bolt. By the way, the name refers to a drink at the Buckhorn Bar and a young lass who was a bit smitten with one of the first ascensionists. **FA:** Paul Piana and Bob Cowan.

2. Mandala★ (5.11a) As you near the top of Flaming Blue Jesus, trend right on the thin crack. Take a few more small cams and nuts if you do this variant.

3. Arch Stanton★★★ (5.12b) 100-plus feet with traverse. Originally an A5 aid line, Todd and Paul freed the arch to an anchor at its end in the early 1980s at 5.11d on tiny brass nuts (and big balls). Paul later returned and added some bolts plus a finish to the top, making it 5.12b. It's still a bit sporty between the bolts at the start, so besides a fistful of quickdraws, you might want a few tiny cams. As for the name, I asked many

Holdout–South East Face

Brian Fabel and Simeon Caskey on Beefeater (5.10b) at the Holdout, Vedauwoo.

years ago and was told it was the answer to "the ultimate Clint Eastwood trivia question." Watch *The Good, The Bad, and The Ugly* for the question. Watch the end of the rope when lowering. **FA:** Paul Piana, Todd Skinner, and later Heidi Badaracco.

4. Wide and Ugly (5.11b) Need we say more? It's the obvious right-trending roof that runs into Bushwack Crack. **FA:** Mike Friedrichs and Dan Moe.

The next four climbs are accessed by 3rd-classing behind the boulder and then doing an exposed move or two onto the ledge. Be careful.

5. Bushwack Crack★ (5.9) 90 feet. A hard start leads to wide hands . . . and a bush. A full range of gear to fist size will be useful.

6. 19th Nervous Breakdown★ (5.10a) Takes all sorts of gear.

7. Down Chimney (5.5) Before the rappel stations this was the descent route.

8. Existential Dilemma (5.8) Offwidth to hands. **FA:** JP Sartre(?).

Holdout—North West Face

This is a clean wall that stays cool late into the afternoon in summer. There are nice views of the Main Wall and central Vedauwoo from most of the routes.

9. Beefeater★★ (5.10b) To get to the goods, you have to do an approach pitch or rap in. The approach from the side (9a, 5.6) is far more preferable than the slimy poop roof under the ledge (9b, 5.10d). Belay from the ledge on a traditional anchor.

The upper crack would get three stars if it weren't for the approach. **FA:** Larry Bruce and Mark Hesse.

10. Mad Cow Disease★ (5.10d) A variant of Beefeater, this route traverses around the arête to the left where Beefeater tips back and right. Thin gear helps get you to and up this lieback flake. **FA:** Zach Orenczak and Mike Bentley.

11. Veggie Eater★ (5.10a) Find this fun little sport climb on the large boulder just north of Beefeater. Three quickdraws to an anchor.

12. Silver Surfer (5.9) A fun little roof to a ledge and anchor 35 feet up. A single set of cams from 0.5 to 3.5 will cover your needs. You gotta do the chimney without the pro. **FA:** Paul Piana and Todd Skinner.

The next two routes extend from the ledge that is the end of Silver Surfer.

13. Pipeline★★ (5.12a) 50 feet. If you like tenuous, thin face climbing, this is your route. From the ledge atop Silver Surfer, go up and right with seven bolts for protection. Last I checked, the rap rings had been heisted off the anchor. If toproping someone from below, watch your ends. **FA:** Mike Lilygren and Steve Bechtel.

14. North Shore (5.13b) 50 feet. A steeper, thinner, and more direct version of Pipeline. Too hard at this angle to be enjoyable, me thinks. **FA:** Steve Bechtel and Bobby Model.

15. Eleven Cent Moon★★ (5.11d) 90 feet. Climb a thin face that steepens into a shallow dihedral. There are two bolts and both are ancient. Gear for the crack is thin wired Stoppers and brass nuts with the odd small

cam. A rap anchor exists above that is shared by Curry's Diagonal. **FA:** Todd Skinner and Paul Piana.

16. Curry's Diagonal★★★ (5.10d) 95 feet.
This is one of the best climbs at Vedauwoo, but the protection in the crux is a bit sketchy. A shallow piton protects the hardest moves. A blue Alien or Lowe Ball would go a long way in backing it up. Be aware. A long sling (for the stump) and hand and thin hands camming units are the gear, plus a couple quickdraws for the pitons. Belay from the anchor at the lip. **FA:** Steve Matous and Doug Cairns.

17. Static Cling (5.12a R) A thin seam that requires a stable mind and stable footwork. Use lots of tiny gear that may or may not stay in. If you want to lead this, you better be technically good. Gravity is unforgiving. **FA:** Todd Skinner and Lisa Schassberger.

18. Reading Raymond Chandler★★ (5.12a)
An easier-to-protect version of Static Cling; you will want plenty of small nuts and tiny cams to protect this. Easier, but not easy, and with minimal gear a fall onto the ledge is possible. There is an anchor up top. **FA:** Paul Piana and Mark Rolofson.

19. Rainbow in the Dark (5.11a) In the trees on the far left of the wall, this climb goes up then follows a large undercling flake. Lots of finger gear protects it well. Finish on Oslunds Delight. **FA:** Sam Lightner Jr. and Bill Walker.

20. Oslunds Delight★ (5.8) Climb a hand crack to a ledge, then onward on finger- and hand-size jams to the top. Large hand pieces work well for an anchor, while most of the route takes finger and thin hands pieces. **FA:** Pete Oslund and Jim Olsen.

Heard in the Wind

Just Kidding

Bolts can be a distressing subject at Vedauwoo, and in the 1980s just saying the words "rap-bolt" might cause a fight. More than once those climbers embracing the future were threatened. One story about a rappel anchor stands out as a display of toughness, if not an example of cowboy under-statement. To protect the rarely innocent, we shall change the names of those involved.

It seems one climber, Lance, had added an anchor to the top of a climb established by another, a man we will call Will. Lance was a third degree black belt in tae kwon do, but Will was infamous and thoroughly respected for his fighting prowess in the Casper oil fields. He'd put the wood to more than one surly cuss in his time, and there wasn't a climber in the country who wanted to stand up to his size 11 hex fists. So one day Lance was standing in the parking area below Fall Wall when Will pulled in.

Will screamed, "You son of a bitch, Lance. You added a couple bolts to my route and now you're gonna pay for it."

Like a snarling grizzly, Will roared across the lot in a bonzai charge. It was clear that Lance would have to fight or die. Lance stepped forward, got in Shotokan position, and then planted the "most perfect front kick ever" (his words) to Will's jaw. Will went from 15 mph forward to 5 mph backward, into the air and onto his back. For a nanosecond everyone thought it was over, but then much to Lance's chagrin, Will threw his feet into the air and shot up, land-ing upright and in fighting position like Johnny Lawrence in *The Karate Kid*.

"What the hell, Lance, I was just kid'n," Will exclaimed while licking blood off his lip. There was a pause as they looked each other up and down. "So was I," Lance replied. Fight finished, the climbing day ensued.

Main Wall

After turning left, paying your fee at the station, and passing the campground, the road drops into a small valley between the Main Wall and the Holdout. It's a bit of a maze of roads, but you want to trend northeast and slightly uphill to find the closest parking spaces to the Main Wall. There are lots of options, none adding more than a minute or two to your walk. There are also a few toilets down here to take advantage of (rather than up at the base of the wall where you can be seen for miles).

Fall Wall

Fall Wall is the right side of the Main Wall buttress. Many of the routes are accessed by bouldering up behind the right side of a giant rock known as the Clam Shell. For the most part these are bolted face climbs, but they are not sport climbs. The difference is they were put up on lead (mostly) and thus tend to be quite runout in spots. Consider a PG rating for virtually everything up here. Sadly, most of the bolts are fairly long in the tooth too.

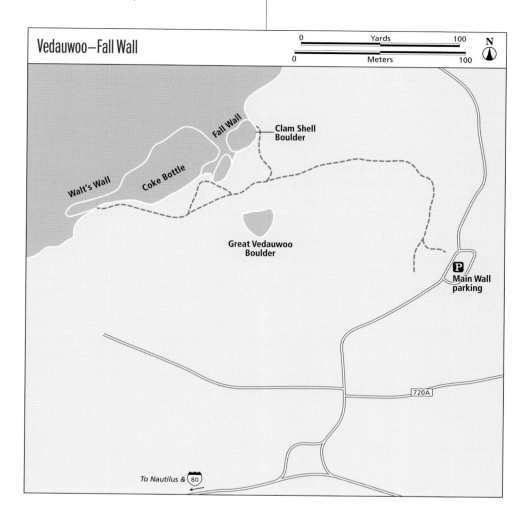

Vedauwoo–Fall Wall

1. Dropzone★ (5.10a) 70 feet. Sadly, this route has been chopped and replaced a few times as people fight to force everyone to their form of fun. At the time of this writing, it took seven quickdraws, but you might want to take eight just in case. **FA:** Skip Harper and John Thomas.

2. Cold Fingers★ (5.8) 70 feet. Traditionally 5.7, this grade seems more in line with where things have fallen out. Four bolts to the anchor. Spicy. **FA:** Peter Koedt and Ken Fisher.

3. Easy Friction★ (5.5) 70 feet. Now we're down to two bolts, but it really is low angle. You'd ski it if the conditions were right. **FA:** Ken Fisher and Peter Koedt.

4. Easy Overhang★★ (5.5) 70 feet. If you want a first trad lead you can stitch up, this is it. Take midsize nuts and finger pieces. **FA:** Rick Horn and Steve Komito.

5. Sport (5.11a) 70 feet. Start up an easy lieback and then move left onto the blunt arête. For years this was a commonly done toprope, perhaps first climbed in the mid-1980s. **FA:** Unknown, but Lightner and Walker likely as a toprope.

6. Gunga Din (5.11a) 70 feet. You can get a small nut or two behind the flake, but mostly this protects by three bolts. It's been toproped a lot over the years and is a bit polished. **FA:** Bob Cowan and Mark Ilgner.

7. 5.11 Crack★★ (5.10a) 70 feet. I'm not sure how this got called 5.11 Crack when it really is only 5.10a with the current level of polish. Getting to the first piece of gear is kind of sketchy. There are a couple bolts but it's mostly tiny nuts in pin scars. It was originally an aid climb (as were many routes at Vedauwoo) that was later freed by Parker and Chapman. On an early ascent a bolt used as a single-point anchor broke, letting

two climbers tumble down the slab. Except for scrapes and bruises they were OK, but spent weeks trying to untie themselves from the tangled lead line!

8. Fear and Loathing★ (5.10a) 70 feet. Start up 5.11 Crack, then break left and follow three bolts to the roof. Use the 5.11 Crack anchors or go left to the Fall Wall anchors for extra pump. **FA:** Layne Kopischka and a host of swimmers.

9. Fall Wall★★★ (5.10a R) 90 feet. I would call this a classic friction pitch. It protects with a #3 cam behind a flake about 15 feet out, then three bolts, then a large finger-size cam under the bulge (with a long sling). Trend back right to the bolted anchor. The pitch above (9a, 5.8) was first attempted by Rex Hoff. He fell and broke both ankles, then Jan Matheisen and Jim Halfpenny established it with the name Falling Hoff. Most people just call it Upper Fall Wall. I give both pitches the R rating, but it especially applies to the first, as a fall at the start, before reaching the cam-flake, would be very disappointing. **FA:** Peter Koedt, Chuck Schapp, Keith Becker, and Jan Matheisen. Upper Fall Wall was Matheisen and Halfpenny. The blank line above the cam-flake was climbed, on lead, by Paul Piana in the early 1980s. He couldn't stop to place a bolt and they left it as is.

The following routes are reached not from the Clam Shell, but from an alcove down and left of the giant boulder. The best way to reach it is to find a trail through the boulders in front of the Clam Shell.

10. Spider God★★ (5.11b R) 110 feet. A stout offering from Mr. Paul, considering not only was it done on lead but also before Boreal rubber (and long before Stealth rubber). Take a couple of micro-cams for the

Fall Wall

horizontals, eight long quickdraws, and a large finger-size piece for the top of Fall Wall. A 60-meter rope will not reach back to the ground. A 70 . . . well, watch your ends. **FA:** Paul Piana and Kelly Thorpe.

11. Fallout★ (5.9) A little face climbing, a hand crack, and some offwidth and chimney work go into an ascent of this. The first anchor, at the ledge, is 110 feet up. Continuing up the seam above at 5.10a requires lots of small gear. Piana and Skinner dubbed that line Neon Cowboy. A better option is Mickey Mantle. It is 50 feet from the anchor above to the ledge atop Fall Wall. **FA:** Paul Piana and Bob Cowan.

12. Mickey Mantle★ (5.10c) A steep water streak protected by four bolts. **FA:** Doug Cairns and John Thomas.

13. Neon Cowboy★ (5.10a R) A thin seam near the giant corner that takes tiny gear

. . . some tiny gear. **FA:** Paul Piana and Todd Skinner.

14. Thomas-McGary Chimney★ (5.6) Find this by going into the cave and then chimneying deep inside the crack that separates the Coke Bottle from Fall Wall. You need large Big Bros to protect it, plus some long slings for tying off chockstones, though it's best to do this if you plan on not falling. A headlamp might be handy too. There is a ledge that breaks it up a little over halfway. **FA:** John Thomas and Frank McGary.

15. Young Guns (5.13b) Ascend from the cave to the obvious ledge via a belly crawl, then stand and trend right on tiny features, clipping eleven bolts along the way. There are a couple anchors at a ledge 120 feet up. Frank was a technical master to get this thing. For slab guys this may deserve a star or two, but I just can't tell when things get this thin. **FA:** Frank Dusl and Steve Bechtel.

16. Space Oddity★★ (5.12a) Another long, thin face climb, but with more substantial holds than its next-door neighbor. Use the same start but then trend up and left, eventually hitting the blunt arête. A dozen quickdraws are your rack. **FA:** Adam Sears, Steve Bechtel, and Frank Dusl.

Coke Bottle

Vaguely resembling an old Coca-Cola bottle in profile, the bulge of the main wall takes on that name. The trail works its way up to these routes from the right. The first five can be accessed by scrambling onto the obvious ledge.

17. Revenge of Nothing★★ (5.11b) Climb through the crux of Main Street then traverse right, passing one anchor, on small edges and crystals. Belay at the second anchor and climb 80 feet to the anchor on the ledge above. You will need two ropes, or to break the rappel into two at the previous anchor, to get down from the ledge. **FA:** Skip Harper and Duff.

18. Never Ending Story★★ (5.11a) Climb Main Street and then traverse to the first anchor. Up from there with seven quickdraws over 80 feet makes it a bit spicy. Again, you'll need two ropes to get down from the ledge above. **FA:** Layne Kopischka, solo.

19. Main Street★ (5.10a) This is good for a wide crack. There is a bolt to protect one crux, but you will need multiple #5s and #6s and some Big Bros for protection. A few more quickdraws help with bolts that can be reached. **FA:** Mark Hess.

20. Panther of the Week★ (5.13a) Climb up and left along the lip of the roof clipping bolts. The second pitch has not been freed yet. **FA:** Todd Skinner and Sam Lightner Jr.

21. Dollywood★★ (5.10c) This line, put in after Panther of the Week, follows bigger holds up to the roof (small cam), then around the corner to the same anchor. **FA:** Zach Orenczak and Rachael Lynn.

22. Bell Crack (5.11a) If you have been bothered by the preponderance of wide cracks, give this one a miss. Wide hands and fists to offwidth and chimney. One of numerous routes first done on aid by the Horn Brothers with 2x4s for pitons.

23. Boardwalk★★ (5.11c, 5.10d obl.) 2 pitches: 5.10b, 511c. A three-star crack that loses one star for its hanging belay (not even a stance!). Pitch 1: Ascend the start of Bell Crack then traverse out left, around the corner at 5.10b, and almost under the obvious splitter to build the belay from finger- to hand-size pieces. Warning: Building the belay directly under the crack could put the next leader in your lap if he/she falls in the crux. Pitch 2 ascends the splitter with large finger to tight hand pieces through the crux. Build an anchor high in the chimney and descend either from the anchor above Main Street or the anchor above Fourth of July Crack. If you are so inclined, Eric Bjornstad, almost infamous for his traversing routes, with Jim Halfpenny and Nancy Westlund, continued on the horizontal crack all the way to Horns Mother at mid-5.10 . . . not sure why. Boardwalk **FA:** Tobin Sorenson and company.

24. Light from Blue Horses★★ (5.11c) Climb Boardwalk to the first pod then traverse left on face holds with bolts to a hanging stance belay. The next pitch continues straight up the water streak and has some distance between the last bolt and the top anchor. Two raps with a single 60-meter rope get you down. **FA:** Paul Piana and Craig Reason.

Coke Bottle

25. Horns Mother★★★ (5.11a) It may not be your favorite kind of climbing, but for its size Horns Mother—consistent, solid, and a long splitter—is a classic. Climb the obvious splitter crack through a bulge and up for 100-plus feet. The first 40 feet can be climbed on large finger to large hand pieces, then it's all #4 Friends and #4 Camelots with a few hand-size pieces at the top. Some people break it into two pitches by belaying in the obvious pod. **FA:** Done on aid by the Horn Brothers and Chuck Schapp with 2x4s for pitons. On the drive up, John Horn leaned out the passenger door of his brother's VW Beetle to grind the boards to a shape he liked. The route was later freed by Dan McClure and Mark Hesse.

26. Silver Salute★★ (5.13b) Todd liked a line of holds . . . they didn't have to go upward. From the pod on Horns Mother, traverse around the arête to the anchor of Light from Blue Horses. Take 10 quickdraws plus whatever you need to get to the pod. **FA:** Todd Skinner, Jacob Valdez, Amy Whistler, and Sam Lightner Jr.

27. Fourth of July Crack★★★ (5.12a) Probably the first 5.12 at Vedauwoo and perhaps the first in the state, this line uses all sizes of gear, fingers to fists. Access it by climbing the first pitch of Satterfields Crack. There is now a bolted anchor on top that will get you down to the anchor on Walt's Wall on a 60-meter rope if you rappel. Plan on doing a bit of swinging to get out to Walt's Wall. **FA:** Todd Skinner and Paul Piana.

28. Satterfields Crack★★ (5.8, 5.8 obl.) 2 pitches: 5.6, 5.8. This is the wide crack that separates the Coke Bottle from Walt's Wall. Pitch 1 is 5.6 and gets your attention at the chockstone. Belay atop that with a traditional anchor. Pitch 2 goes from wide fists to chimney, then another chockstone. Climb around the chockstone to the belay ledge and bolts on Walt's Wall. Named for Chuck Satterfield, who did it on toprope like a billion years ago. **FA:** Jerry Sublette and Skip Hamilton.

Mandy Fabel on the finishing moves of Edwards Crack (5.7), Walt's Wall, Vedauwoo.

Walt's Wall

The far left side of the Main Wall area, virtually every square foot of Walt's Wall has been climbed on at one time or another. We try to cover the better routes for you here. This is a great place to go for your first leads.

29. In Through the Out Door★ (5.10c)
Accessed from the giant chockstone midway up Satterfields Crack, this is a slippery friction line in and just right of the obvious water streak and left of Satterfields Crack. **FA:** Will Laurue, Chris Cox, and Zach Orenczak.

30. The Water Streak★★ (5.10a R)
A fun friction pitch running more or less directly from the top of pitch 1 to the top of pitch 2 on Walt's Wall. A fistful of quickdraws and solid nerves will get you there. **FA:** Layne Kopischka or Steve Matous.

31. 5.7 Cracks★ (5.8 R)
Hard to protect on tiny wires and micro-cams, most just toprope this slit in the rock. **FA:** Likely Layne Kopischka.

32. Walt's Wall★★ (5.4)
A great first lead that is broken into three pitches. A mixed rack of cams to hand size, plus some nuts and a lot of long slings and quickdraws for the odd bolt will work for gear. Pitch 1 goes up and left to a bolted rappel anchor. Pitch 2 goes out left on the ledge, then up and back right to another anchor. This is a good place to learn about using slings to limit rope drag. Pitch 3 into the corner, then when you feel comfy come out onto the slab and friction

Walt's Wall

to the rappel anchor atop the wall. It's only 5.4 up here, but runout. Two single-rope rappels get you down. A more straight-up version of pitch 1 is known as The Mantle Route. It's 5.9 and very runout—most just toprope it. **FA:** Walt Sticker.

33. Friction Slab (5.9) A bit of pulling, then true friction takes you to the ledge breaks on Walt's Wall. There are a couple of bolts on it for what passes as "safety." **FA:** Unknown.

34. Jacquot's Face (5.7, 5.7 obl.) 3 pitches: 5.4, 5.7, 5.6. Climb the first pitch of Walt's Wall. On the second pitch, where W.W. goes back right, go left toward the top of pitch 1 of Edwards Crack. For pitch 3, ignore the obvious splitter that is Eds Crack and venture back out onto the Achilles-straining slab, making your way to a broken dihedral. Pass this and traverse off the top, or just ignore it and do Edwards Crack. **FA:** Ray Jacquot, Rex Hoff, Jerry Edwards, and Bob Frisbay over an eight- to ten-year period.

35. Edwards Crack★★★ (5.7, 5.6 obl.) 2 pitches: 5.7, 5.7. This line stands out so well you can see it from I-80. Maybe from space. Pound for pound it's the best route at Vedauwoo and the line I would call the best 5.7 in Wyoming. Granted, it was originally only a 5.6 . . . but we migrate in our grading. Climb the steep hand crack and corner to a ledge on wide hands and a bit of off-width technique. From the ledge do a couple of not too bad friction moves to reach the crack, then continue on to a nice ledge for a belay you build yourself. Pitch 2 continues up the crack and through the roof at its top using a number of different climbing skills. Continue on easy ground and belay at a comfy spot under a tree. A double set of cams to fist size, some nuts, and some long slings are the proper rack. If it's your first lead, you might want a few extra midsize pieces. To get down, traverse across the formation to the . . . WAIT! Take in the view. OK, now traverse climbers-right to above the Coke Bottle, then back left to the Walt's Wall rappels that can be done in two on a single 60-meter rope. Edwards Crack can be led as one big pitch with a 70-meter rope. **FA:** Jerry Edwards and Ray Jacquot.

36. Whistling Jupiter★★ (5.12b) The west face of the Great Vedauwoo Boulder has a worthy slab sport climb. A bouldery start gets you on, then keep your head together to an anchor on top. Five quickdraws cover the pro, and a stick clip might save your ankles. **FA:** First climbed by Chuck Schapp, Jim Halfpenny, Peter Koedt, and Stevenson with innovative hooks, later freed by Paul Piana, Skinner, and Dan Michaels.

FREMONT CANYON

■ OVERVIEW

Wyoming is a state of stand-out scenery. Devils Tower juts from the prairie so starkly it has become an icon not only for Wyoming, but also science fiction. The beauty of Yellowstone so inspired visitors of the nineteenth century that they made it the world's first protected national park. The Tetons, picturesque and stunning as an abrupt mountain range, have been used for tourist brochures in Canada! In a state filled with incredible beauty, the spectacular narrows of Fremont Canyon fit right in.

The canyon takes its name from frontiersman and explorer John C. Fremont, who led an expedition through the West and down the North Platte in 1842. A cool, shady river canyon on the unforgiving Wyoming prairie was no doubt a more comfortable way to transit the dry plains. Descending into the narrows, however, with no means of retreat and not knowing whether there was a waterfall or Blackfeet village around the next bend, must have been a bit nerve-racking.

The canyon formed through millions of years of the North Platte River grinding away at 2-billion-year-old granite. Though the rock walls are some of the oldest in the United States, the flow of the river that formed them has recently been altered by man. The North Platte has its headwaters in the Park Range of northern Colorado. Its largest tributary, the Sweetwater, begins its flow at the southern end of the Wind River Range near Wild Iris. In 1905 the newly formed Bureau of Reclamation began work on the Pathfinder Dam in an effort to capture more water for Wyoming and Nebraska agriculture. The facility was built with cement hauled by horse teams from Casper some 47 miles away. One team had twenty-two horses and towed a wagon with 31,000 pounds of cement, while another was actually towed by sheep. At a total cost of 2.2 million dollars, the project was huge by early twentieth-century standards. It was completed in June 1909, creating a reservoir that holds some 1 million-plus acre-feet of water. The dam's state-of-the-art construction from the early 1900s led to it being placed on the National Register of Historic Places in 1971.

A couple of pinnacles are detached from the main rim of the canyon, and it appears climbers took notice of them sometime in the 1950s, though there is no official record of an ascent. In the 1970s climbers like Pat Parmenter, Steve Petro, and Arno Ilgner laid the path for Steve Bechtel and Micah Rush—all of whom laid paths for us. Thank you for that, fellas.

The Climbing and Gear

The granite in Fremont Canyon tends to be solid and clean with plenty of vertical and horizontal cracks. It is featured enough with edges and pockets to be a good place for both crack climbers and non-crack climbers. Obviously there are a lot of options.

In most climbing areas, setting up a toprope on a route can be a pain in the butt, and leading is just the easiest way to get the rope up there. The opposite is true at Fremont, and it is a toproper's heaven. For most climbs there are bolted anchors or a tree to use as an anchor, but they are not always exactly where you want them, and rarely are they right at the rim. Most locals bring an extra-long cordelette (30 feet) to set up rappels or engineer topropes. You might also have to build an anchor with traditional gear, or build a directional from the nearest bolted anchor. In any event a long cordelette helps get your rope to the rim.

Heard in the Wind

The Most Likable Outlaw

Of all the outlaws and ruffians to wander the plains and mountains of Wyoming, none have been more popular or admired than Butch Cassidy. He robbed banks and trains in Utah, New Mexico, Colorado, South Dakota, and Idaho, and because of his likable character was applauded for it. Butch actually cut his teeth as an outlaw rustling cattle in the Cowboy State. Though he broke the law in virtually every state west of the Continental Divide, it was Wyoming where he spent most of his time and seemingly where he called "home."

Butch was born Robert Leroy Parker in Circleville, Utah. He was raised Mormon by British-born parents who had migrated across the United States towing a hand cart (see the Granite Mountains chapter). He worked as a jockey in Telluride, but had to leave town on the race-horse after robbing the San Miguel Valley Bank. At some point he ended up on the right side of the law in Rock Springs, Wyoming, where he worked as a butcher. It's thought this is where he took on the nickname Butch, adding the last name of his mentor, a Mr. Mike Cassidy, who was a Utah rancher also known for borrowing other people's bovines.

Butch bought a ranch near Dubois, Wyoming, off the proceeds of the San Miguel robbery, but the fun of robbing banks, and the interesting company that came with it, drew him back to that line of work. He ran a collection racket in Wyoming and was eventually arrested for stealing horses in Lander. For this he had to sit a spell in the Wyoming State Prison, which was considered a good break compared to what was usually done to horse thieves in Wyoming—and remains on the books to this day (yeah, you steal a man's horse and we might hang ya).

It was common for western towns and their sheriffs to turn a blind eye to a man's brushes with the law in other places, provided the outlaw did not break the law nearby. Wyoming stands alone as being an entire state that did this, at least in Butch's case. He was let out of prison early after promising Wyoming's Governor Will Richards that he would not break the law in his state again.

Butch hooked up with Harry Longabaugh, a man who commonly went by the nickname Sundance after being arrested and spending time in the Sundance, Wyoming, jail. Together they formed the backbone of a group known as The Wild Bunch, who robbed banks and trains in states around Wyoming. Known to all—including those he robbed—as affable and gregarious, his exploits were regaled in the eastern press as something more akin to a comic strip than grand theft. The group would meet at their favorite hideout, about halfway between Fremont Canyon and Ten Sleep Canyon. They would rob something, separate for a given time, then meet back up again to plan another robbery. This continued until Butch screwed up and robbed a Union Pacific train outside of Tipton, Wyoming, breaking his agreement with the governor and starting a manhunt.

Butch, Sundance, and the latter's girlfriend, Etta Place, then fled to Argentina. The same line of work came easy to the gringos while in South America. They actually had their biggest robbery ever at a bank in southern Chile, and were known to hang out in the cow towns of Patagonia.

Though in the award-winning film *Butch Cassidy and the Sundance Kid* (highly recommended), the two outlaws die in a shootout with the Bolivian Army in 1908, there is no real evidence that the men shot were Butch and Sundance. In fact, there is plenty of evidence the two men came back to the United States, with Butch living as an auto mechanic in Spokane, Washington. Numerous people claim Butch returned to his beloved Lander, Wyoming, to search the Mary's Lake area (5 miles north of Sinks Canyon) for gold and cash he had stashed away. Among others to have seen him was his doctor, Francis Smith, who claimed to have given the man a physical and recognized a bullet wound he had stitched up years before. A number of other people claimed to have spent time with Butch, and the general consensus was he died a happy old man in Johnnie, Nevada, around 1945.

Micah Rush jamming his way up Dillingham Blues (5.10b), Bridge Area, Fremont Canyon.

A typical rack for a traditionally protected route starts with a single set of cams, from micro to 3.5, and nuts, micro to large. From there you can add depending on the description, as in hand crack for hand size and so forth. Slings and quickdraws will help eliminate any drag. The standard default is two sets of cams and a set of nuts. For the routes near the bridge, a single 60-meter rope will suffice. If you want to rap into the Honemaster Wall, you will either need to do multiple raps or bring two ropes to get down in one big rappel.

Obviously, as you are already at the top, it is tempting to simply toprope the route rather than lead. It's your choice, but if you want to lead, the standard method is to fix a rappel line to the anchor and take a separate lead line for the climb out. This not only negates the problem of pulling your rope and having it drop into the water, but also gives you a handy support line if you find the route beyond your abilities. Keep in mind you will likely need a second cordelette, or do some jiggery-pockery with the extra bit of fixed line, to build your anchor when you get down to the start of the climb. Oh, and the starts of many of the climbs require you to build an anchor at a ledge or stance above the waterline, so remember that a few extras of various sizes go a long way.

There are a few key points we should make in the matter of safety. The rim of the canyon is abrupt and in some places almost unnoticeable until you are right on it. Pay attention and don't accidentally take one extra step. The same goes for building the anchor; don't forget about the 100-foot void behind you.

The answer to that one question you immediately had is "usually not deep enough." Murphy's Law often applies: If you want to wade across, it's often too deep, but if you want to deep water solo, then it usually isn't deep enough. In some spots there are holes that drop 30 or 40 feet deep, but you cannot be sure your route is above a deep spot. There are often boulders or ledges a foot or two under the surface, and without swimming or wading around, it is almost impossible to tell. The flow of the river changes according to the snow level the previous winter and the amount of water the dam is releasing. This changes daily, so there is no fixed depth anywhere.

Also, keep in mind that a fall from the rim would likely be fatal even if you landed in deep water. For this reason I also consider this a bad place to bring your dog or your toddler. If you do bring the pooch, keep it on the leash. More than one excited dog has run right off the rim. Finally, pay attention when you are building that anchor on top, as rattlesnakes are common here.

One more thing: Due to the limited space to cover all variations on a topo, what you see here covers only the best and most popular of these walls at Fremont Canyon. There are linkups and routes between the lines covered here that are not popular, so don't assume you are off-route when you see a variant bolt out on a blank face. Also, don't assume you got a first ascent because you chose the lower-angle, munge- and mud-filled crack. That route was likely done forty-five years ago and seldom since.

Trip Planning Information

General description: Traditional and sport climbing on granite above the North Platte River in a picturesque gorge

Location: Sandwiched between Pathfinder and Alcova Reservoirs, 35 miles south of Casper

Land managers: Bureau of Land Management (BLM) and Bureau of Reclamation

Fees: None

Climbing seasons: Spring, summer, fall

Camping and hotels: Casper is Wyoming's second-largest metropolis with just over 60,000 people, so it has a host of hotels and motels to take advantage of. There are no hotels near the canyon.

For years people camped along the road between the Bridge Area and the dam, but much of this land along the north side of the road, though not fenced, is owned by the Pathfinder Ranch, and they do not tolerate camping. If you see a sign, heed it, or you might meet with the sheriff. There are BLM open camping spots on the south side of the road in a few places, but if you see a sign saying camping is not allowed, you better go to an official campsite. There are campsites at Wolfpoint Campground on Pathfinder Reservoir or the Weiss Campground near the marina and Honemaster Wall. These sites are inexpensive, and there are kiosks that allow you to self-pay. There is a dumpster and toilet at the Bridge Area parking, and another toilet at the Honemaster/Pathfinder Dam parking area. You are allowed to camp in your car in both lots. Look for something cozy, then please utilize the toilets at the above locations rather than dig a hole in the prairie.

The closest store to the area is Sloanes at the corner of WY 220 and Kortes Road. It has some basic necessities, but for most items you will need to stock up in Casper. As you come into town, WY 220 becomes Cy Avenue, one of the main thoroughfares in the city. There are numerous grocery stores and restaurants on this road. To rinse off that sticky-stinky that comes with camping and climbing, there are showers for a minimal charge at the 5150 Climbing Gym in Casper, or you can swim in one of the reservoirs.

Food: Some supplies can be purchased at Sloanes (see above), but you will want to stock up in Casper for the bulk of your supplies. Casper also has dozens of restaurants if you are sick of cooking.

Guidebooks and other resources: Micah Rush has a very thorough guidebook, *Fremont Canyon and Dome Rock*, to all the routes in the canyon. It can be purchased in Casper at Mountain Sports or at 5150 Climbing Gym. Fremontcanyon.com has some topos, but it is quite dated. As always, Mountain Project has information, though it tends to be more opinion and less topographic, which is not that useful at a rappel-in crag.

Nearby shops and guide services: The climbing shop in Casper is Mountain Sports at 543 S. Center. The climbing gym, 5150, is at 408 N. Beverly and has a somewhat limited amount of gear available. However, the folks that work there are good for information.

As the climbing is accessed from above, it is often difficult to know with certainty where you are along a wall. For this reason a guide makes sense even if you feel qualified to climb at a particular grade. If you think a guide might be useful, then you are in luck. Micah Rush is an AMGA-certified guide, Exum guide, and search-and-rescue team trainer. He is also the author of the definitive guidebook to the area and knows the rock climbs like the back of his hand. Micah can be reached at (307) 267-4815 or wyoboulder@hotmail.com.

Emergency services: Cell service is almost nonexistent in the canyon, but at various places along the rim, you can get a bar or two. Casper and Natrona County have a search-and-rescue group that are best reached with 911. If you need the Natrona County Sheriff's Department, they can be reached at (307) 235-9282. If you are looking for a hospital, the Wyoming Medical Center is at 1233 E. 2nd St. near the center of town.

Restrictions and access issues: Fremont Canyon is managed by both the BLM and the Bureau of Reclamation. Currently there are no restrictions on access for the areas covered in this guide. The Pathfinder Ranch owns much of the land you would be tempted to camp on and does not condone camping.

Finding the cliffs: Fremont Canyon is 35 miles southwest of Casper, which has an airport served by a couple of nationally recognized airlines. The usual car rental companies are there, and if you are flying in, you will need a car to reach the climbing area. There is no public transportation going out to the canyon.

To reach Fremont Canyon by car from Casper, follow WY 220 southwest toward Alcova Reservoir. About 20 miles out of town, depending on where you got on WY 220, take a left onto Kortes Road (#407). Follow this for about 7.5 miles and trend right, then go another 2.7 miles to the obvious bridge over the gorge. Park in the parking area on the north side of the bridge for all of the Bridge Area climbs. The Honemaster Wall is another 3.7 miles west of the bridge and can be reached from a pullout referred to as the Dam Overlook.

If you are coming from the southwest, like from Lander or Laramie, follow US 287/WY 220 en route to Casper. At Muddy Gap Junction, 80 miles from the Lander Bar, set your speedometer to zero. Go 36 miles and take a right onto Pathfinder Road (#409), then go approximately 6 miles to Fremont Canyon Road (#408), where you take a hard left. (A right takes you to the marina for Pathfinder Reservoir and the

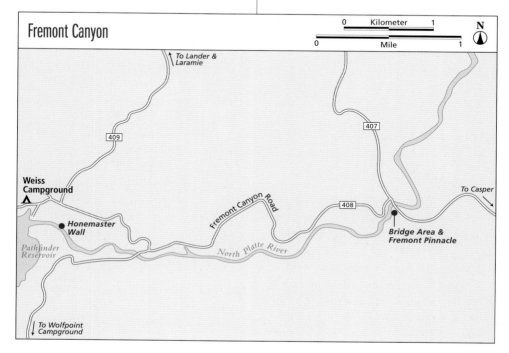

Fremont Canyon

To Lander & Laramie

409

407

Weiss Campground

408

To Casper

Honemaster Wall

Bridge Area & Fremont Pinnacle

Pathfinder Reservoir

North Platte River

Fremont Canyon Road

To Wolfpoint Campground

Weiss Campground.) After 0.1 mile is a right that goes to the Dam Overlook and Honemaster Wall parking. To get to the Bridge Area, continue on Fremont Canyon Road for 3.7 more miles. The parking is obvious on the north side of the bridge.

The Classics

Stone King (5.10a)
Dillingham Blues (5.10b)
Greystoke (5.10d)
All Time Loser (5.11b)
Honemaster (5.11c)
Superman (5.12a)
Gleaming the Cube (5.12a)
Dead Cat in a Top Hat (5.12a)
Winner Take Nothing (5.12a)

Bridge Area

Bridge Area South Face

The following routes are found by walking out to the overlook across the parking lot from the toilet. Go over the railing and look for anchors near the edge. If one isn't there, you will need to build it. When you get to the bottom, you will likely need to build another anchor to ascend from. The routes are listed from right to left as you look into the canyon, or as a climber from left to right.

1. Peterman Variation★★ (5.7) 50 feet. Build an anchor on the west end of the overlook and rappel to a ledge 50 feet below. Climb the broken crack system that leads up and to the left.

2. Peterman Route★★ (5.6) 50 feet. Climb over the west side of the overlook railing

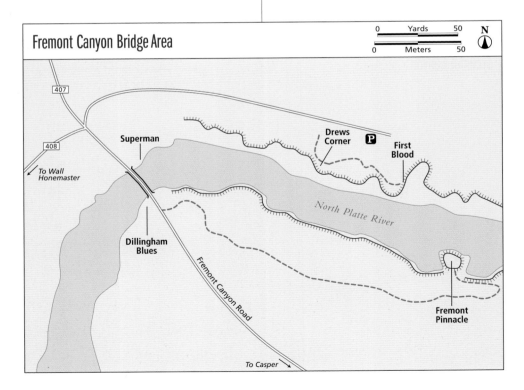

Fremont Canyon Bridge Area

0 Yards 50
0 Meters 50
N

407

408

To Wall
Honemaster

Superman

Dillingham
Blues

Drews
Corner

P

First
Blood

North Platte River

Fremont Canyon Road

Fremont
Pinnacle

To Casper

and rappel to a large triangular ledge. Fun climbing up a crack in a dihedral.

3. Walk on the Wild Side★ (5.11c) 75 feet. Rappel to a large ledge near the waterline, then ascend a corner. Clip a bolt to reach an arête and then work over small overhangs to the top. The route going left, Ingin' Scout, is easier at 5.10a, but sparse on gear (as in X). **FA:** Kelly Moore.

4. Easy Day for a Lady★★ (5.9) 75 feet. Rap to the lowest point below the obvious wide crack. The rack is 3.5 to #5 or #6, but the climbing is not pure offwidth. Use various holds to get out.

5. Drews Corner★★ (5.9) 50 feet. Rap from the front of the railing to a thin horizontal crack halfway down the wall. Climb the crack and arête to the top. Begins with small nuts and micro-cams and widens to hands. Unique.

6. Going, Going, Gone★ (5.12c) 80 feet. Rap from the east front corner of the overlook to a small ledge just above the waterline. Climb thin cracks on bolts and gear. **FA:** Steve Bechtel.

7. Nubus★ (5.10c) 80 feet. Rappel from the top of #6, trending rappelers right to a ledge just above waterline. Climb through cracks and edges trending left at the top. Can be dirty. **FA:** Paul Piana and Steve Petro.

8. B-25★★ (5.9) 80 feet. Find the bush 50 feet east of the overlook to build the rappel anchor, then rap from bolts to a large ledge slightly right. Ascend the corner on hands, then move back right to the rim.

9. Scrape With Death★★★ (5.10b) 80 feet. Instead of trending left to the tree on B-25, trend right in a splitter crack for the better finish. **FA:** Steve Petro.

Bridge Area Central

10. Broken Hand Fitzgerald (5.11b) 80 feet. From the B-25 ledge, climb up and right for 40 feet to a ledge, then continue on with a thin crack to the top. Originally done in two pitches. **FA:** Steve Petro.

11. Stone King★★★ (5.10a) 75 feet. Build an anchor above a large corner (Hemeteria Left) that is about 50 feet right of the bush above B-25. The gravel from the parking lot comes close to the rim here. Rap 80 feet to a large ledge. Climb up and left to the arête, where you will find a hand crack that takes you to a ledge and then to the rim. **FA:** Arno Ilgner.

12. Captain America★ (5.11d) 75 feet. From that same ledge climb straight up to a thin crack that splits the face. Takes lots of small wires and micro-cams. **FA:** Arno Ilgner.

13. Hemeteria Left★★ (5.8) 50 feet. Jam and lieback up the obvious dihedral from a ledge.

14. Hemeteria Right★ (5.9) 50/80 feet. Ascend from the previous route's ledge or from the ledge at the base of Stone King and Captain America on edges with a crack for protection.

15. Ghost Buster (5.10c) 80 feet. Build an anchor 10 feet east of Hemeteria Right above a large corner, then rappel to the large white ledge. Ascend the left crack in the corner. This one can be dirty.

16. Greystoke★★★ (5.10d) 80 feet. One of the classics of the area. Ascend the face climbers-right of Ghost Buster to a large corner. Follow this dihedral to the rim, putting you about 10 feet right of the rappel. Use thin gear low, then larger nuts high. **FA:** Arno Ilgner.

17. Wild Flower Arête (5.11d) 80 feet. Climb the thinly protected face to the base of the Greystoke dihedral, then move right to the arête, clipping just three bolts to reach the rim. A little spicy.

The following two routes are just out of sight on the topo, but are not difficult to find and follow.

18. First Blood★★★ (5.10b) 85 feet. Thirty feet east of the top of Greystoke, find a bolted anchor in a notch for First Blood. Use this to get to the talus field just above waterline. The line follows the overhanging hand crack in the corner. **FA:** Arno Ilgner.

19. Gleaming the Cube★★★ (5.12a) 80 feet. A Fremont classic. From higher on the talus, climb up and left, then straight up the face. A #2 and #3 cam helps, plus one wide hand-size piece to reach the first bolt, then seven quickdraws. **FA:** Steve Petro.

Bridge Area Right

Bridge Area North Side

The following routes are under the bridge on the north (south-facing) side of the canyon. Most people use a steel crossbeam as an anchor and feel little need to back it up. Again, routes are from right to left as you look down into the canyon.

20. Morning Sickness★★★ (5.11d) 85 feet. You can rap off the bridge and do a traversing pitch (short) to reach this route and the next two, or you can build an anchor above and rap to the ledge. For Morning Sickness descend below the ledge for a short traverse pitch, then climb over a bulge and up the crack. This is the crux. Most people build a belay on the small ledge and do the obvious wide crack from there. Once even with Flare to Meddling, most people use both cracks, so it's not as offwidthy as you might think. A rack of fingers to offwidth is needed. **FA:** Arno Ilgner.

21. Flare to Meddling★★ (5.11b) 70 feet. From the ledge ascend the finger crack just left of the arête. **FA:** Steve Petro.

22. Donkey Kong★ (5.9) 70 feet. Better than it looks, but can be dirty after a big rain. Climb the obvious dihedral from the ledge. Hand- to offwidth-size gear.

Bridge Area North Side

23. Starman 8 (5.10a) 70 feet. Directly below the bridge find a hand crack coming up from a small ledge. This route can be dirty after the winter runoff.

24. Superman★★★ (5.12a) 70 feet. Very popular double finger crack. Though the photo is a bit distorted, you can reach the base rapping from the bridge. Take a 3.5 Friend and plenty of fingers and micro-cams. You begin from a large ledge that has no bolted anchor. **FA:** Steve Petro. (Trivia: Moments after Petro did the first ascent, his belayer, Todd Skinner, followed; on-sight free solo in the mid-1980s.)

Bridge Area South Side

The following routes are on the north-facing side of the canyon directly across from the previous five climbs. They can be dusty after a big rain or the spring melt. Again, the bridge beams make a nice anchor point.

Note that a few of the climbs exceed a doubled-up 60-meter rope for the rappel.

25. Prince of Darkness (5.10a) 120 feet. Follow the corner, climbers-right, through a couple overhangs. **FA:** Steve Petro.

26. Seven Heroes (5.11b) 120 feet. The corner just right of Prince of Darkness. Use lots of finger-size gear. **FA:** Steve Petro.

27. All Time Loser★★★ (5.11b) 75 feet. Rap to a ledge with a single bolt that can be backed up with a 2.5-inch cam. Climb out the roof and up the right crack, using finger, hand, and fist technique. **FA:** Arno Ilgner.

28. Dillingham Blues★★★ (5.10b) 75 feet. Another Fremont classic. Use finger- and hand-size gear to climb the double cracks. **FA:** Arno Ilgner.

29. Escape Route (5.8) 85 feet. If you find yourself intimidated by the previous two,

Bridge Area South Side

traverse left and up the corner that is Bridge Route.

30. Short 'n Sassy★★ (5.11d) 125 feet. From the ledge traverse right to a finger crack, then follow it to the next ledge where you can meet up with Bridge Route. Takes small wires and micro-cams, plus a quickdraw for a bolt. **FA:** Steve Petro.

31. Bridge Route★ (5.8) 125 feet. From the ledge just above the water, climb up and then trend right to the dihedral.

32. Bushwacker★★ (5.9) 125 feet. Again start from that low ledge but trend left to a thin crack on a face. Lots of medium wired nuts are useful.

33. Raw Deal★★★ (5.13b) 125 feet. An amazing finger crack that angles into the wall. If the water is high, you will have to start from a hanging belay, but often you can just rappel from a boulder to the talus slope right

above the water. The route is just around the arête and thus not pictured. There is a bolted anchor above the business, so you can work it without doing the easy finish to the rim. **FA:** Steve Bechtel.

Fremont Pinnacle

Fremont Pinnacle was likely the first feature climbed in Fremont Canyon. Reach it by skirting the fence then walking along a trail near the south rim of the canyon. The obvious cleft in the wall behind the pinnacle can be 4th-classed to the bottom of the canyon and base of the spire. There are also rappel bolts that allow you to reach the base of the South Chimney route. Locals like to rig a static across the span and Tyrolean to get out (you best learn how to do that before trying it here). Reach Dead Cat in a Top Hat and Silver Heels by rappelling to the start from the summit.

Karl Rigrish and Micah Rush on Dead Cat in a Top Hat (5.12a), Fremont Pinnacle, Fremont Canyon.

34. South Chimney (5.8) 70 feet. This route follows the obvious weakness of large holds and blocks that faces the main rim of the south side. The easiest way to get to many of the routes on the north face of the Pinnacle is to climb this route (mixed rack) and rap in from the top. This was likely the first climb established in Fremont Canyon.

35. Dancin' on the End of a Rope★★ (5.11d) 80 feet. Traverse behind the pinnacle almost to the water's edge to find this face and arête. Small wired nuts supplement the four bolts for protection. **FA:** Ken Driese.

36. Dead Cat in a Top Hat★★★ (5.12a) 85 feet. Rappel off the west side of the pinnacle's summit to a small ledge. Nine or ten bolts, plus a #2 and a couple micro-cams, are the gear. **FA:** Steve Petro.

37. Silver Heels★★★ (5.12b) 90 feet. Rappel off the north side of the pinnacle to a ledge just above the waterline. There are multiple bolts on the pitch, but you will want micro- to midsize cams and midsize nuts to go with those quickdraws. **FA:** Arno Ilgner.

38. North Face★ (5.10a) 90 feet. Traverse the ledge system from the east end of the pinnacle to a large ledge, then climb the hand crack in the corner to the summit. Take lots of midsize cams and small to mid-size nuts. **FA:** Kevin Moore.

39. Active Duty (5.11b) 80 feet. Climb a varied line with a mix of bolts and small gear to the summit. **FA:** Kevin Moore.

Fremont Pinnacle

Descent

34

XX

39

38

37

XX

36

35

Micah Rush and Mandy Fabel on Honemaster (5.11c), Honemaster Wall, Fremont Canyon.

Pathfinder Dam
(aka Honemaster Wall)

This wall is just below the Pathfinder Dam and can be somewhat photogenic when large amounts of water are being released from the reservoir. To find it, drive west from the bridge about 3.7 miles to a parking lot on the left. If you reach the four-way intersection you have gone too far. Park and follow the Overlook Trail for a hundred yards, then pick up a faint climber's trail that goes about 120 yards to the rim. As a point of reference, there is currently a solar-powered camera, owned by the Bureau of Reclamation, aimed at the dam from the top of Honemaster. The top

of these routes are about 75 yards southeast of the official overlook point that comes complete with seats and railing.

40. Caffeine Crack★ (5.9) 40 feet. Starting from a ledge high on the wall, climb the obvious hand crack. Fun but short.

41. Winner Take Nothing★★★ (5.12a) 40 feet. Again short, but if you link it with Blazing Saddles, you get an incredible 5.12 pitch with the sting at the end. Takes small nuts and tiny cams. **FA:** Steve Bechtel.

42. Blazing Saddles★★ (5.11b/5.12a) 140 feet. Originally broken into three pitches, we list it as one biggie. Lower all the way down the wall with fourteen quickdraws and a light

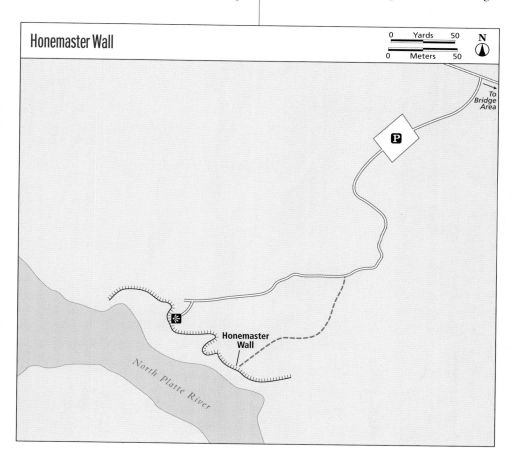

Honemaster Wall

Honemaster Wall

rack to a #3 cam, but add a few hand pieces to finish Caffeine Crack or tiny stuff to finish Winner Take Nothing. **FA:** Paula Piana.

43. Golden Staircase★★ (5.11b) 90 feet.
Find a couple bolts just over the rim and climbers-right of the top of the previous three routes. There is a single-bolt anchor on a ledge to begin from about 90 feet down. **FA:** Micah Rush.

44. Honemaster★★★ (5.11c) 150 feet.
Another classic from Paul Piana and Arno Ilgner. Find bolts on the wall behind the small tree, or build an anchor and rap down the obvious corner. The route was originally broken into three pitches, but is now done in two. There is an anchor at the halfway point, making it possible to do this with a single 70-meter rope. Take a couple quickdraws and lots of gear from micro to hand size. **FA:** Paul Piana and Arno Ilgner.

45. Combat Challenge★★ (5.11b) 75 feet.
Rap to the anchor at the ledge halfway down Honemaster, then climb back up on the right side of the arête. A dozen quickdraws will suffice. **FA:** Micah Rush.

46. Turtlehead Trauma★★ (5.11d) 150 feet.
If you have to go, go now, then find rappel bolts 30 feet climbers-right of Honemaster. Rap to the bottom of the wall, either with two ropes or stopping at the Honemaster belay. Ascend the first part of Honemaster, then move right on bolts. Again use the Honemaster belay ledge but climb right past eight bolts to another small ledge. Belay here and climb the crux pitch past five bolts on the headwall. **FA:** Eric Meade and friends.

47. Pacing the Cage (5.11b) 150 feet.
Forty feet climbers-right of Honemaster, this route begins below a couple roofs. The first pitch climbs through the roofs then up a large corner to a ledge halfway. There are five bolts, but you'll need plenty of midsize nuts and small cams. The second pitch continues straight up using a hand crack. Take a double set plus a few extra hand-size cams.

48. Looking for a Place to Happen★ (5.10b)
120 feet. Another 20 feet uphill of Pacing the Cage is this two-pitch climb. It can be dusty over here. Pitch 1 stems up a bolted corner then over a small roof using a hand crack to a bolted anchor. Continue on in the same crack for the second pitch. Take half a dozen quickdraws and small nuts to hand-size pieces. **FA:** Kevin and Marni Seibke.

GRANITE MOUNTAINS

■ **OVERVIEW**

At almost the geographic center of Wyoming are a cluster of domes and rock outcroppings collectively known as the Granite Mountains. At an estimated 2.5 billion years old, the Granite Mountains are likely the oldest rocks in the world that climbers use for recreation. The Granites are actually one of the larger ranges in the state, and it's common for people to break them into separate sections of Split Rock, Hells Gate, and Dome Rock. The areas covered here, Lankin Dome and Cranner Rock, are commonly referred to as Sweetwater Rocks.

These monoliths served as major milestones to the pioneers on the Oregon Trail. In the mid–1800s an estimated 400,000 immigrants, bound for Oregon, Washington, California, and the Great Salt Lake Valley, passed through the dangerous Wyoming Territory. Almost all of them came through the Granite Mountains, crossing the Sweetwater River a number of times en route to South Pass and the various divides that came farther along the trail. The Granite Mountains, then referred to as Split Rock, were a place to fill tankards with water, let the stock graze on thick grass, and, with the wagons circled, perhaps get a little rest.

For climbers the area is a place to get a little exercise. The climbing varies from low-angle friction to incredibly steep crack and face climbing. Despite the fact that one of the two crags is "roadside," this area is a great place to get away from crowds. In a book that is about far-flung climbing locations in the nation's least populous state, this is probably the most remote area. Other than Yellowstone, there is no region in Wyoming that has fewer people per square mile than the Granite Mountains. Cell service is almost nil, and passersby can be measured in days, if not weeks. There may be a ranch house 8 miles away, but the travel to get to it might require 30 miles of rough driving. If you get stuck or have an accident, you are in a bit of a mess. Best to just keep your wits about you and not screw up.

One reason there are so few people here is the harshness of the climate. Winter nights go well below zero, summer afternoons soar into triple digits, and thunderstorms abound with hail and lightning. This may be the windiest place in the windiest state in the union, and the summit of Lankin Dome is likely the windiest spot in this place. On any given day it can snow or the temperature can be above 100°F. That said, bring plenty of water and shorts, plus a hat and down coat, because anything is possible on any outing.

Also of note, ticks are common in the spring, mosquitoes can swarm in early summer, and prairie rattlesnakes can carpet the area on a warm day. Again, keep your wits about you, and remember that this knowledge is not a reason avoid the area. To the contrary, it is what draws us, and few others, to these wild places.

The Climbing and Gear

This is granite slab and crack climbing. Most routes on Lankin require at minimum a single set of cams to 3 inches and nuts, plus quickdraws and some long slings. A double set is often useful so that you have the exact right piece for that key placement. Expect lots of smearing on those toes and for the bolts to be spaced out. Oh, and about that . . . the bolts are ⅜-inch diameter, but most are over twenty years old and showing the years in the elements. Keep in mind that Lankin Dome is not a place you want to be with thunderstorms in the area. Not only is

Climbers on Planet Earth (5.11c), Lankin Dome, Granite Mountains.

it a giant lightning rod, but the runout slabs could be deadly with a thin layer of water.

At Cranner Rock you usually can get by with a double set of cams plus a few extras of your favorite size. A single 60-meter rope is enough to get you down.

Trip Planning Information

General description: Granite face and crack climbing, sometimes with long runouts, with few others at the crag

Location: The very middle of Wyoming, north of US 287

Land manager: Bureau of Land Management (BLM) Lander Field Office

Fees: None

Climbing seasons: Late spring, summer, early fall

Camping and hotels: There are no hotels within 50 driving miles of the Lankin Dome or Cranner Rock. Camping is free on BLM land for up to two weeks. For Lankin Dome most people camp at the trailhead in Nolen Pocket to get an early start. For Cranner Rock it is actually possible to camp in the meadow just north of the crag. From the highway find a BLM access road about half a mile west of the Cranner Rock parking area. Go north, and after 0.25 mile take your first right onto the unmarked Oregon Trail. Drive east and then pull off when you get near the rock. Don't drive too far on this road or you will end up on Split Rock Ranch property, and they do not want you there. If you have a dog, keep it on a leash or nearby as cowboys have the right to shoot any dog disturbing their cattle. Also watch for snakes; snout bites are common when our fuzzy friends go poking around the sage.

Food: There are no food services of any kind within 60 miles of this area. Before going to the Granite Mountains, you should stock up on supplies in Casper, Rawlins, or Lander.

Guidebooks and other resources: The book in your hands is the only source in print. Greg Collins and Vance White put a section on the Granite Mountains in *Lander Rock*, but it has gone out of print. Mountain Project has a small database of the thousands of climbs that exist in the area.

Nearby shops and guide services: The closest shop is Wild Iris Mountain Sports in Lander. If you want a guide, Micah Rush from Casper, who works with Exum Mountain Guides, is the best. Micah can be reached at (307) 267-4815 or wyoboulder@hotmail.com.

Emergency services: You are on your own. Cranner Rock is evenly split in Fremont County and Natrona County, while Lankin Dome is in Fremont County, but you cannot get cell reception to call for a rescue from the base of either rock. You can get Verizon access from the top of Lankin Dome. If you are not on the summit of this high point, your best bet is to get to Jeffrey City, half a dozen miles west of the area, and contact Fremont County from there at (307) 332-5611. Jeffrey City has a volunteer fire department, if that helps. Honestly, don't get hurt out here.

Restrictions and access issues: There is an enormous amount of existing climbing and climbing potential in the Granite Mountains, but much of the access to the area is via private land. The private land is intermingled with Wyoming state land and federal BLM land. Signs are often posted that read "public and private lands beyond this sign are open for recreation," but then later the landowner has second thoughts and recreationists get a bad name for trespassing. In short, there are access issues concerning private land that have not been resolved. For that reason, we recommend you only climb on Lankin Dome and Cranner Rock until these issues can be settled.

Also, following the road system described here for getting to Lankin Dome has so far proven to be an access-friendly approach. However, the Nolen Pocket road briefly passes through private land. If you come across a sign that says No Trespassing, change your plans. To boot, taking a direct route toward the south face of the dome from the highway will likely get you a meeting with the sheriff. Please abide by the landowners' requests.

Nolen Pocket, where the parking location described below is located, lies on BLM land and is legal for camping up to fourteen days. Lankin Dome is in the Split Rock Wilderness Study Area, which means all the "wilderness area" rules apply without congressional approval (hmm). Among those rules is one that says you are not allowed to use a power drill.

Getting there: This is another area where you will need a car. Actually, you might want to make it a four-wheel-drive car. The Granite Mountains are 58 miles east of Lander, 65 miles north of Rawlins, and 65 miles southwest of Casper. The closest thing to a town nearby is Jeffrey City, which does not have a grocery store but does have a bar (this is Wyoming, after all). The directions to Lankin Dome specifically are below.

The Classics

Lankin Dome

The Sky Route (5.10b, 5.8 obl., R)
Venus and Mars (5.10a, 5.9 obl., R)
Red Nations (5.11c, 5.11a obl., PG.13)
Planet Earth (5.11c, 5.10d obl., R)

Cranner Rock

Jaw Bone (5.7)
Owl Corner (5.10a)
Geophysical (5.11d)
Cranner Roof Crack (5.13a)

Lankin Dome

The smooth, clean faces of Lankin Dome rise some 1,200 feet above the surrounding prairie (7,621 feet in elevation). This rock is a long ways from nowhere, but as Lander is the most likely alternative climbing destination in the general area, we will give directions from its most prestigious location.

From the Lander Bar, drive south 8.2 miles to the junction of US 287 and WY 28 and go east toward Rawlins on US 287 for 56 miles (64.2 miles from the Lander Bar), watching for Agate Flats Road on the left. Take Agate Flats Road northeast, passing over the unmarked Oregon Trail, Pony Express Route, Sweetwater River, and a few cattle guards. At 5.2 miles from the highway, take a hard right just after a cattle guard. The road goes east for 0.2 mile and then turns 90 degrees left. Keep following, passing a fence, creek, and water tank at 6.9 miles from the highway. The creek is the driving crux. Also make sure you leave the gate as you found it. Keep on the road for another 0.5 mile (7.4 miles from the highway), passing a right

Heard in the Wind

The Oregon Trail and the Handcarters

The 2,200-mile Oregon Trail has become synonymous with the growth of the United States. Between 1830 and 1870, almost half a million people passed beneath Lankin Dome and the Granite Mountains en route to the new American territories of California, Washington, Utah, and Oregon. The hardships of this trek were great for all involved, but no group suffered even close to the level of the Mormon Handcarters.

The Mormons, for reasons real, fabricated, and always unconstitutional, were pretty heavily persecuted in Illinois and Missouri. After the murder of their founder, Joseph Smith, their new leader, Brigham Young, began looking for other parts of North America that would be safe for his people to call "home." In 1847 Young led about 2,200 Mormons on the trail that had been laid out by people immigrating to Oregon Territory. There is a lot of evidence that Young intended to make Vancouver Island the new homeland, but the hardships of the trek through Wyoming took a toll on the Mormons.

By the time they reached Fort Bridger (west of Wild Iris), Young could see his people had been through enough. He turned to a more southern route, recently followed by the Donner Party, and then decided on the banks of the Great Salt Lake as their homeland. Young sent word back to the rest of the Mormons that he had found "the place," and with that 45,000 more immigrants made their way west to the planned country of Deseret (later to be called the state of Utah, but that's another story).

Of those 45,000 immigrants, there was a group of about 3,000 who were too poor to afford horses, mules, or oxen. This group has become known as the Handcarters, and there is a monument and museum dedicated to them about 18 miles east of Lankin Dome. The Handcarters essentially built smaller wagons that they could pull across the country themselves. A sick relative or infant was thrown in the cart with the dishes, bedding, and farming tools that would be useful when they reached the promised land. Those able then pulled and pushed the cart across the prairie. Through mud and snow, up steep hills and braking down the other side, the people were the beasts of burden.

Two groups, the Martin and Willie companies, left St. Louis later in the summer than was recommended. They ran low on supplies near Fort Laramie, then after going south at Fort Caspar (Casper, Wyoming) were caught in an October blizzard. Crossings of the Sweetwater River near Lankin Dome were particularly hard as blocks of ice cut the skin and the wet, muddy conditions added cases of frostbite and hypothermia.

A rescue party was sent from Utah with clothing, wagons, and fresh food, but it took weeks to make it through the 2-foot-deep snow. The rescuers eventually met the Handcarters somewhere near South Pass (Wild Iris). The Handcarters were placed into wagons, finally reaching Salt Lake City on November 30, 1856. Of the 400 or so members of the Martin and Willie companies, most were frostbitten and a number lost limbs. In total 145 died in the Wyoming blizzard on the banks of the Sweetwater River.

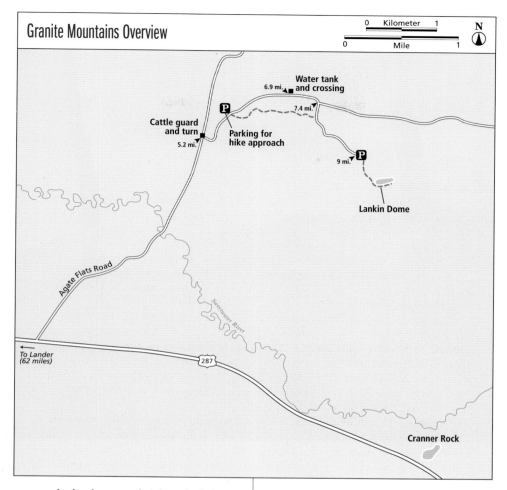

0 Kilometer 1

0 Mile 1

N

Water tank
6.9 mi. and crossing

P

7.4 mi.

Cattle guard
and turn

Parking for
hike approach

5.2 mi.

9 mi.

P

Lankin Dome

Agate Flats Road

Sweetwater River

To Lander
(62 miles)

287

Cranner Rock

turn, and take the second right, which lines you up with Lankin Dome. Follow this into Nolen Pocket, trending right after another 1.2 miles and then park in the trees. If you see a No Trespassing sign at the aforementioned fence or water tank, or if you don't want to make the stream crossing in your Prius, park 0.25 mile back down the road and walk to Nolen Pocket by skirting around the rocks to the south. This adds a little over a mile to the approach. Do not park in the middle of the road.

Keep in mind that "four-wheeling" across the sage is illegal and could cost access to this climbing area. For what it's worth, the

majority of this route is passable in a two-wheel-drive car, provided you don't worry a lot about your two-wheel-drive car and it doesn't rain while you are in there. The water tank at 6.9 miles, where things can get tricky with private property, tends to be the crux. If it's been rainy, you could be out of luck.

From the parking location in Nolen Pocket, hike up granite slabs through scrubby pine, aiming for the saddle between the west end of Lankin Dome and the prominent rock outcropping to its right (west). There is no obvious trail, but it's easy route finding if you walk on the slabs. Obviously, sticky-rubber approach shoes help. The gap between

Lankin Dome.

the west end of Lankin Dome and the rock outcropping is also where the descent route (aka Cowboy Route) ends, so you will likely come back to this point and could rack up and leave packs here. However, there is still a quarter mile or so of hiking, so you will want to carry at least your approach shoes with you.

Pass through the gap and descend along the base of the wall in a scrub-filled gully. Getting away from the wall on granite slabs south of the gully makes for easier walking. At the first real clearing, you are below The Sky Route. Another hundred yards and you are at the base of Tree Route and other climbs.

1. Cowboy Route (4th class) This is the west ridge of the dome. It's 4th class, with the most difficult portion, the only portion where you might touch your hands to the rock, being in the first couple hundred feet (last couple hundred when descending). After that it's exposed walking along the ridge to the summit. "Cowboy Route" is likely a misnomer for the first ascensionists of the dome. A better name would have been "Prehistoric Route," as people have probably gone up this ridge for the last 12,000 years. **FA:** Ugg and Uhmpapka.

2. The Sky Route★★★ (5.10b, 5.8 obl., R) 7 pitches: 5.5, 5.6, 5.7, 5.8, 5.5, 5.8, 5.10b.

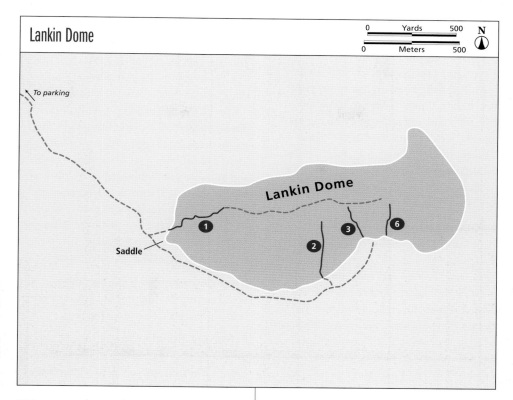

To parking

Lankin Dome

Saddle

1   3   6

2

This is a great route that goes straight to the summit of the dome. The pitches are quite runout by modern standards, sometimes 40 feet or more, but the cruxes tend to have a bolt nearby. There are only a total of twenty-three bolts in the route's 600-plus feet of climbing, but if you have climbed in Tuolumne or Joshua Tree, you won't be rattled. There are ledges or large stances at all the belays, and all the anchors except the summit are bolted. A rack of a single set of camming devices from 0.5 to 3, plus a few Stoppers, along with eight quickdraws and a few long slings is sufficient. Find the first pitch, the shortest of all at about 100 feet, at a right-facing corner with three cracks. There is a tree up and left of the pitch, about 85 feet up the wall. The route goes more or less straight up from the top of pitch 1. Pitch 5 passes through the roof to the left of the belay, and

the last pitch has an alternative 5.4 finish (left to the corner) rather than the straight up 5.10. There are a number of cracks and fissures at the summit to build a belay in. The descent is to the west (climbers-left) on the Cowboy Route and is 4th class. Sticky rubber on your approach shoes will help a lot, or just do it in your rock shoes. **FA:** Greg Collins, Sue Miller, and Mike Wood.

3. Star Jumper★★ (5.9, 5.9 obl., R) 5 pitches: 5.8, 5.8, 5.8, 5.9, 5.9. Find the start to this climb left of a large flake that vaguely resembles an elephant reaching forward with his trunk (much like the stars look like Cassiopeia). Though the climbing is mostly protected by bolts, some of the belays require gear. Take some long slings and a single rack up to hands with a few small nuts. Expect runouts for some of the more difficult moves. A rope less than 60 meters in length might require a bit of simulclimbing. **FA:** Richard and Catherine Collins.

There are a host of pitches bolted, and partially bolted, between Star Jumper and Rat-Route, though none are recommended. The following routes begin by hiking up into the cleft in the center of the dome. This gradually gets steeper to 4th class (has been ascended to the big limber pine by a Labrador retriever). The second pitch of the next three routes begins at the big tree.

4. Rat-Route (5.10, 5.10b obl.) 3 pitches: 4th class, 5.10c, 5.10a. Wide crack climbing with a good supply of guano. Ascend the 4th class to the tree. For the very long pitch 2, continue up the cleft then out a ledge system to the left. Climb the crack up and back right. Bring lots of slings and wide gear. Belay on a ledge in the crack. Pitch 3 continues on easier but wide ground to broken rock near the summit. **FA:** Phil Powers and friends.

5. Tree Route★★ (5.9, 5.9 obl.) 4 pitches: 4th class, 5.7, 5.9, 5.7. This route follows the crack and chimney that splits the dome in half. Climb the 4th class to the pine tree, then get technical. Lots of hand-size and some wide gear is useful. If it is near your limit, take more than a double set of cams, as you will be building anchors as well as protecting the climbing. A #5 cam (or two) can be useful on the third pitch. Climb the chimney to a ledge. Pitch 4 ascends easier ground to the summit. The route can be rappelled using chockstones and such. The rappels move a bit from time to time and often need to be rebuilt.

6. Red Nations★★★ (5.11c, 5.11a obl., PG13) 3 pitches: 4th class, 5.11b, 5.11c. Everyone who has done this route loves it. Ascend the 4th class to the tree, then get on with the long second pitch by going up and right into

a corner system right of the Tree Route. Go straight up for many bolts and a few gear placements, including a wide hand-size cam placement under a small roof. Find a three-bolt anchor on a small ledge. Pitch 3 is another rope stretcher and the crux. Trend up and left clipping many bolts. Belay on the large ledge with your own anchor. Take a set of nuts, a set of cams to 3 inches, and at least sixteen quickdraws. A 70-meter rope is advised. The route can be rappelled with two 70s, but it requires some swinging around. Better to rap the Tree Route or walk off on the Cowboy Route. **FA:** Greg Collins and Sue Miller.

The following routes begin on the easy and well-featured slab right of the 4th-class cleft used for the previous three routes.

7. Mercury Rising★ (5.10+, 5.10b obl., R) 4 pitches: 5.0, 5.10b, 5.10d. 5.8. Climb the featured but unprotectable slab to a ledge shared by Planet Earth. There is a tree and a 3.5-inch crack to build the belay from. Pitch 2 climbs up and slightly left past well-spaced bolts to a small ledge. Pitch 3 continues on with a crack on steeper ground. The crux is above the crack. Belay at a stance and then climb the final runout pitch to the right side of the large block. An easy scramble around this puts you on top. **FA:** Peter and Molly Absolon.

8. Planet Earth★★ (5.11c, 5.10d obl., R) 4 pitches: 5.0, 5.7, 5.11c (A1), 5.9. The third pitch is three stars of engaging climbing, but the other pitches are so much easier that the lack of consistency makes it a two-star climb. Ascend the easy slab to a ledge shared by Mercury Rising and protect with a wide hand-size cam and the tree. Climb the shallow corner above on small gear, then run it out to the bolt and on to the next ledge. Pitch 3 hits hard at the start. The first ascensionist says 5.11a and we say 5.12a,

Lankin Dome

← 4th Class

P2 anchor

Approach

The bottom portions of the climbs are obscured by the ridge between the photographer and the base of the dome.

so we will settle in between with 11c. Do the hard move into the dihedral, then work up it with various thought-provoking and sometimes spacey gear placements. High in the second dihedral of the pitch, clip a bolt and move onto the face, which has some very committing moves. After the third bolt (that's five total) on the face, move up and left and onto a comfy ledge. A double set of cams with extra 0.5 micro-cams and eight to ten slings is recommended. The final pitch climbs 5.9 right off the belay, then a bolt is clipped and a long runout ensues. A micro-cam gets you to the second bolt, and a 5.8 move 30 feet above keeps you on your toes. Belay off gear just below the summit. **FA:** Greg Collins and friends.

9. Venus and Mars★★★ (5.10a, 5.9 obl., R) 4 pitches: 5.5, 5.9, 5.10a, 5.8. Perhaps the most consistent of all the routes on the right side of the dome. Find the start about 60

feet left of the large block leaning against the wall. This climb requires a solid head for climbing above your gear at the grade. Make sure your rack includes micro-nuts. A bolt (about 25 feet up) protects a move down low on pitch 1, then climb to a ledge with a bolted belay. Pitch 2 climbs over a bulge with some bolts, then makes a long unprotected run into a bowl right of a strange area of featured rock. Protect in the roof and climb left to a natural belay in the broken ground. Pitch 3 climbs up and right over bulges with bolts not always where you would like to have them (nearby). Get some gear in a thin crack and move up and left to a double bolt belay on a ledge. Pitch 4 continues on runout ground with small gear in places and big runouts in most. Belay below the big block above. If you are bothered by exposed 3rd class, belay a short pitch around the corner to the right. The straight up crack is 5.8. **FA:** Greg Collins and Rob Hess.

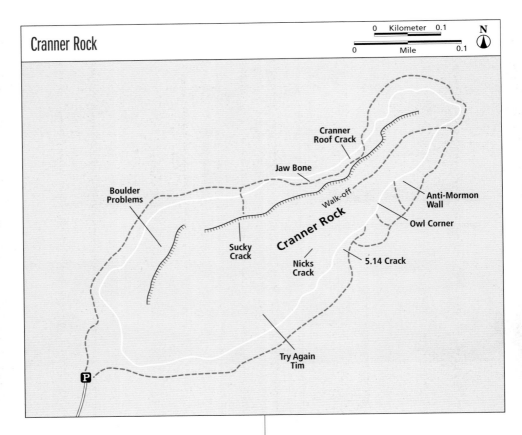

Cranner Roof Crack

Jaw Bone

Boulder Problems

Walk-off

Cranner Rock

Anti-Mormon Wall

Owl Corner

Sucky Crack

Nicks Crack

5.14 Crack

Try Again Tim

Cranner Rock

Like Lankin Dome, Cranner Rock is part of the Granite Mountains and was a stop on the Oregon Trail and later the Pony Express. It also became the site of a stage stop and official US post office for the ranchers of central Wyoming. The rock is the same high-quality granite as Lankin Dome, but the climbs are all short, single-pitch affairs and usually a bit steeper than the bigger climbs on Lankin.

This small dome is obvious from the Split Rock rest area and historical marker off the north side of US 287. Find it about 8 miles west of Muddy Gap Junction or 7.5 miles east of Agate Flats Road. Unmaintained trails circle the dome. Watch for snakes.

Carry a double set of cams and some Stoppers, plus slings and a fistful of quickdraws, and then pick your rack according to what you see on the crack. Throwing a few extra hand-size pieces in won't hurt. The climbs are short enough that a small load of gear usually suffices, but remember that some of the routes do not have anchors on top and thus require you to have some spare stuff to build one. Take a stick clip, if for no other reason than to lift rattlesnakes away from your pack. The standard descent is to walk off to the east.

Vance White sails off Cranner Roof Crack (5.13a), Cranner Rock, Granite Mountains.

North Side Climbs

Getting shade until late afternoon, these routes are often climbed in midsummer. From the parking area, walk to the information plaques then continue on, hopping over the fence and onto BLM territory. The boulders making up the base of the rock to the right of the "trail" have a number of fun problems. The cow/climber/pronghorn trail fades at times, but it's easy to just wander through the sage trending toward the crag.

The routes on the northwest face of Cranner Rock go into the sun in midafternoon.

Ty's Corner Area

1. Sucky Crack (aka Ty's Corner)★★ (5.11b) 50 feet. This is the obvious flared hand crack that runs up the right side of the wall in a corner next to a blunt arête. Take hand and thin hands pieces plus nuts. **FA:** Ty Mack.

2. Ali Babba and the Forty Thieves★ (5.11d) 50 feet. Beginning with a V4 boulder problem, climb into the finger- to hand-size crack that trends up and right to an anchor. It's best to stick clip the one bolt to protect the problem. Finger- and hand-size gear after that. **FA:** Tom Rangitsch.

3. Matt's Finger Crack (5.12d) 50 feet. A Matt Wendling testpiece. The opening section is protected with a bolt, then it's flared fingers and thin hands to the anchor. Bring lots of small wires and micro-cams. **FA:** Matt Wendling.

Cranner Roof Crack Area

4. Crack 1 (5.9) 65 feet. Up a left-trending corner for half its length, then follow a crack back right. Mostly hand-size gear.

5. Wild Jennies Crack★ (5.8) 65 feet. Climb the right-trending hand and finger crack just right of the large corner system.

6. Cranner Corner (5.7) 65 feet. Ascend into a short chimney, then climb the crack that trends to the left to a ledge and on to a higher set of ledges. Build your own anchor for this one and walk off to the east.

7. Mormon Rut (5.10a) 65 feet. Climb the steep hand crack into the corner then up and left to easier ground.

8. Bush of Ghosts (5.11b) 65 feet. Climb out the big flake, taking care to not get the rope stuck in your cam lobes as you pull onto easier ground. Wide hand- and fist-size cams for the start. **FA:** Mark Stanley.

Cranner Roof Crack Area

9. Springfield Nuclear (5.12a) 50 feet. Running straight up the face right of Jaw Bone to that route's anchor is this thin slab protected by six bolts. **FA:** Vance White and Jason Sloan.

10. Jaw Bone★★★ (5.7) 50 feet. One of the better routes at Cranner and a good novice trad lead if you have plenty of hand-size gear. Traverse into the obvious crack on the ledge—a really fun hand crack that takes hand and wide hand pieces. There is a double ring anchor just right of the crack just below the top.

11. Skeletor (5.10d R) A thin face to a flaring hand crack. Gear is tricky, so most people toprope it off the higher ring anchor. **FA:** Greg Collins and Reave Castenholz.

12. Generic (5.11a R) Forcing yourself farther left—and it is a force—is this thinner, shorter crack with more thin face. Toprope it if you must.

13. Where the Antelope Play★ (5.11a) 75 feet. Ascend on good edges with one distinct crux low, then up a crack that takes solid off-finger and thin hands pieces. Lower from the ASCA anchor above. **FA:** Sam Lightner Jr. and Elyse Guarino.

14. Half-life Arête★ (5.11c) 45 feet. Powerful crimping on the arête leads to an anchor (not seen in the topo). **FA:** Sam Lightner Jr. and Elyse Guarino.

The following routes are in a large alcove between Jaw Bone and the steep wall that is Cranner Roof Crack. In the very back of the alcove is a 5.0 ramp that traverses up onto the ledges above the previous routes. It could be protected with some large cams (#6s), or you could tell yourself it is 4th class. Be careful if you use it to access the top.

15. Western Nuclear★★ (5.11b) 50 feet. On the east face of the alcove, do a boulder problem with some small wires for gear, then move into a flared finger and thin hands crack that arches to the left. Protection is thin and difficult to get in at the start, and with a low crux you could get hurt if one piece popped. Be careful. **FA:** Greg Collins and Phil Peabody.

16. Nucleonics★ (5.11c) 60 feet. Eight feet right of the obvious U-238, climb broken ground with some small cams and a thin hands piece to a line of five bolts that ascends a steep headwall into a dihedral. **FA:** Vance White.

17. U-235 (5.12b) 30 feet. A boulder problem that radiates insecurity. Shares the anchor with the better, and obvious, U-238. **FA:** Greg Collins and Mark Rolofson.

18. U-238★★ (5.11a) 30 feet. A nice finger crack that would get loads of stars if it just continued. There is a double ring anchor directly above it where the arching HEET meets the crack. Takes small wired nuts and mini-cams. **FA:** Greg Collins and Mark Rolofson.

19. HEET★ (5.12b) 35 feet. A flaring, arching crack that takes small gear and then opens to take a few hand-size pieces. Shares the anchor with U-238. **FA:** Greg Collins and Rob Hess.

20. Cranner Slab Crack (5.10d) 80 feet. Thin boulder problem crack to low-angle incipient cracks that are hard to protect.

21. Bushwacker★ (5.10b) 80 feet. A crack in a corner that sometimes requires a vegetable-pull to get through the crux. Find this thing about 20 feet before the obvious, striking line that is Geophysical. It goes up and left, then straight up. Use lots of hand-size and wide hand gear. **FA:** Tony Jewell and Rob Hess.

22. Bushwacker Face★★ (5.10d) 80 feet. About 45 feet up Bushwacker, trend right onto the featured face. There are five bolts to protect you on the way to the anchor shared with Bushwacker. **FA:** Matt Wendling.

23. Geophysical★★★ (5.11d) This is the best route on the dome, and the one that will catch your eye. There is a boulder problem to get you into this crack. Prepare to use all techniques, but mostly hand crack climbing. Two sets of cams will suffice. There is an anchor on top. **FA:** Likely Greg Collins and Reave Castenholz.

24. Skinner Project North (no grade) 50 feet. Start just left of Geophysical and move left into a horribly flared crack, then over a roof to an anchor on the face. Open.

25. Cranner Roof Crack★★★ (5.13a) By all accounts one of the best 5.13 crack lines in the country, and our vote for best 5.13a in the state. Use plenty of small cams and nuts in the start; a 3.5 Friend fits well at a pod. A bolt in the roof keeps your rope out of any cam lobes. Expect to place a few hand or finger pieces after pulling the lip. There is a double bolt station on top to descend from. **FA:** Greg Collins and Reave Castenholz.

26. Darkness (grade unknown) 80 feet. If you like chimneys, and if you are not bothered by raven poop, this one is not to be missed. Like The Outlaw and Josey Wales, two hard face climbs listed below, the start to this is obscured on the topo by the large boulders. Climb about 45 feet before reaching a bulging hand crack. Gear is sparse below that.

27. Gone Fishin'★ (5.13a) 35 feet. Obviously a boulderer's delight, this powerful line begins with a tiny dihedral about 15 feet left of the chimney. Five bolts to a shared ring anchor. **FA:** Steve Babits.

28. Critical Mass★ (5.12d) 35 feet. Another bouldery climb with five bolts to a shared anchor. **FA:** Steve Babits.

29. Juniper Groove★ (5.8) 80 feet. A long hand and wide hand crack in a groove about 40 feet left of the Darkness chimney. Build an anchor on the slabs above and walk off.

About 100 yards east of Juniper Groove, on a wall up the incline with a nice ledge at its base, are two more difficult face climbs.

30. The Outlaw★ (5.12a) The route on the right starts easy and then goes into two distinct cruxes. **FA:** Vance White.

31. Josey Wales★ (5.12c) The left line starts steep, then up a dihedral, then big moves on patina edges of the upper face. **FA:** Vance White.

South Face Climbs

These routes are generally climbed in winter, though in warmer months they do go into shade late in the afternoon. Again, the trail is often indistinct, but wandering through the sage is easy. Walk due east out of the parking lot for about a quarter mile to reach 5.14 Crack Area. Another 150 yards gets you to Owl Corner.

5.14 Crack Area

32. Try Again Tim (5.12c) 30 feet. A hand crack through a roof that tightens to thin hands at the lip. This climb is actually about 100 yards west of the 5.14 Crack. **FA:** Tim Toula.

33. Kirks Corner (5.9) 40 feet. Kirks Corner takes small gear at the bottom, then steepens with good gear in a widening crack. The chimney to its left, Kirks Crack, has been

5.14 Crack Area

downclimbed—not sure if anyone bothered to go up. There is no anchor on top. **FA:** Kirk Billings.

There are multiple runout 5.11s on the slab to the left of Kirks Corner. Farther left is a bolted, open project on a steep red wall.

34. Larry, Curly, and Mo★ (5.11d) 65 feet. Mantle, stem, crimp . . . do what it takes to go up and right past a few bolts with some varied gear placements. You'll have to build an anchor on top.

35. Unanswered Call (5.11b) 60 feet. There can be a lot of poop on this and the next route. Thin nuts help up high.

36. Ravens Mess★ (5.11a) 60 feet. If the raven isn't home, this is a fun crack of varied sizes; the gear, mostly hands and wide hands, is pretty obvious from below.

37. Claim It!★ (5.9) 50 feet. Ascend the obvious lieback/hand crack, then make a hard turn left on large footholds and gritty crimps. Pretty much straight up from there. A couple hand pieces in the start, then a mix of stuff from a 3.5 Friend down. Bring long slings and belay off a natural anchor at the back of the large ledge. **FA:** Sam Lightner Jr. and Elyse Guarino.

38. 5.14 Crack★★ 60 feet. An open project of a crack climb. Many years of trying by hard men have still not opened its secrets. Despite many attempts by 5.14 climbers, it has not been redpointed. We may have to rename with a higher number.

39. Skinner Project South★ (grade unknown) 60 feet. Another orphaned route from the master. It goes out a roof then onto an arête and up the face. The powerful lip move has yet to be ticked. Open.

40. Zanzibar★ (5.11d X) 60 feet. Climb the smooth dihedral out the roof then up the runout face above to an anchor shared with the project above. There is a spot on the face to get in some small gear, but it's really just for emotional support. You will deck from the high moves. **FA:** Steve Bechtel.

41. Railer (5.10b) 30 feet. Climb a corner to an obvious horizontal crack that runs up and to the right. Downclimb the slabs to get back to earth. **FA:** Todd Skinner.

42. Nicks Crack (5.9) 30 feet. This splitter can be found by climbing onto the ledge system behind Claim It!, either by that route or one of the bouldery chimneys that allow access. There is a rappel anchor atop the crack. Take a few hand-size pieces. **FA:** Nick.

Anti-Mormon Area

About 75 yards farther east are a couple of big blocks separated from the main wall. The bases of all but the last of these routes are found in the corridors. The name stems from anti-Mormon grafitti found in the corridor. Route names followed suit with tongue in cheek.

43. Owl Corner★★ (5.10a) 60 feet. A cool corner that starts with a little loose wide stuff but tapers down to fingers and hands. You can get by with a couple of hand and thin hands pieces plus finger and off-finger stuff. Efforts to dislodge the obvious guillotine flake have proved unsuccessful, but you should be careful just the same. Good anchor atop the crack.

44. A Hoot!★★ (5.10a) 60 feet. The arête right of Owl Corner. Start from the alcove and go up ledges to progressively steeper face climbing. Hard move to the anchor. **FA:** Sam Lightner Jr. and Elyse Guarino.

Anti-Mormon Area

45. Bring'em Young★ (5.11a) Outside the corridor, this route angles up to a single ring anchor.

46. No Man Knows My History (5.11d/5.9) 30 feet. Inside the corridor on the right (main wall) side is this technical seam. Takes thin wires and micro-cams. **FA:** Tom Rangitsch.

47. Poly-jammy (5.11a/5.8) 30 feet. The mirror route of Bring'em Young in the corridor. A hard little thing if you don't stem back to the wall behind you . . . do that and it's like 5.7. Thin gear. Rap from a couple anchors on top. **FA:** Todd Skinner.

48. Crack-in-Slot (5.11c/5.8) 30 feet. Just inside the corridor on the right (main wall) side. The grade reflects getting British and treating it as an eliminate route where the back wall is off-limits. Climb back to the boulder to find a rap anchor. **FA:** Todd Skinner.

49. Copper Tablets★★ (5.12a) 30 feet. The best of the bunch. An arête with four bolts for protection. **FA:** Todd Skinner.

Liz Lightner on her route Frogger (5.8), Killer Cave, Sinks Canyon.

SINKS CANYON

■ OVERVIEW

Lander, Wyoming, which is the common denominator for the Sinks Canyon and Wild Iris climbing areas, once promoted itself as "where the rails end and trails begin." The town lies near the geographic center of the state and is the quintessential Wyoming community. It is bordered by one of the country's largest mountain chains, the Wind River Range, and the North American Great Plains. To the north lies the Wind River Indian Reservation, and to the south is uninhabited mountains and desert. Lander, or actually the area Lander sits on, was the site of two of the famed rendezvous of trappers and Indians in 1829 and 1838. The economy focuses on mineral extraction, ranching, and outdoor recreation. Lander is so much the epitome of Wyoming that the state symbol, Stub Farrow on the bucking bronco Steamboat, is taken from Lander. Stub was born and raised in Lander and served as undersheriff in the 1950s. In short, if you want a taste of all things Wyoming, you need to visit Lander.

The town began with peaceful intentions. Chief Washakie of the Shoshone helped draw up and then signed a treaty with the United States in 1868 that would grant the Shoshone the Wind River Valley, but required assistance from the US Cavalry for protection from the Sioux, Arapaho, and Cheyenne. To fulfill this side of the contract, the US Army built Fort Auger. The town that grew up around Fort Auger was later named for the explorer who helped lay out the Oregon Trail, General Fredrick Lander. It was incorporated as a town in 1890, the same year Wyoming was granted statehood.

The Lander area has been surviving off the land for much longer than the town has been in existence. The Shoshone, through Chief Washakie, recognized they had the pot at the end of the rainbow and were thus willing to accept it as the terms of the treaty. In the late 1860s the South Pass area near Wild Iris was the site of a gold rush. At one point South Pass, mostly a re-created tourist site now, was the second-largest town in Wyoming with a population of over 3,000. Cattle ranches have thrived in the region since the early settlers, and oil, gas, and other minerals, including uranium, are a windfall for the region and the state.

Lander, and not Boulder, Salt Lake, Bishop, or Chatanooga, is the best town for climbers in America. In the rain shadow of the Wind River Range, Lander has over 300 days a year of good rock climbing weather. Despite the Wyoming winters, Lander is often sunny and dry through the darker months, making even cold days climbable on the south-facing walls. In the summer months, Lander climbers can hide from the heat by driving 30 minutes south to Wild Iris. At 9,000 feet above sea level, the base of that crag's white dolomite walls is typically 20 degrees cooler than town. And if you are sick of pulling on pockets or crimping edges, an hour's drive east puts you on the slabs and cracks of the Granite Mountains. Wait, there's more. If you just want to get away from it all, load up your pack and head into the Wind River Range, where you can go weeks without seeing another climber. Tie all that together with the easy, comfortable camping in Lander City Park and the best climber bar in the world, and you have the best town in America for climbers.

Hunting has been a mainstay of Lander for the last 18,000 years, but became a popular form of recreation in the early twentieth century. It remains so today, but Lander is also home to the National Outdoor

Heard in the Wind

Gold Rush

With the discovery of gold at Sutter's Mill, California, in 1849, every man in America began to wonder if he might be the one to stumble onto the next El Dorado in the remote and dangerous western territories. Anyone coming west was tempted to look around the next ridge or creek bed knowing they could possibly find rivers of wealth. Such was the case with Major Noyes Baldwin and Captain John Skelton, who were stationed at nearby Fort Bridger in 1864. Tasked with leading a regiment in the protection of the brand-new trans-American telegraph lines that ran over the South Pass, they spent many a day watching the potentially gold-filled ground pass under the hooves of their mounts. In 1865 they and two hired men, W. Shoemaker and J. James, searched the rugged terrain between the Little Popo Agie and South Pass, deciding that a small tributary of Beaver Creek would be the first claim.

They found gold. Not a lot, but enough to inspire thousands of others to come to the area. Placer and shaft mines went in all over the South Pass area, and a camp grew up where ten years before few men would have considered spending a night. Despite the harshest of winter conditions, and a number of raids by Sioux, Arapaho, and Cheyenne warriors, a town grew. A cavalry regiment was garrisoned near the town to ensure safety. More prospectors were inspired as East Coast newspapers proclaimed "slathers" of gold in what were commonly referred to as the Sweetwater Mines. Sawmills, general stores, a post office, gaming halls, saloons, and of course brothels came to be South Pass City, and by 1869 it was Wyoming Territory's second-largest city with some 3,000 inhabitants. Secondary towns, like Atlantic City, Lewiston, and Miners Delight, popped up like suburbs to the big city.

And then, as fast as it came, it disappeared. A large take from the Carissa in 1867 made a few men rich, but for the most part the mines were turning out so little gold that it wasn't worth a miner's time. By the late 1870s, prospectors were tripping over each other to get to other gold rushes in places like southern Colorado, central Montana, or the Black Hills of South Dakota. South Pass City, a place that had challenged Cheyenne for the territorial capital, became a ghost town.

The boom or bust cycle has actually come to the South Pass area a number of times. If the price of gold is very high, it doesn't take much gold to make a season of work worth it. About a hundred years after the first big rush, in the summer of 1988, a woman named Holly Skinner decided to prospect around the old Sweetwater Mines. She searched the upper tributaries of Beaver Creek and made a claim, but sadly found little gold. She did, however, find a cliff that looked like something her brother, Todd, would be interested in. She called him and described the pocketed walls as akin to those found in the famous climbing area of Buoux, France. Todd and his friends visited the cliffs of upper Beaver Creek and immediately saw its potential. No one would get rich, but it was the El Dorado they had been searching for. With that, there was another boom, a gold rush of a different kind. The new group of prospectors decided to name the cliff after Holly Skinner's claim on Beaver Creek; they called it the Wild Iris.

Leadership School, which teaches outdoor skills (like climbing) to people all over the world. NOLS was formed by climber Paul Petzoldt in 1965, and now employs over a thousand people in various locations across the globe. In the late 1980s a couple of NOLS instructors, notably Greg Collins and Sue Miller, began developing sport climbs in Sinks Canyon. About that time Todd Skinner and his gypsy clan, as well as climber Richard Collins, stumbled across Wild Iris. With that, Lander began to grow as a climbing community. It is now home to dozens of climbers and visited by thousands every year. With the amount of climbing in the area, and with locals just beginning to develop cliffs like Wolf Point, Lander is one of the great climber towns of the world.

The Climbing and Gear

Back in the day, Wyoming climbers just accepted that they had to go south for the winter months. January and February nightly temperatures are often below zero, and the constant snow never sticks, it just blows to Nebraska. Then, on a seemingly rare warm afternoon, a couple of climbers decided to bolt a route on the brown dolomite walls of Sinks Canyon. You know, for spring when it warmed up. After prepping the route, they were surprised to find it was actually warm enough to climb it. Shockingly, they were able to climb the next day as well, despite the temperature in town being in the 20s. It turns out that the south-facing walls of Sinks Canyon creates their own little microclimate that provides some of the best winter cragging in the country.

The climbs of Sinks Canyon are on Bighorn dolomite, a sedimentary rock that differs from limestone only in that it contains magnesium. Bighorn dolomite is the same rock we climb on at Wild Iris and a dozen other crags around Lander, as well as at Ten Sleep Canyon, South Piney Creek, and in Corbet's Couloir above Jackson Hole. Bighorn dolomite was laid down approximately 450 million years ago, at which time North America was centered close to the equator; thus the shallow sea had warm temperatures and was full of marine life. Look close enough on virtually any rock climb in Sinks Canyon and you will likely find a fossil.

The dolomite of Sinks Canyon saw more water erosion than that of Wild Iris, so it is a bit more edgy and less pocketed, and a darker brown than Wild Iris's alabaster faces. The walls are higher and steeper than most of the other areas, making for routes that are more about endurance and less about power. However, don't let that fool you; most of the grades here are considered to be a little sandbagged, and that is often because there is a powerful move thrown into that 80 feet of overhanging crimps. The easiest routes on Main Wall are in the 5.7 range, with most climbs being 5.11 or harder. If you need a 5.13 or 5.14, great, 'cause there are plenty to go around. Though a few of the routes were once ascended with traditional gear, virtually all the climbs on the dolomite are bolt protected. Most routes at Wild Iris can be climbed with ten quickdraws, and fifteen quickdraws will get you up everything at Sinks.

Despite the fact that sunny-day temperatures make Sinks a good winter climbing area, you can climb here in the summer as well. Granted, it's way too hot to climb all day, but the wall goes into the shade around 3:30 p.m. Give it an hour or so to cool down, and you can get in a late day session. Spring and fall are obviously great as well. The Sinks Canyon Main Wall is one of those rare crags that can be climbed all year if you get the right conditions.

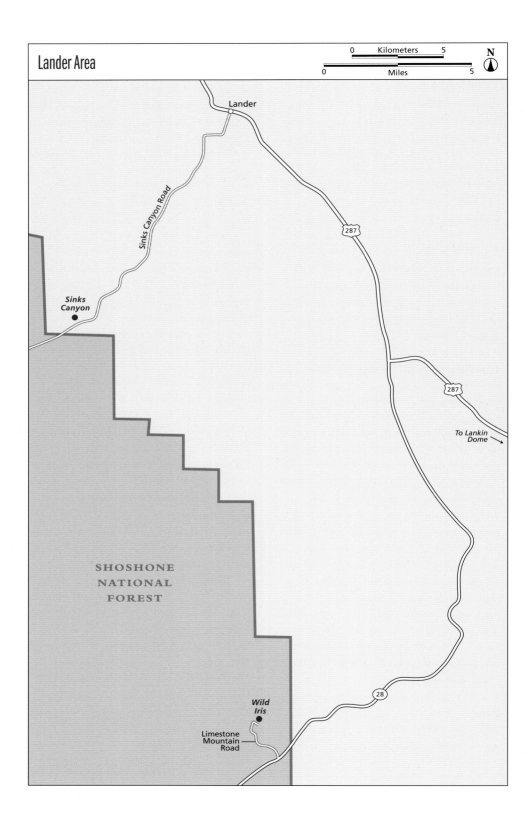

Lander Area

0 Kilometers 5

0 Miles 5

N

Lander

Sinks Canyon Road

287

Sinks Canyon

287

To Lankin Dome

SHOSHONE NATIONAL FOREST

Wild Iris

Limestone Mountain Road

28

Trip Planning Information

General description: Single-pitch sport climbing on pockets and edges with bouldery cruxes

Location: Two areas in central Wyoming on the eastern flank of the Wind River Range

Land managers: Shoshone National Forest and Sinks Canyon State Park

Fees: None

Climbing seasons: Year-round

Camping and hotels: It's hard to imagine a better deal than camping in Lander City Park. The park is under mature cottonwood trees that provide cool shade in the summer. Campsites are wherever you want, on well-maintained bluegrass growing around a meandering stream. There is a communal space to cook in, under a roof, and there are men's and women's restrooms in the south parking lot. The best part? It's all free to visiting climbers. OK, there are no showers. Sorry about that, but they are available for a minimal fee at Elemental Performance + Fitness, the climbing gym located one block north of the Lander Bar. Lander City Park is at 405 Fremont St., the road you take out of town to get to Sinks Canyon.

If in-town camping isn't what you want, Sinks Canyon State Park operates a couple campgrounds along the Middle Popo Agie (pronounce po-po jah) River. Sites are inexpensive and within walking distance to Sinks Canyon's Main Wall. There is also a US Forest Service campground a couple miles farther up canyon that offers sites at a reasonable rate. Up at Wild Iris, which is 30 minutes south of Lander, the Forest Service maintains a simple series of campsites within walking distance of the crags. This campground is free, but it does come with resident bears and cold nights.

Keep a clean camp with all your food stored so you don't meet Waffles the grizzly bear in the middle of the night.

If you want a hotel, Lander sports the usual chains, with Holiday Inn Express having the nicest pool. The Best Western is closest to the Lander Bar and coffee shops.

Food: Every climber should stop in the Lander Bar and Gannet Grill for dinner and beer. Don't talk smack in here—your bartender climbs 5.14. Next door is Lander's finest dining establishment, the Cowfish. Great food, and again, don't talk smack for the same reason. Half a block farther west is the Lander Bakery with great coffee and baked goods, and another half a block down on the left is a great breakfast place, The Middle Fork.

There are two grocery stores in Lander: Mr. D's on Main Street in the middle of town, and Safeway, also on Main at the west end of town. Both have liquor stores, but if you want beer, just fill a growler (or water bottle) at the Cowfish or Lander Bar.

Guidebooks and other resources: Steve Bechtel believes there are over 4,000 rock climbs in the greater Lander area, so obviously this book only touches the surface. His book, *Lander Sport Climbs*, does an excellent job of covering the established climbing on the dolomite, sandstone, and granite. David Lloyd and Ben Sears have written a wonderful guide to the region's seemingly endless bouldering called *Bouldering in the Wind River Range*. As always, you may find information on Mountain Project.

Nearby shops and guide services: Wild Iris Mountain Sports is the climbing shop for central Wyoming. Not only do they stock everything you need, but the people working there are an excellent resource for information.

If you need a guide, contact Micah Rush at (307) 267-4815 or wyoboulder@hotmail.com. Micah knows the area intimately, including a lot of the outlying crags that are not covered here. Another option is Jackson Hole Mountain Guides or Exum Mountain Guides, who occasionally send guides over to Lander to meet clients.

Another source of information, as well as a spot to get a workout during a rainstorm, or a shower after a hot day, is Elemental Performance + Fitness. Elemental, owned by Steve and Ellen Bechtel, is located at 134 Lincoln St., exactly one block north of the Lander Bar.

Emergency services: The Fremont County Sheriff's Department can be reached at (307) 332-5611. You can get an ambulance by calling (307) 332-3241, or just call the Lander Regional Hospital at (307) 332-4420. Lander Search and Rescue, essentially the Sheriff's Department, is best reached by just dialing 911.

Restrictions and access issues: Sinks Canyon's Main Wall falls under the management of two different agencies. The east end, where the Scud Wall and Killer Cave are located, is managed by Wyoming State Parks. The park is totally receptive to climbers, but doggies are required to be on a leash. They do watch from the road, so be a good ambassador and follow the rule. The west end of the wall, where Addiction and Square Top are located, falls under the jurisdiction of the US Forest Service. There are no special rules here for climbers or our furry friends.

In spring, summer, and fall, the rattlesnake population is quite noticeable. Be careful, and be careful with your pet. Climbers and dogs have been bitten at the crag. In a number of places, there is poison ivy along the base of the wall, so watch for that too. Finally, wildfires have wiped out a bit of the foliage along the rim of the cliff, so after rain and snowfalls there can be rockfall. You might want a helmet for the belay.

You may notice a strong presence of brand-new glue-in anchors at Sinks Canyon's Main Wall. This is part of the rebolting effort put forward by BARF (Bolt Anchor Replacement Fund), which is a division of the Central Wyoming Climbers Alliance. That is the organization that puts on the International Climbers Festival every July. BARF is a volunteer organization that spends a huge amount of money replacing and updating bolts and anchors. If you stop into Wild Iris, consider giving a donation to BARF so it can continue its work. You can also find BARF via the Central Wyoming Climbers Alliance website and the BARF Facebook page.

Finding the cliffs: To reach the Main Wall in Sinks Canyon from Lander, go south from Main Street on 5th Street for about eight blocks to Fremont Street. Turn right onto Fremont; it becomes WY 131, also known as the Sinks Canyon Road. Follow WY 131 for about 8.5 miles, the last 3 miles being in Sinks Canyon. After crossing a cattle guard, you will see a parking lot on the right with an outhouse-style toilet. Park here and find the trail next to the toilet. After 28 feet of hiking, you'll come across a kiosk and a fork in the trail. To get to Killer Cave and the Scud Wall, take the right fork for 10 minutes, or until you reach the unbelievably cool overhanging walls. For Addiction Buttress, go left at the kiosk and hike for 14 minutes. The wall is right in front of you where the trail from the parking lot meets the trail that traces the base of Sinks Canyon's Main Wall.

The best way to reach Square Top Boulder is to park about a quarter mile farther

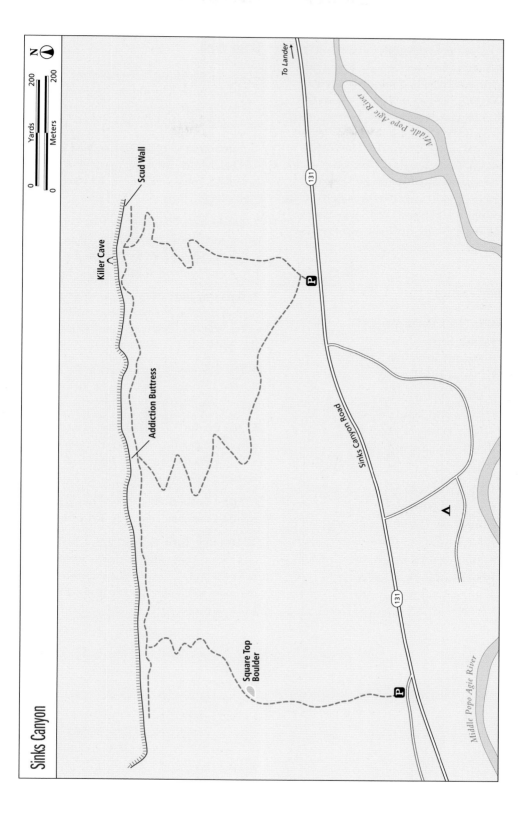

Sinks Canyon

Scud Wall

Killer Cave

Addiction Buttress

Square Top
Boulder

Sinks Canyon Road

131

131

To Lander

Middle Popo Agie River

Middle Popo Agie River

N

Yards   0   200
Meters   0   200

up canyon from the main parking area. This small dirt pullout on the right side of the highway is noted by a four-wheel–drive road that continues through it and up the hill. Park here, not blocking the four-wheel–drive road, and find a climber's trail on the right side of the parking lot. The boulder is obvious after you crest the hill above the lot. It takes about 5 minutes to get there. For what it's worth, the trail continues on to the base of the Sinks Main Wall and connects with the trails that reach the wall from the main lot.

The Classics

- Go West, Young Man (5.7)
- Frogger (5.8)
- Elmo's Fish (5.10d)
- Corner Drug (5.11a)
- Brown Trout (5.11c)
- Boys From Brazil (5.11c)
- Drug Enemy (5.12a)
- Blue Moon (5.12a)
- The Road to Dushanbe (5.12b)
- Bush Doctor (5.12b)
- Cartoon Graveyard (5.12d)
- Addiction (5.12d)
- Mr. Majestyk (5.13a)
- Samsara (5.13b)
- Endeavor to Persevere (5.13c)
- Bus Load of Faith (5.14a)

Scud Wall

The Scud Wall has a large percentage of moderate routes. Get to it by following the trail to the right after reaching the base of the wall at the right side of Killer Cave.

1. Iron Dome★★ (5.10d) 65 feet. Find the start behind the tree. Long moves lead to a large flake (solid) and a bulge. **FA:** Sam and Liz Lightner.

2. Bombs over Crag-bag★ (5.10b) Ten feet left of Iron Dome, this is fun climbing, but it is not cleaning up like we thought it would. **FA:** Mandy and Brian Fabel.

3. Girls Day Out★ (5.7) 65 feet. In a cleft right of the large boulder start, scramble up to the wall. The first bolt is kind of high. **FA:** Mike and Laura Lindsey.

4. Mei Day (5.6) 60 feet. Begin in the boulder chimney, then hand crack in the large corner. **FA:** Mei and Jim Ratz.

5. You Go, Girl★ (5.11a) 45 feet. Start in the corner just past the obvious arête. Climbs a slightly overhanging wall. **FA:** Heidi Badaracco and Paul Piana.

6. Boy, I Gotta Go★★ (5.10b) 45 feet. A fun route on the blunt arête. **FA:** Jeff Leafgreen.

7. Atta Boy, Girl★ (5.9) 50 feet. Climb up and left on big holds to a shared anchor with Climb Like a Girl. Continue on over the route to bump it up one grade. **FA:** Mark Howe.

Scud Wall

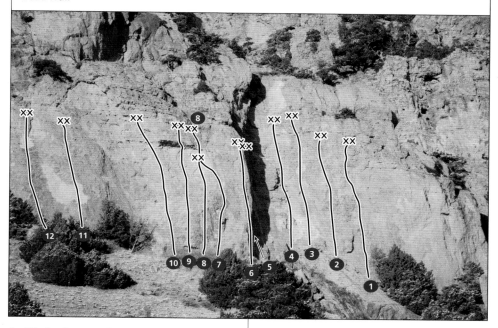

8. Climb Like a Girl★ (5.10b) Slightly thinner, slightly harder, and slightly more straight up version of Girls Day Out. **FA:** Jeff Leafgreen.

9. Stud Alert★ (5.10c) 50 feet. Easily recognized as the route that passes over the low roof and then the high roof. Stick clip recommended. **FA:** David Doll.

10. Duck Soup★★ (5.9) 55 feet. Perhaps the best 5.9 in the canyon, this route climbs jugs and flakes just left of the high roof. The start is just right of the tree. **FA:** David Doll.

11. Banoffee★ (5.10a) 50 feet. This route is on the wall left of the main buttress, climbing through a large spall of lighter-colored rock. Hard move at the start to good holds. **FA:** Jeff Leafgreen.

12. Doggin' Dude★ (5.9) Just right of the tree, this follows a low-angle seam then up the slab. **FA:** Jeff Leafgreen.

Killer Cave Area

Ninety feet high, and overhanging as much as 40 feet at its center, Killer Cave is an impressive venue for climbing. It stays in the sun until about 3:30 in the afternoon, at which time you can either begin climbing in the shade (in summer) or scamper to the left to find sun (in winter).

There are linkups from one route to the other all over the cave. Some of them are shown here, but not all, as the minutiae of directions becomes confusing and does not necessarily create better rock climbs. Suffice it to say that if there are holds between one line of bolts and another, someone has found a way to climb it. You will need a 70-meter rope for some of the longer routes in the middle of the cave.

13. Endeavor to Persevere★★★ (5.13c) 80 feet. Generally thought of as the best 5.13c in the canyon, this route climbs from a boulder through the large, low roof, then up the obvious arête. **FA:** Craig Reason and Hassan Saab.

The following six routes share a start on a boulder and climb into an awkward corner.

14. Jimmy Wings Not Included★ (5.12c) 80 feet. Climb to the awkward roof, then traverse left across the bolts of Stud Alert and to an anchor above a small roof. **FA:** Paul Piana and Heidi Badaracco.

15. Dr. Endeavor★★ (5.13a) 80 feet. This fun line goes up the corner to the roof just like Jimmy Wings, but then goes up the arête of Endeavor to Persevere.

16. Clown Stabber★ (5.12d) 80 feet. Climb to the awkward roof then over the bulge and straight up to an anchor shared with Endeavor to Persevere. **FA:** Paul Piana and Heidi Badaracco.

17. Bloodline★★ (5.11d) 80 feet. Climb to the roof then around left to a straightforward dihedral. When it steepens, traverse right to the overhanging corner that is the upper bit of Clown Stabber.

18. Bush Doctor★★★ (5.12b) 80 feet. This is the original line in the corner. Start from the boulder, go up to the awkward roof, and traverse left, then up the dihedral. Move slightly right and up a steep prow with a roof. **FA:** Trey Warren.

19. Ring of Fire★ (5.12c) 80 feet. Follow the last few routes, then go straight up the overhanging face above the dihedral. **FA:** Peter Absolon.

20. The Urchin★ (5.13b) 45 feet. A very powerful climb through a roof and up a deceptively steep face. Popular with the bouldering crowd. **FA:** Greg Collins and Frank Dusl.

The following climbs begin in the steep corner to the left of The Urchin.

21. Zero Degrees★ (5.13c) 80 feet. Climb into the corner and to the anchor for Baghdad at about 75 feet, then straight out the big roof, trending right at the top. **FA:** BJ Tilden.

22. Cannonball★★ (5.12c) 95 feet. Follow Zero Degrees, but trend left to an anchor above the roof. **FA:** Steve Bechtel.

23. Deadmans Ranch (5.12d) 95 feet. Breaks left from Zero Degrees and Cannonball just after a rest flake, then joins Cannonball over the roof. **FA:** Steve Bechtel.

24. Baghdad★★ (5.12d) Climb the corner and then move out left on big holds, getting pumped out of your skull. **FA:** Greg Collins.

25. Basra (5.12c) 80 feet. Same as Baghdad, but traverse even farther left and straight up. **FA:** Greg Collins.

Killer Cave Right Side

26. House of God (5.13a) 100 feet. Same as Basra, but go all the way to the black streak and straight up. **FA:** Greg Collins.

The following routes begin near the middle of the cave where a steep start is usually aided with a rope ladder (fixed). The start has been freed, but not many people enjoy the climbing. It's best to stick clip one of the bolts at the start and be hoisted up while also climbing the ladder.

27. Kingdom of Jah★★ (5.12d) 80 feet. Tram up to the start, then hang a hard right. This route trends up and right to an anchor near the black water streak. **FA:** Greg Collins.

28. Nirvana★★ (5.13a) 90 feet. Same start then right, but not as far as Kingdom of Jah. **FA:** George Squibb.

29. Samsara★★★ (5.13b) 95 feet. A classic from brewmeister Kirk Billings. Climb up and right through the bouldery crux that Jah and Nirvana share, then straight up for 95 feet of pump. **FA:** Kirk Billings.

30. Cartoon Graveyard★★★ (5.12d) 90 feet. Much of this route is shared by Samsara. Where Samsara goes slightly right, trend straight up through the steep headwall. **FA:** Paul Piana and Heidi Badaracco.

31. Exodus★★★ (5.13c) 100 feet. This route is a three-bolt extension to Cartoon Graveyard, taking that line onto the headwall above. **FA:** Vance White.

32. Stronger than Reason (5.13c) This is the line that goes straight up from the A0 start. Shallow pockets and thin edges make it quite difficult. **FA:** Matt Lund.

33. Mr. Majestyk★★★ (5.13a) 95 feet. Climb through the start of Killer. At the end of the angling seam, trend slightly back right and up, going through the headwall to reach an anchor shared with Stronger than Reason. **FA:** Steve Bechtel.

34. Sweet Bro★★ (5.13a) 95 feet. This route follows Killer to the big roof, then trends up and right to the anchor shared by routes Stronger than Reason and Mr. Majestyk. **FA:** Steve Bechtel.

35. Killer★★ (5.12d) 90 feet. Do the A0 start shared by the previous routes, trending up and left along a seam feature with very technical footwork. Step left at the end of the seam and go straight up, through the big roof, to an anchor high in the headwall. **FA:** Greg Collins and Frank Dusl.

36. The Successor★★ (5.13b) 90 feet. Start off a cheater stone to thin, powerful moves on edges and pockets to an anchor left of the Killer anchor. **FA:** Greg Collins.

37. The Throne★ (5.13b) 90 feet. A very bouldery first 30 feet make this a hard tick. **FA:** Greg Collins.

38. Wield the Sceptor (5.13b) A hard start traversing into The Throne and to that anchor.

39. Bus Load of Faith★★★ (5.14a) 65 feet. One of the testpieces at Sinks. Hard the whole way. **FA:** Frank Dusl and Greg Collins.

40. Moonstone★ (5.13b) 70 feet. Follows a gold streak on stellar rock. A variation, Sister Ray (5.13a), climbs the first few bolts of Moonstone and then traverses to the anchor of Bus Load. **FA:** Greg Collins.

41. Blue Moon★★★ (5.12a) 80 feet. An excellent climb following a large flake and then moving onto a steep face with good but spaced-out holds. The anchor is at the horizontal break in the cave. **FA:** Keith Lenard.

42. Brown Trout★★★ (5.11c) 75 feet. Much maligned for its naturally slick rock, this

Killer Cave Center

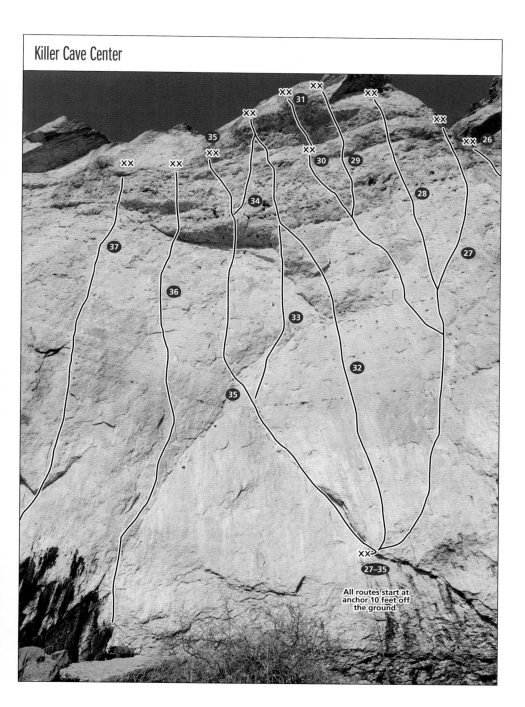

All routes start at anchor 10 feet off the ground.

Kyle Vassilopoulos in the crux of Bus Load of Faith (5.14a), Killer Cave, Sinks Canyon.

route climbs the brown flake, traverses around the arête, and then follows steep ground for a solid pump. An extension, not that good, goes from this anchor at 5.11d. **FA:** Greg Collins.

43. Whirling Disease★★★ (5.10d) 75 feet. A fun new route on the left side of the cave that goes through a couple bulges and along a corner/arête. **FA:** Sam and Liz Lightner.

44. Sign of the Times★ (5.11c) 75 feet. Technical crux down low, then better holds. From the anchor you can climb up and left of the roof for a technical 5.13a. Be careful lowering as it's 110 feet long. **FA:** Frank Dusl.

45. Powderfinger★ (5.11a) 60 feet. Climb to a flake then to the horizontal crack on good holds. **FA:** Steve Bechtel.

46. After the Goldrush★★ (5.11c) 60 feet. Technical moves to big holds. **FA:** Steve Bechtel.

47. Harvest Moon★★ (5.11a) 60 feet. A popular, thus somewhat polished climb. It was one of the early routes on the Sinks Main Wall. Look for a right-trending flake at the start. **FA:** Richard Collins, 1989.

48. Sunspot★ (5.11d) 60 feet. Polished crimpers have made this technical climb a bit less desirable. **FA:** Sue Miller and Greg Collins.

49. Firecracker Kid★ (5.10b) 55 feet. Find the large flake for the start then work up an obvious corner. Perhaps the first route on the dolomite in Sinks. **FA:** Tim Rawson, 1984.

50. Elmo's Fish★★★ (5.10d) 60 feet. Climb the corner, then traverse left on steeper ground with good holds. Pumpy. **FA:** Heidi Badaracco.

51. Pocket Calculator★ (5.12b) 60 feet. Due to the ease of toproping this line from Elmo's Fish, there is a fair bit of polish. Still, the moves are fun. **FA:** Greg Collins.

52. Sam I Am★ (5.9) 50 feet. A nice line of holds, but gets runoff from the top so it can be dirty. After a rain or snowstorm, it's best to avoid this line, as rocks do come down the channel above. **FA:** Steve and Ellen Bechtel.

53. Global Warm Up★★ (5.10d) 50 feet. Technical and pumpy crimping. **FA:** Ellen and Steve Bechtel.

54. Frogger★★★ (5.8) 55 feet. Stem up a chimney past four bolts then onto a blunt arête for another three bolts to an anchor above the roof. **FA:** Liz and Sam Lightner.

Killer Cave Left Side

Addiction Buttress

Seventy-five feet of overhanging perfection. Virtually every route on this wall is great. Find the Addiction Buttress by walking about 300 yards left of Killer Cave or by hiking directly up from the parking lot, taking the left fork at the kiosk. The wall is just right of where this trail joins the trail that traverses the base of Sinks Canyon's Main Wall.

55. Dewalts Challenge (5.11d) 30 feet. Not the best route on the wall as it's often dirty, but if you want a really bouldery 5.11d, this works. It is just out of sight on the topo. **FA:** Trey Warren.

56. The Black Hole (5.12d) 35 feet. Powerful moves using a large black pocket. **FA:** Greg Collins.

57. The White Dwarf★★ (5.12c) 35 feet. The best of the right three routes. This is an interesting route despite its length. **FA:** Greg Collins.

58. Corner Drug★★★ (5.11a) 50 feet. Very popular, and showing it with some polish, but an excellent climb. **FA:** Greg Collins.

59. I Want a New Drug★ (5.12c) 55 feet. Climb Corner Drug, then move left at the break and go up the first line of bolts. **FA:** Vance White.

60. Drug Enemy★★★ (5.12a) 60 feet. The linkup of Corner Drug and Public Enemy that avoids the slabby boulder problem of the latter. Climb the first three bolts of Corner Drug, then traverse left and go over a bulge. **FA:** Greg Collins and Gary Wilmot.

61. Public Enemy★ (5.12b) 60 feet. A very difficult start takes you into an interesting bulge. **FA:** Gary Wilmot.

Addiction Buttress

62. The Gathering★ (5.13c) 75 feet. Hard, thin climbing with a couple of bouldery cruxes. **FA:** Frank Dusl and Greg Collins.

63. Pretty Hate Machine★★★ (5.13b) Considered by many to be the best 5.13b in Sinks Canyon. This route shares an anchor with Dogs of War. Find the start directly behind the tree. **FA:** Frank Dusl.

64. Dogs of War★★ (5.13a) Lots of 5.12 climbing with a hard boulder problem midway. Find the start of this climb just left of the tree. The climbing trends slightly right. **FA:** Frank Dusl.

65. Addiction★★★ (5.12d) 75 feet. The best route of its grade in this book. Start from the high ledge and climb right, then straight up to a memorable finish. **FA:** Frank Dusl.

66. Surplus Fusion Reaction★★ (5.13a) 70 feet. Same start as Addiction, but straight up off the ledge using holds on either side of a blunt arête. **FA:** Frank Dusl.

The next three routes begin in a cleft with a crack.

67. The Road to Dushanbe★★★ (5.12b) 70 feet. Begin in the cleft and follow good holds in and around the crack. At the bulge step right and climb a pocketed face with interesting moves. **FA:** Sam and Liz Lightner.

68. Soul Finger★★ (5.11a) 75 feet. Follow the crack into the dihedral. Pumpy, then technical. **FA:** Steve Bechtel.

69. Mezzmerie (5.12c) 65 feet. Climb the crack in the cleft, then force yourself out of the dihedral and onto a difficult face and arête to its left. **FA:** Paul Piana.

70. Go West, Young Man★★★ (5.7) There are few routes at this grade in the canyon, but this one is worth the walk. Follow the obvious crack up and right (west) for 55 feet. **FA:** Kirk Billings.

71. Soup Sandwich★ (5.9) 55 feet. Technical climbing with some interesting moves. It shares an anchor with Go West, Young Man. **FA:** Steve Bechtel.

72. A Beautiful Life★ (5.9) 50 feet. Named for Jim Ratz, who was killed while climbing at Sinks, this is the farthest left line on the buttress. **FA:** Tom Hargis.

Square Top Boulder

Not the tallest venue, but the climbing is steep and fun, and it just so happens to be the closest crag to the road. The routes on the south face are characterized by big moves to big holds. The few routes on the west face of the boulder are not listed because they aren't as much fun. The south face of Square Top goes into the shade in late afternoon in the summer.

The best way to reach Square Top Boulder is to park about a quarter mile farther up canyon from the parking area for Main Wall. This small dirt pullout, on the right side of the highway, is noted by a four-wheel-drive-only road that continues up the hill. Park here, not blocking the four-wheel-drive road, and find a climber's trail on the right side of the parking lot. The boulder is obvious after you crest the hill above the lot. It takes about 5 minutes to get there. For what it's worth, the trail continues on to the base of the Sinks Main Wall and connects with the trail that traverses the cliff.

73. German Girl★ (5.12b) 35 feet. The obvious steep arête on the right side of the cliff. The top is a little sharp. **FA:** Greg Collins and Sue Miller.

74. American Man Meat★ (5.12a) 35 feet. Fun, but slightly squeezed, as you can start

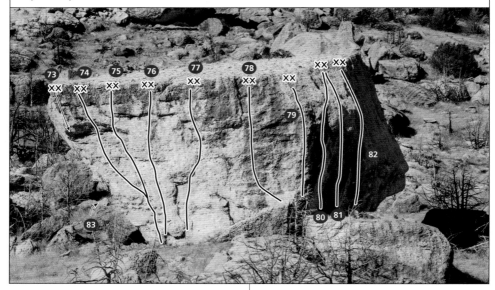

on German Girl or Burly to reach the upper goods. **FA:** Jesse Brown and Vance White.

75. Burly★★ (5.11d) 35 feet. Another early route in Sinks dolomite climbing, this is pumpy with a fun boulder problem. **FA:** Greg Collins and Sue Miller.

76. Hurly★★★ (5.12a) 35 feet. A steep gem on positive holds. **FA:** Sam Lightner Jr. and Liz Lightner.

77. Boys From Brazil★★★ (5.11c) 35 feet. Another steep line with good holds that will pump you up despite the length. **FA:** Unknown. An excellent new line went in between Boys From Brazil and Isolate and Dominate right as we went to press; therefore it is not drawn on the topo. Lunch Break (5.11a) goes straight up the face on great holds. **FA:** Mike Lilygren and Sam Lightner Jr.

78. Isolate and Dominate★ (5.11a) 30 feet. A little sharp up high, but still a fun climb. Best to stick clip the bouldery start onto the ledge. **FA:** Brian Dunnohew.

79. Walk the Line★★ (5.11d) 30 feet. A super steep arête that never lets up. **FA:** Sam Lightner Jr. and Mike Lilygren.

80. Full Iterations★ (5.12a) 35 feet. It actually climbs longer than it looks. Fun, technical climbing on good pockets. **FA:** Greg Collins.

81. Zion Train★★ (5.12b) 35 feet. A bit harder than Full Iterations, with longer reaches. Lots of fun. Watch for poison ivy at the base of these climbs in summer. **FA:** Greg Collins.

82. Steel Pulse (5.11a) 35 feet. It looks good, but somehow a weird couple of moves on sharp holds are disappointing. **FA:** Vance White.

83. Original Route (5.10a) 30 feet. This route is the easy access to the top of the boulder. Look for a bouldery move into a dihedral on the back side. The trail passes right by it. **FA:** Unknown.

WILD IRIS

■ OVERVIEW

Wild Iris was first noticed by climbers in the late 1980s. For a while it was referred to as "Todd Skinner's Secret Area," a name that made it forbidden fruit and seemingly enhanced its popularity. By the early 1990s it was being visited by climbers from all over the world.

　　The climbing is unique in the United States in that most of the holds are pockets, the routes tend to be short, and the moves are extremely powerful. If I were to compare it to any crag in the world, I would say its closest relative is the Frankenjura in Germany. The rock is bright white Bighorn dolomite, which is the same stuff you find in Sinks Canyon, Ten Sleep Canyon, and Corbet's Couloir in Jackson. However, those areas tend to have longer climbs with far more edges, as well as bigger holds that give them a decidedly "endurance" feel.

The Climbing and Gear

Wild Iris is actually three or four crags spread across a ridge. These areas cover a lot of land and could comprise their own guidebook. We cover some of the Main Wall and OK Corral, the two best known and easiest to access crags. The very thorough Bechtel guidebook, *Lander Sport Climbs*, available at

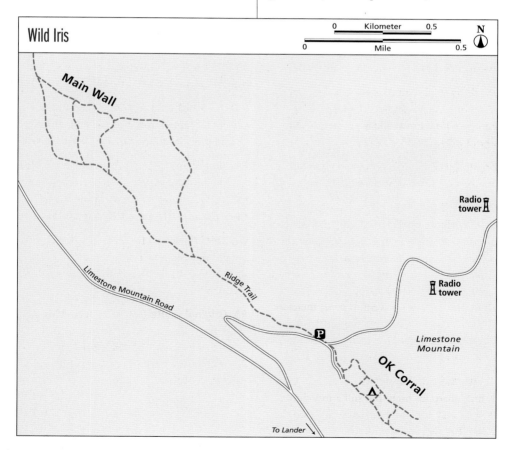

Wild Iris

Liz Lightner leading Mike Lilygren up Ryobi Ranger (5.10b) at Five-Ten Wall, Wild Iris.

Wild Iris Mountain Sports, can get you to the outlying areas.

There are a lot of trees at these areas, with OK Corral being particularly heavily forested. This makes it difficult to create good topos of all the routes. Use both the written description and the topos to figure out which route is which.

Finally, the gear. Leave the rack in the car and don't carry more than a dozen quickdraws. Like Sinks Canyon, Wild Iris is going through an extensive rebolting process, and the exact number of bolts changes according to anchor placement and so forth, but you are safe in assuming that very few routes have as many as ten bolts, and most are around six.

Trip Planning Information

General description: Single-pitch sport climbing on pockets and edges with bouldery cruxes

Location: Central Wyoming on the eastern flank of the Wind River Range

Land manager: Shoshone National Forest

Fees: None

Climbing seasons: Year-round

Camping and hotels: The Forest Service has primitive campsites in the trees below OK Corral (just uphill and to the right from the parking lot). This is a wonderful place to camp, but be on your best bear behavior. You are in grizzly country, and we don't need human-habituated bears. Keep your food inaccessible and your bear spray handy. Also, campfires should only be used in wet years. This area is on the edge of the Red Desert and thus can be very combustible— you don't want to be the one who burned down the forest!

If you want a hotel, Lander sports the usual chains, with Holiday Inn Express having the nicest pool. The Best Western is closest to the Lander Bar and coffee shops.

Food: There are no services at Wild Iris. Your best bet is to stock up in Lander for camping, or make the daily commute and eat at the Lander Bar and Cowfish each night.

Guidebooks and other resources: Steve Bechtel's *Lander Sport Climbs* thoroughly covers this crag and many others in the area.

Nearby shops and guide services: Wild Iris Mountain Sports, on Main Street next to the Cowfish and Lander Bar, is the best climbing equipment shop in Wyoming. They can put you in touch with a guide, but you can also contact Micah Rush at (307) 267-4815 or wyoboulder@hotmail.com. He is an excellent guide who knows the area inside out.

Emergency services: The Fremont County Sheriff's Department can be reached at (307) 332-5611. You can get an ambulance by calling (307) 332-3241, or just call the Lander Regional Hospital at (307) 332-4420. Lander Search and Rescue, essentially the Sheriff's Department, is best reached by just dialing 911.

Restrictions and access issues: Wild Iris is in the Washakie District of the Shoshone National Forest. The local climbing community has a great relationship with the Forest Service, and there are no restrictions on climbing.

Finding the cliffs: *See map page 68.* To reach Wild Iris, drive south from Lander on Main Street/US 287/WY 28. This road eventually climbs up South Pass, and the view of Red Canyon is stunning. At 23 miles take a right onto Limestone Mountain Road. Go up along the southwest face of Limestone

Mountain for about 1.2 miles and take the higher, right–trending fork. Find a large parking area on the left about a quarter mile after the hairpin turn. There is a primitive toilet just uphill at the entrance to the campsites.

The Classics

Big Jake (5.8)
Red Rider (5.10a)
Claim Jumper (5.10c)
The Devil Wears Spurs (5.11a)
Winchester Pump (5.11b)
Tribal War (5.11b)
Hot Tamale Baby (5.12a)

Saddled Dreams (5.12a)
Ruby Shooter (5.12b)
Bob Marley (5.12b)
Bobcat Logic (5.12c)
Genetic Drifter (5.14c)

OK Corral

This is the wall behind the campsites and east of the Wild Iris Main Wall parking area. It is best to park in that lot and not in the campsites, so you do not block a potential camper. The wall faces southwest, but the spruce and pine trees along its base keep many of the routes in the shade through the day. A series of trails run from the road through the campsites to the base of the

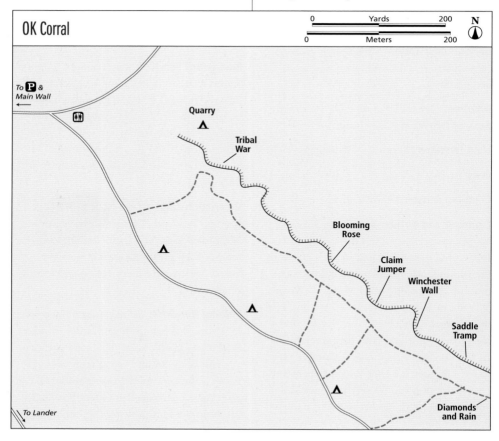

Trey Warren on the headwall of Tribal War (5.11b) with Wild Iris Main Wall in the distance.

various walls. In 2014 the Central Wyoming Climbers Alliance and the Forest Service placed signs at the start of the trails directing climbers to the walls.

Tribal War Area

Named for its best route, this is the farthest left of the climbing venues at OK Corral.

1. Rope the Moon★★ (5.11a) 60 feet. Starting from a ledge on the very left side of the crag, climb a low-angle slab to the big bulge. The crux is not where you think it is! **FA:** Jeremy Rowan.

2. Western Front (5.11d) 65 feet. A somewhat sharp and dirty climb that would likely get a star or two if the description was not so fitting. **FA:** Tim Roberts.

3. Tribal War★★★ (5.11b) 65 feet. A great climb ascending the face just left of the obvious wide-crack dihedral. Pumpy finish. **FA:** Pat Perrin.

4. Stirrup Trouble (5.12a) 45 feet. Climbs the wall right of the big crack, starting right and trending left. Thin. **FA:** Unknown.

5. An Unkindness of Ravens★ (5.11b) 50 feet. Starting just right of Stirrup Trouble,

Tribal War Area

climb up the left edge of the blunt arête.
FA: Sam Lightner Jr. and Liz Lightner.

6. Stone Ranger★★ (5.12b) 50 feet. Found
25 feet right of An Unkindness of Ravens. A
thin start leads to a powerful move over the
obvious overhang.

7. Deputized★★ (5.11d) 50 feet. Just right of
Stone Ranger, a hard boulder problem gets
you onto easier ground. **FA:** Jeremy Rowan.

8. Urban Cowboys★★ (5.10b) 40 feet. A fun
little climb on a clean wall. **FA:** Eric Horst.

Blooming Rose Wall

This wall is approximately 200 yards right of Tribal War Area. The climbs tend to be shorter than those at Tribal War and closely packed together.

9. Iron Horse with a Twisted Heart (5.9) 35 feet. A thin slab that tends to hold dirt. **FA:** Pete Delannoy.

10. Give My Love to Rose★ (5.12a) 40 feet. Up the dirt slope, just right of the obvious crack, is this vertical, technical testpiece. Be careful at the second clip. **FA:** John Hennings.

11. Red as a Blooming Rose★★ (5.11a) 45 feet. Pumpy pocket pulling on good stone. **FA:** Pete Delannoy.

12. Roll in the Hay★ (5.10d) 45 feet. A couple thin moves and then a technical corner. **FA:** Pat Thompson.

13. Stacked Deck★ (5.10c) 45 feet. Progressively smaller holds on the blunt arête. **FA:** Pete Delannoy.

14. Matilda's Last Waltz (5.10d) 45 feet. Farthest right before the obvious cleft in the wall, this climb is a bit slabby and slimy in the crux. **FA:** Pete Delannoy.

Blooming Rose Wall Left Side

15. Cowboys Are My Only Weakness★ (5.11a) 40 feet. A blunt arête 10 feet right of a large cleft and corner in the wall. **FA:** Cindy Tolle and Tom Hargis.

16. Aces and Eights★ (5.10b) 50 feet. Bill Hickok's hand when he was shot. **FA:** Pete Delannoy.

17. Never Sit with Your Back to the Door★★ (5.10b) 45 feet. Bill Hickok's position when he was shot. A difficult start with long moves to good pockets. **FA:** Pete Delannoy.

18. Brown Dirt Cowgirl★★ (5.10a) 40 feet. Found just left of the double corner. Another tricky start. **FA:** Pat Thompson.

19. Phat Phinger Phrenzy★★ (5.8) 50 feet. Climb the double corner, or pocketed stem box, using every skill in the book and clipping six bolts. While belaying, contemplate a good way to describe this feature. **FA:** Pat Thompson.

20. Dogfight at the OK Corral (5.11d) A rounded, somehow overhanging slab of an arête. **FA:** Pete Delannoy.

Not pictured, but about 100 feet right of Dogfight, is a right-trending flake on a clean wall. This feature is quite distinct and thus hard to miss. There is a route on either side of it.

21. Chubs 4 U (5.6) 25 feet. This short slab is just left of the distinctive Claim Jumper.

22. Claim Jumper★★★ (5.10c) Technical and powerful. Climb the right-leaning crack/flake up and through a fun headwall. Very interesting feature. **FA:** Jim Stegal.

23. Annie Get Your Drill★ (5.9) Follows an incipient crack about 20 feet right of Claim Jumper. **FA:** Jim Stegal.

Blooming Rose Wall Right Side

Winchester Wall

Two hundred feet right of Blooming Rose, just after the point where a trail comes up from the road and the White Buffalo (V11) boulder problem, is a buttress with a steep headwall. There are two good routes here. A third was chopped by a confused vagrant a few years ago. The White Buffalo has been bolted and there are bolts on top of the boulder to toprope from, if you can get to them.

24. Sharps 50 (5.11a) Chopped, but to be repaired.

25. Winchester Pump★★★ (5.11b) 55 feet. Excellent climbing up steep rock. **FA:** Dave Doll.

26. Red Rider★★★ (5.10a) 55 feet. Many feel this is the best 5.10a at Wild Iris. Flakes and pockets to a steeper headwall. **FA:** Dave Doll.

Winchester Wall

Saddle Tramp Wall

Found 100 feet right of Red Rider on the Winchester Wall, this short wall gets lots of shade from the surrounding trees. Another trail coming up from the road and campsites meets the trans-cliff trail at this crag.

27. Back in the Saddle★ (5.10c) 35 feet. From the large ledge left of the arête, climb on slightly sharp holds past four bolts. **FA:** Pete Delannoy.

28. Saddled Dreams★★★ (5.12a) 40 feet. This route shares a mono-start with Saddle Tramp, then moves up and left using holds on either side of the arête. **FA:** Vance White and Jeremy Rowan.

29. Saddle Tramp★ (5.12a) 40 feet. Pull through a powerful start, then go up and right along a flake under a bulge to a powerful move onto the headwall.

30. Whips, Chaps, and Chains★★ (5.11d) 40 feet. Climb up and right, getting far more pumped than you thought you would on a route this short. **FA:** Pete Delannoy.

Saddle Tramp Wall

Diamonds and Rain

Just 100 feet right of Saddle Tramp are these longer lines.

31. Doob Lube (5.10b) 60 feet. Climbs the long buttress/crack feature then onto a heavily pocketed wall and out the bulge. **FA:** Ben Sears.

32. Clean Slate (5.12d) 40 feet. Starting just right of the crack, this is a difficult, thin line that trends right on vertical to slightly overhanging terrain. **FA:** Ben Sears.

33. Diamonds and Rain (5.12a) 40 feet. Another technical route that keeps you on your toes. **FA:** Eric Horst.

34. When the Man Comes Around (5.12d) 35 feet. A very difficult bouldery route right of the crack and about 20 feet right of Diamonds. **FA:** John Hennings.

Diamonds and Rain

Wild Iris Main Wall

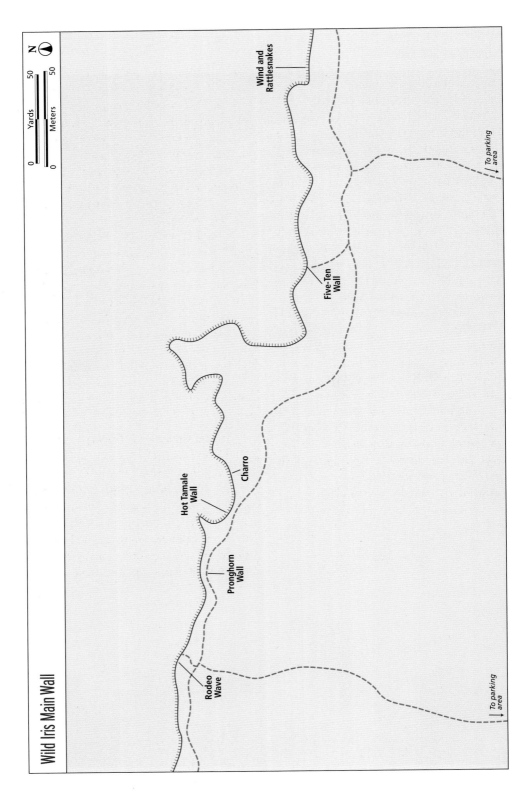

Rodeo Wave

Pronghorn Wall

Hot Tamale Wall

Charro

Five-Ten Wall

Wind and Rattlesnakes

To parking area

To parking area

N

Yards
0   50

Meters
0   50

Wild Iris Main Wall

This is the line of blazing white dolomite that sailed a thousand ships, or at least a thousand Subaru and Toyota trucks. The climbing tends to be short—often no more than five bolts long—but with very powerful moves. Be ready to isolate those fingers.

To reach Main Wall from the parking area, follow the obvious trail running northwest just right of the ridge. Three trails break off to the right, all leading to the Main Wall. The first goes to an area less visited and not covered here, known as Cowboy Poetry. You want to take the second or third branch, both found after descending a hill east of the ridge. The first trail reaches the Main Wall at the far right end between Wind and Rattlesnakes Wall and the Five-Ten Wall. The third branch reaches the Main Wall at the Rodeo Wave, the left-most crag covered here. A trail running along the base of Main Wall connects all the segments described in this book.

Keep in mind that the trees along Main Wall often obscure the routes. This makes it difficult to clearly show all routes on the photographic topos. Use the topos as a reference, knowing that often a particular route could not actually be shown.

Rodeo Wave

Overhanging at the most difficult angle, about 45 degrees, this is one of the best walls for the hard men. The climbs are all fairly short, getting no higher than 65 feet off the ground, but unless you are special you will find it very pumpy. The easiest route on this wave of rock is 5.12b. One great thing about this wall is that even though it faces due south, the rock itself sees very little sun. It's just too steep.

Most people belay at the far right end and allow the leader to ascend the ramp to his or her chosen line. This is made easier on the belayer by clipping a bolt right above the belayer to hold the line of pull directly above the belay. Or, have the belayer stand in front of the slab at the base of the chosen line and simply flip the rope along the slab until you clip the first bolt on your route. You may want a stick clip for the first move on many of these routes, as they start way off the ground.

1. Ground from Upside Down★★ (5.13a)
This is actually left of the bolt line that is Bobcat Logic. Chalked jugs mark the line. It's a boulder problem that is 65 feet long, starting in the base of the slot and topping out over the rim. You need a spotter to move the crash pad along, and perhaps to shove you into the slot if you pop off the top. **FA:** BJ Tilden and Tom Rangitsch.

Rodeo Wave

2. Bobcat Logic★★★ (5.12c) An excellent line near the far left of the wave (right of the boulder problem starting deep in the slot). Find the start between two dark water streaks. **FA:** Heidi Badaracco and Paul Piana.

3. Bob Marley★★★ (5.12b) This is a linkup of Bobcat and Cow Reggae. Climb past the first three bolts of Bobcat, then traverse right to finish on Reggae. **FA:** Jacob Valdez and Heidi Badaracco.

4. Cow Reggae★★ (5.13b) One of the more popular 5.13bs in the area, this is just right of Bobcat. **FA:** Frank Dusl, Jacob Valdez, and Sam Lightner Jr.

5. Babalouie★★ (5.12c) A linkup of Reggae and Atomic Stetson. There is one hold that requires split-finger power to "live long and prosper." **FA:** Dan Michael and Jacob Valdez.

6. Atomic Stetson★★ (5.13c) A very powerful climb following a faint water streak. **FA:** Paul Piana and Todd Skinner.

7. Atomic Cow★★ (5.13d) A linkup of the crux of Stetson and Reggae. **FA:** Paul Piana and Heidi Badaracco.

8. Rodeo Free Europe★★ (5.14a) Starting at the base of the wave, where everyone belays, and going up the darkest streak. **FA:** Jason Campbell (stolen) and Todd Skinner.

9. Genetic Drifter★★★ (5.14c) One of the hardest routes covered in this book, the route links the cruxes of Rodeo, Stetson, and Cow Reggae. The name was given by Todd Skinner, who first began work on it. **FA:** Jason Campbell and Tiffany Levine.

10. Rodeo Active (5.14a) The right-most line on the wave, this climb is very bouldery and rarely done. **FA:** Andy Skiba.

Two Kinds of Justice

Found right of the Rodeo Wave, this buttress becomes the Pronghorn Wall and Wild Horses Wall. Most of the climbs in this sector are 40 feet long or less.

11. Six Impossible Things★★ (5.12c) A jump start puts you on a steep wall. It ain't over till it's over. The start is obscured on the topo by the boulder. **FA:** Kyle Vassilopoulos.

12. NFR★ (5.13c) Seriously powerful line that took years to see a redpoint. **FA:** BJ Tilden and Todd Skinner.

13. Two Kinds of Justice★★ (5.12c) Popular. On you from the start. **FA:** Porter Jarard and Sam Lightner Jr.

14. Gored By Inosine★ (5.12d) This route is noted by a large, dark pocket and is just left of a dihedral (In Todd We Trust). **FA:** Todd Skinner.

15. In Todd We Trust★ (5.11d) An interesting dihedral with a hard finish. **FA:** Vance White.

Two Kinds of Justice

Pronghorn Wall

Pronghorn Wall

The following routes lie in a sector that takes its name from the first route established, even though that climb is at the far right end.

16. Limestone Cowboy★★ (5.12a) 50 feet. On the wall closest to the dead whitebark pine (damn beetles). Powerful crux. **FA:** Joe Desimone.

17. Hip Boot Romance★ (5.11a) 50 feet. Greatly improved by BARF's rebolting effort, this climb boulders into a slight dihedral then out a bulge and on to good holds. **FA:** Steve Scott.

18. Star Spangled Rodeo★★ (5.10c) 50 feet. Found on the wall where the large block has dropped away. Climb from the block over the bulge onto the small ledge, then upward with good holds. Stick clip is advised. **FA:** Sam and Liz Lightner.

19. Pronghorn Tamp★★★ (5.10b) 50 feet. A fun climb starting just right of Star Spangled's block and about 20 feet left of the obvious large dihedral (The Prospect). **FA:** Sam and Liz Lightner.

20. Pronghorn Love (5.11d) 50 feet. A tweaky, less direct version of Pronghorn Tamp. **FA:** Steve Scott.

21. The Prospect★★ (5.10d) 55 feet. Climb the crack in the dihedral then onto the face. This may have been the first route bolted at the Wild Iris Main Wall. **FA:** Probably Richard Collins.

Wild Horses Wall

The following routes cannot be seen in the photo topo, but are easily found at the base of the steep gully left of Big Jake on the Hot Tamale Wall.

22. The Devil Wears Spurs★★★ (5.11a) 55
feet. Arguably the best climb on the Main Wall, the start is just right of the large pine tree. **FA:** Carol and John Gogas.

23. Posse on My Tail★
(5.11d) 60 feet. Thin and techy, but fun. The first bolt is kind of high . . . old school. **FA:** Jacob Valdez and Sam Lightner Jr.

24. Wild Horses★ (5.11a) 60 feet. Start in the
corner then climb onto the wall higher up, following the bolt line. Another stick clip–recommended route. **FA:** Jacob Valdez and Sam Lightner Jr.

25. Jackalope and Boomslang (5.10a) 40
feet. Another technical route that keeps you on your feet to the very end. Find it on the buttress just right of the large crack. **FA:** Glenda Lanais.

Wild Horses Wall

Hot Tamale Wall

26. Big Jake★★★ (5.8) 80 feet. Right of the obvious large gully, this route starts next to a low overhang and goes up a blunt arête, then trends left to an anchor. **FA:** Sam and Liz Lightner.

27. Big Whiskey★★ (5.11c) 60 feet. Down a step and a few feet right of Big Jake, this route pulls onto the wall from a bulge, moves right, and then hangs on through the roof and steep ground. Shares an anchor with In God's Country. **FA:** Sam and Liz Lightner.

28. In God's Country★ (5.12c) 60 feet. Powerful, thin moves on the vertical wall and through the bulge. Shares an anchor with Big Whiskey. **FA:** Eric and Lisa Horst.

29. Ruby Shooter★★★ (5.12b) 65 feet. A stiff start, then a pumpy finish. Excellent rock climb. **FA:** Heidi Badaracco and Paul Piana.

30. Hot Tamale Baby★★★ (5.12a) 65 feet. Pumpy. Big holds. Start just left of the crack and later work two sides of a blunt arête. **FA:** Heidi Badaracco and Paul Piana.

31. Hey, Mr. Vaquero★★ (5.12b) 70 feet. Find it 10 feet right of the crack. Goes out a steep bulge to a very tricky vertical wall. **FA:** Paul Piana and Heidi Badaracco.

Hot Tamale Wall Left

32. Mexican Rodeo★★ (5.12d) 70 feet. Very difficult pulls in the bulge, then a hard vertical wall above. **FA:** Paul Piana and Heidi Badaracco.

33. Charro★★★ (5.12b) 70 feet. Big holds, though they don't all face the right way. Tricky slab higher. **FA:** Paul Piana and Heidi Badaracco.

34. Caballero del Norte★ (5.11d) 50 feet. Thin and technical. Hard slab. **FA:** Chris Oates and The Bear.

35. Windy City★★ (5.10a) 50 feet. Starts in a faint corner and crack, then works its way up then right to a shared anchor with Popa Agie Pocket Pool. **FA:** Jeff Leafgreen.

36. Popa Agie Pocket Pool★★ (5.10b) 50 feet. Find it behind and left of the cool-looking dead tree. Trends up and left to the shared anchor with Windy City. **FA:** Rick Thompson.

37. Distant Early Warning★ (5.10d) Just right of Pocket Pool and left of the dead tree. Bolted for a very powerful move (5.12a) that is usually bypassed left. Shares anchor with Osita. **FA:** Sam and Liz Lightner.

38. Osita★ (5.11b) 45 feet. Find this route just right of a large burned tree that leans away from the wall. A very hard start to more enjoyable climbing. For an extension with the same grade, you can finish on a headwall with a mantle onto a ledge. **FA:** Judy Barnes and Chris Oates.

39. Digital Stimulation (5.10c) 45 feet. Find this around the corner and facing east. It looks good, but somehow isn't that much fun. **FA:** Jeff Leafgreen.

On the small wall just right of Osita are two fun climbs that are not shown on the topo.

40. The Shootist★★ (5.10b) 40 feet. The left route, starting just right of the wall with Distant Early Warning. Good holds to a tricky finish. **FA:** Steve Scott.

41. Wind River Rose★★ (5.9) 45 feet. Climbs the slabby, blunt arête to a bulge just right of The Shootist. **FA:** Steve Scott.

42. Jake and the Neverland Cowboys★★ (5.6) 40 feet. Perhaps the best first lead at Wild Iris, and maybe in this book. Climbs the low-angle rock to the right of Wind River Rose. **FA:** Sam and Anabel Bechtel.

Hot Tamale Wall Right

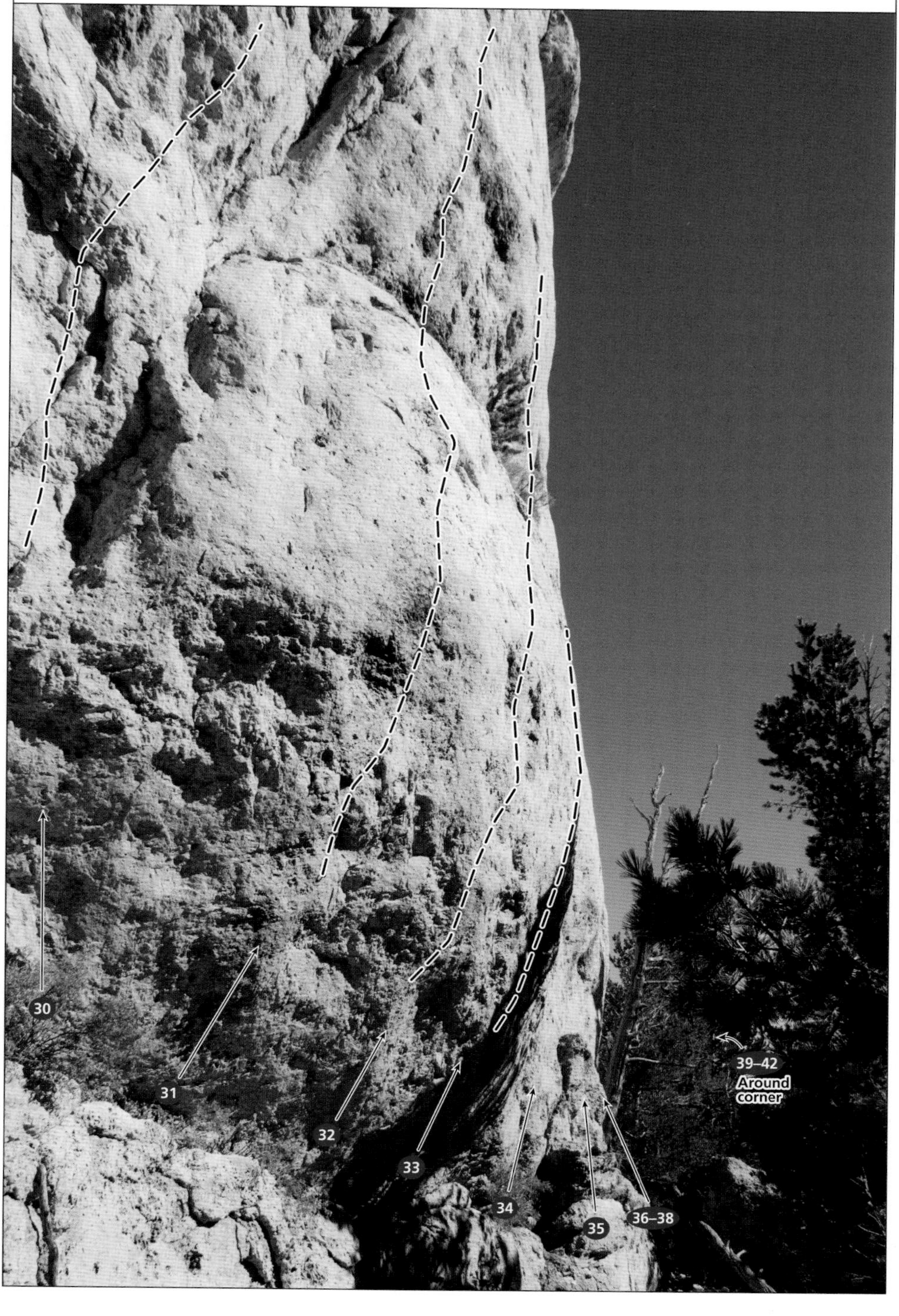
30
31
32
33
34
35
36–38
39–42
Around corner

Five-Ten Wall

The Five-Ten Wall is about 80 yards right of the Wind River Rose route. As the name implies, there are plenty of moderates here. The wall is split into two main sections, with the Stonehenge Boulder being the visual divider.

43. Ryobi Jr.★ (5.10b) 40 feet. At the far left end of the wall is a ledge. This route begins on the left end of the ledge. **FA:** Pat Perrin.

44. Ryobi Rustler (5.11a) 40 feet. Find this route off the middle of the previously mentioned ledge. Bouldery start and a little sharp. **FA:** Pat Perrin.

45. Ryobi Wrangler★ (5.11a) 40 feet. Starts on the right end of the ledge. Not quite so sharp as its neighbors. **FA:** Pat Perrin.

46. Ryobi Ranger★★ (5.10b) 50 feet. The most popular of the Ryobi routes, and rightfully so. Long moves on good holds. **FA:** Pat Perrin.

47. Indian Country/Big Country★★
(5.10b/5.11c) 50 feet. Start from a small ledge and move up and left on progressively better holds. For the harder finish climb through three bulges on good holds with five more bolts for protection. **FA:** Jacob Valdez, Gerald Whistler, and Sam and Liz Lightner.

48. Dynamitic★★★ (5.9) 45 feet. Maybe the best 5.9 sport climb in this book. Ascends the faint corner on big holds. **FA:** Rick Thompson.

Five-Ten Wall Right

49. Sacajawea (5.10c) 45 feet. There is a large boulder stack, commonly called the Stonehenge Boulder, beneath the middle of the Five-Ten Wall. This thin climb begins directly behind the boulder. **FA:** Elaine Chandler.

50. Pistol Pete★ (5.11a) Just right of the Stonehenge Boulder is this powerful start with large holds to finish. **FA:** Pete Delannoy.

51. Wild Horses Keep Dragging Me Away★ (5.10c) 45 feet. Hard pulls low to technical stuff. **FA:** Shepard Vail and Todd Skinner.

52. You Picked a Fine Climb to Lead Me, Lucille★ (5.10a) 45 feet. Another thin start to longer moves on better holds. **FA:** Gerald and Lucille Whistler.

53. Latex Cowboy★★ (5.10c) 45 feet. Perhaps one of the better 5.10s on the wall, this route is 10 feet left of the bush- and tree-filled crack.

54. Good Hearted Woman★★ (5.8) 45 feet. A great first sport lead, this climb starts just left of the bushy crack and follows good holds to an anchor 4 feet right of the top of Latex Cowboy. **FA:** Liz and Sam Lightner.

55. T & T★★ (5.10c) 40 feet. Over near the large slot and chimney with the giant chockstone is this pumpy line. It didn't make the topo photo. **FA:** Rick Thompson.

Rode Hard Area

Fifty yards east of Five-Ten Wall are the roof routes of Rode Hard. These climbs face the same direction as the others on the wall, but due to trees and steepness they tend to be shadier.

56. Jones on the Juke Box (5.13d) 30 feet. Kind of a boulder problem in the sky, this giant roof of pockets is always shady. Shares an exit with Ewe on My Mind. **FA:** BJ Tilden and Todd Skinner.

57. Ewe on My Mind★ (5.12a) 55 feet. The left-most route under the roof, this climb goes up the "slab" then passes the roof on the far left to a shared anchor. **FA:** Sam and Liz Lightner.

58. Full Circle★★ (5.13a) 55 feet. Shares a start with Copenhagen Angel, then goes left through the roof to an anchor at the skyline. **FA:** Matt Wendling.

59. Copenhagen Angel★ (5.13b) 60 feet. Up the white face and out the roof. Many people climb the lower portion, which is 5.11, and then lower off a large glue-in bolt. **FA:** Todd and Amy Skinner.

60. Phony Express★★ (5.12c) 60 feet. Climb Rode Hard on the lower wall, then move up and left through the bulge on holds that work a little better than those of Rode Hard. **FA:** Paul Piana and Heidi Badaracco.

61. Rode Hard and Put Up Wet★★ (5.12d) 60 feet. Up the white wall and out the roof. This is one of the first routes bolted at Wild Iris. **FA:** Todd Skinner and Jacob Valdez.

62. Nine Horse Johnson★★ (5.11d) 60 feet. Climb a large flake about 10 feet left of the big crack. Go out the roof with Cirque du Soleil moves and up the slab to the anchor. **FA:** Steve Bechtel.

63. Windy West★★ (5.12b) 50 feet. Begin in the big crack that is the start of Wind and Rattlesnakes. Climb out the bulge then go west (left) at the fourth bolt, continuing on the steepest terrain. Feel the pump. **FA:** Steve Bechtel and Jeremy Rowan.

64. Wind and Rattlesnakes★★★ (5.12a) 55 feet. The classic of the area. Begin in the large broken crack, then climb out the bulge and straight up on somewhat heady and very pumpy terrain. **FA:** Amy and Todd Skinner.

65. Tomahawk Slam★ (5.12a) 55 feet. Very popular despite a powerful and potentially injurious move. Starts on flakes just right of Wind and Rattlesnakes. **FA:** Heidi Badaracco and Paul Piana.

66. Easy Ridin★★ (5.10d) 55 feet. Up large pockets through the overhang just right of Tomahawk Slam. **FA:** Diedre Burton.

Rode Hard Area

JACKSON HOLE

◼ OVERVIEW

The valley known as Jackson Hole is one of the most beautiful places in America. The "hole" formed by the Teton, Gros Ventre, and various smaller mountain ranges is about 40 miles long and a dozen miles wide. The valley floor averages about 6,500 feet above sea level and has a comfortable climate in the summer months. Wildlife abounds in the region, to the level that it's actually difficult to *not* see bison, elk, deer, and moose.

Jackson Hole has a very rich and colorful history. Prior to the trapper era of the early 1800s, the valley fell inside the territory of the Shoshone, though there were very few, if any, Native Americans who lived in the harsh climate year-round. The valley was named after trapper Davey Jackson, who made it his home during the warmer months of the 1820s. It wasn't until the 1880s that settlers were able to eke out an existence in the area, and even then it was a special breed who took on the challenge. The valley was actually noted as being one of those places in the West where former murderers and horse thieves could hide from the law, provided they didn't come out of retirement, and this reputation held true well into the twentieth century. A 1956 *Fortune Magazine* article called Jackson the "second toughest town in America" (it lost out to Butte, Montana), and most locals only took offense at the distinction because they "got second."

The hardships of the winter climate and ranching culture are difficult to imagine now. Coffee shops and boutiques have replaced the liveries and saddle shops, and Range Rovers and Audis crowd roads that were once only used by pickup trucks and herds of cattle. Wyoming has no state taxes, and that combined with the beauty of Jackson Hole has changed the demographics of Teton County. Almost all the ranchland has been bought by semi-retired millionaires and billionaires, or encompassed within the boundaries of Grand Teton National Park. What was once a place too hard to live year-round is now the wealthiest county, per capita, in the United States.

For climbers the region is known more for alpine climbing in the Tetons than cragging in the valley. The Tetons in the 1920s to the 1950s saw groundbreaking achievements in American mountaineering. In fact, the North Face of the Grand Teton was considered to be the most difficult climb in America in the 1930s. Times change, and somehow the mountains get smaller. Today the Tetons are thought of more as a bastion of difficult ski-mountaineering terrain than cutting-edge alpine climbing, but that doesn't mean they won't test your mettle. If you want to climb on the larger peaks, and I recommend it, get a copy of Richard Rossiter's *Best Climbs Grand Teton National Park* (previously called *Teton Classics*) or Renny Jackson and Leigh Ortenberger's *A Climbers Guide to the Teton Range*. For those wanting to do just a bit of cragging, there are half a dozen cliffs around the valley, the best of which are covered here.

One thing to note, so the locals don't mock you too much. The name Jackson Hole is the name given to the area by French trappers, with the word "hole" being synonymous at the time with "valley." The largest community in the valley is the town of Jackson, not to be confused with the name of the valley. So the town of Jackson is at the southern end of the valley known as Jackson Hole. Now if you want to impress the locals, mention that Jackson Peak is actually named after famed horse thief "Teton" Jackson, not Davey Jackson and not the town of Jackson.

Bison and Mount Moran in Grand Teton National Park, Jackson Hole.

The Climbing and Gear

We have put three separate crags of distinctly different styles in the Jackson area. One is a "quick-hit" sport crag, while the others are a bit more involved in the approach and will eat up much of the day. If you want to climb in the Tetons but don't have much time, then Rock Springs Buttress is the perfect option. If you want to crimp hard and utilize that perfect footwork with an amazing view, Blacktail Butte is a great option. Corbet's Couloir is a little of both.

Trip Planning Information

General description: Vertical sport climbing with an amazing view, and alpine traditional and sport climbing

Location: Northwest Wyoming; one area in Grand Teton National Park and two more at Jackson Hole Mountain Resort

Land managers: Bridger-Teton National Forest and National Park Service (NPS)

Fees: None at Blacktail Butte; pricey ticket to ride the tram to the crag at the resort

Climbing seasons: Spring, summer, fall

Camping and hotels: There are numerous campgrounds in Grand Teton National Park, most requiring reservations in advance during the summer months. The US Forest Service maintains campgrounds in Curtis Canyon, near Slide Lake in the Gros Ventre Range, and also in Hoback Canyon. All of these locations are a reasonable drive from the climbing areas. Finally, there is the

Virginian Campground in town, though it caters more to the RV crowd, and the Jackson Hole Campground, about halfway between Jackson and Teton Village.

Hotels abound in Jackson Hole, from Motel 6 to The Four Seasons. None are cheap, but there is a very nice standout for climbers. The Alpine House, run by climbers Hans and Nancy Johnstone, is not only a nice place with a great location, but it's also the place to get the scoop on new routes and climbing conditions in the area. If you want to be in the park, and don't want to break the bank, the Grand Teton Climbers Ranch, run by the American Alpine Club, is the best alternative. It's economical and within walking distance of the Grand, but you will need a car to reach the cragging areas.

Food: Jackson Hole is many things, some enjoyable and some annoying, but I think everyone would agree it is the culinary capital of Wyoming. There are all sorts of restaurants catering to all wallet sizes. A few I like are Pica's for Mexican food, King Sushi for sushi, and, if you want to go all out, the Snake River Grill is exceptional. The best climber hangs are the Snake River Brewpub and, of course, the climber-icon Dornan's Bar in Moose. I highly recommend the latter for pizza, wine, and an exceptional view.

There are three large grocery stores in Jackson: Albertsons, Smiths, and the Jackson Whole Grocer. If you want all organic and such, the last of the three is your place. All are in the west end of Jackson. Smaller, shall we say "specialty" (ergo expensive) grocery stores are in Teton Village, Wilson, and Dornan's at Moose.

Guidebooks and other resources: Wesley Gooch's *Rock Climbing Jackson Hole and Pinedale* does an excellent job of complete coverage of the cliffs around Jackson. Also,

the founder of MountainProject.com lived in Jackson for a while, so that database tends to be pretty thorough. If you decide to venture into the mountains, I highly recommend you purchase Renny Jackson and Leigh Ortenberger's *A Climbers Guide to the Teton Range*. Richard Rossiter's *Best Climbs Grand Teton National Park* (formerly *Teton Classics*) accurately covers the best of the range. There is also a digital guidebook on DVD called *Teton Rock Climbs* by Aaron Gams. Finally, if you want to learn about the interesting history of Jackson Hole, *Roads Through Time: A Roadside History of Jackson Hole* by Sam Lightner Jr. (me) is considered by many to be the most accurate and readable book on the area.

Nearby shops and guide services: Teton Mountaineering, on Cache Street in Jackson, is the best climbing shop in the area. Moosely Seconds, across from Dornan's in Moose, also has climbing gear and outerwear.

If you need a guide, you came to the right town. Exum Mountain Guides and Jackson Hole Mountain Guides both operate in the area. You can find JHMG next to the Smiths grocery store in town, and Exum is found at Jenny Lake near the base of the Grand Teton.

If you just need exercise and time is of the essence, check out the artificial bouldering park at the base of Snow King Mountain in Jackson—it's an easy place to get a workout.

Emergency services: St. Johns Hospital, on East Broadway in the east end of Jackson, is the only hospital in the region and can be reached at (307) 733-3636. If you need a cop, call the Teton County Sheriff's office at (307) 733-4052. These guys can get you to search and rescue for Teton County as well. The Grand Teton Search and Rescue,

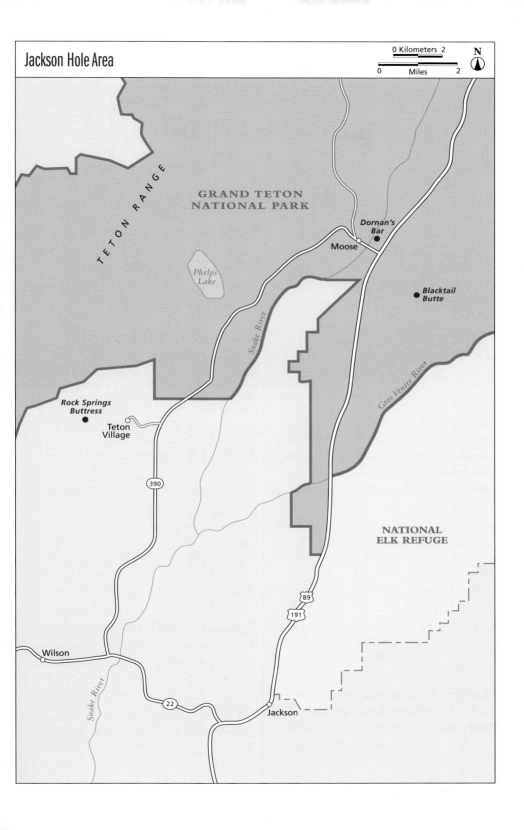

Jackson Hole Area

0 Kilometers 2
0 Miles 2

N

TETON RANGE

GRAND TETON
NATIONAL PARK

Phelps
Lake

Dornan's
Bar

Moose

Blacktail
Butte

Snake River

Gros Ventre River

Rock Springs
Buttress

Teton
Village

390

NATIONAL
ELK REFUGE

89

191

Wilson

Snake River

22

Jackson

Anthony Menolascino finishing up Inconceivably Busted (5.11a), Blacktail Butte, Jackson Hole.

which only operates in the park, is based at the Jenny Lake Ranger Station and can be reached at (307) 739-3343. They also operate a website with lots of good info: teton climbing.blogspot.com.

Getting there: Jackson has the busiest airport in Wyoming, with jet service to cities all over the United States. There is bus service between the town of Jackson and the Jackson Hole Mountain Resort, but no bus between the airport and town. Despite the local bus service, for most endeavors you are going to need a car, and there are car rental companies at the airport.

Jackson is about 3 hours from Lander and 5 hours from Salt Lake City. Going from Devils Tower to Jackson is an all-day affair.

Blacktail Butte

Blacktail Butte has been called the most scenic crag in the United States. The Madison limestone wall, turned almost dead vertical, sits 5 miles east of the Grand Teton and offers incredible views of the Teton Range, Snake River, and everything in between.

The season is spring, summer, and fall. Most people like to avoid the sun in the summer months, and the wall does stay shady until around 1 p.m. After that, on a hot day you can go down and around the corner to the two routes on the northwest face and stay in the shade until late in the day.

Restrictions and access issues: Blacktail Butte lies in the very heart of Grand Teton

Liz Lightner pulling hard on Stiffy (5.11a), Blacktail Butte, Jackson Hole.

National Park, so all the usual restrictions exist (no power drills, no dogs, etc.).

Finding the cliffs: To reach the main wall, park in the parking lot on the right side of US 89/191 about a mile north of the highway's intersection with Teton Park Road. This is also about a mile northeast of the "town" of Moose. From the parking lot, follow the NPS trail that switchbacks up to the obvious wall above. Total hiking time is about 8 minutes. To reach the North Wall, find the game trail on the north end of the lot and follow it, paralleling the road, for about 250 yards. Look for a climber's trail ascending into the trees for about 150 feet to the base of the wall.

One thing to note is that this wall was the only easy-access local cragging for years, so virtually every inch of rock has been climbed. There are many variations and toproped routes that are not covered in this guide, as they would clutter the topo. If you want to know more, get Wes Gooch's book.

The Classics

Inconceivably Busted (5.11b)
The Arch (5.12a)
The Waterstreak (5.12c)

Main Wall

The climbing on the main wall is characterized by steep crimping and highly technical edging moves. In other words, it's a vertical slab. For this reason it has fallen from favor, as climbers tend to want overhanging jughauls, but for this type of climbing Blacktail is excellent. Two things are certain for a day at this cliff: You will have an incredible view, and your footwork will improve. Most of the routes at the main wall are between 5.11d and 5.12c, with a few stragglers at either end, so unless you are in 5.15ish shape, you will get pumped. All the climbs but one are bolt protected, so a dozen quickdraws and a 60-meter rope will suffice.

1. Leftovers★ (5.10c) 40 feet. The obvious corner and arête at the far left end of the wall. **FA:** Greg Miles and Trevor Bowman.

2. As You Wish (5.11d) 40 feet. Seriously thin. **FA:** Sam Lightner Jr. and Eric Gabriel.

3. Inconceivable★ (5.11a) 40 feet. Up and left. **FA:** Sam Lightner Jr. and Eric Gabriel.

4. Inconceivably Busted★★ (5.11a) 70 feet. Climb Inconceivable, but before clipping the anchor move up and right to a line of bolts, then to an anchor at the top of the

Blacktail Butte Main Wall

wall. Perhaps the best route on the wall, and certainly the steepest. **FA:** Greg Miles and Trevor Bowman.

5. Raven Crack (5.10d) 70 feet. Not my favorite route. The Raven Crack can be climbed on gear, though doing the routes left and right of it will get you almost the same moves but with better gear. By the way, the crack's ascent predates the sport routes, but the disparity of quality between the sport routes and the crack line obliterates the need to keep the crack pure. **FA:** Rex Hong.

6. Do the Right Thing (5.11c) 70 feet. Start up Inconceivable, hang a right after the first bolt, then go on to anchors right of the crack. **FA:** Joe Sottile and friends.

7. Waterstreak Direct (5.13a) 70 feet. At about the fifth bolt, the original route trends right. This is the straight up variant. **FA:** Rex Hong and Sam Lightner Jr.

8. The Waterstreak★★ (5.12c) 70 feet. An excellent technical route with multiple cruxes, trending up and then slightly right, then back left. Try and imagine doing the last moves ropeless as Alex Lowe did in 1991. **FA:** Rex Hong, Mike Fisher, and Sam Lightner Jr.

9. Arch Direct (5.12d) 70 feet. Just right of The Waterstreak following the obvious lower arching flake. **FA:** Rex Hong, Sam Lightner, and Mike Fisher.

10. The Arch★ (5.12a) 70 feet. A more direct version of the "direct" route, this one is also more pleasant on the fingers. One of the better routes on the wall. **FA:** Sam Lightner Jr. and Rex Hong.

11. Kehoe Cling★ (5.12c) 70 feet. First toproped by Mike Kehoe in the mid-1980s, this route was eventually bolted and redpointed by Rex Hong.

12. Jingus Road★ (5.12b) 70 feet. Interesting moves make this a worthy climb. **FA:** Rex Hong, Mike Fisher, and Sam Lightner Jr.

13. Higher Education (5.12a) This route passes over a couple of topropes and runs to the anchor up and right. **FA:** Debatable.

14. Gill Crack (5.11b) 65 feet. Legend has it, and there is photographic proof of said legend, that John Gill solo'd this route in 1959. You need a few finger- and off-finger-size cams, some tiny stuff, and a bold mindset to lead this. **FA:** John Gill.

15. Time Flies When You're Alive (5.10c) 65 feet. The right-most sport climb on the wall, this is probably the easiest way up. **FA:** Joe Sottile and friends.

Blacktail Butte North Wall

North Wall

1. Junior★ (5.11b) 40 feet. Just a smidge harder than its brother to the right. **FA:** Sam Lightner Jr. and Forest Dramis.

2. Stiffy★ (5.11a) 40 feet. Shares an anchor with Junior. Both routes are steeper than those on the main wall. **FA:** Sam Lightner Jr. and Forest Dramis.

Jackson Hole Mountain Resort

Opened in 1965 with only one chairlift, the Jackson Hole Ski Resort came to be known as the most challenging ski area in the country. The aerial tram, which opened in 1966, gave access to uniquely difficult and dangerous terrain that could only be compared to the big mountain resorts of Europe. In fact, the 1967 World Cup Downhill, which began just below Corbet's Couloir, was deemed "too dangerous" by many of the competitors. Over the years the resort has upgraded lifts and terrain, and is now recognized for its summer activities as well as skiing in winter. Climbing, of course, is one of those summer activities, with the tram offering access to both Corbet's Couloir and Rock Springs Buttress.

The climbing season for Corbet's is really only while the tram runs in summer, generally between Memorial Day and Labor Day. If you want to hike up, keep in mind that in spring the snow is melting and keeping the walls wet, and fall can be a very short season at 10,000 feet above sea level.

Rock Springs Buttress is different. Locals enjoy both the spring and fall, though the tram is not available and they have to hike up. At least a few hardy souls have rock climbed on the south-facing wall in midwinter, and mixed climbs are regularly ascended on the terrain right of Munger Crack and left of Clowns and Jokers when conditions warrant. You can actually ski right to the crag until the lifts shut down in April.

Restriction and access issues: The Jackson Hole Mountain Resort leases the land from the US Forest Service, so climbers are there at their pleasure. Follow the various rules they have posted around the resort or you may get us all in trouble. Dogs are not allowed on the tram.

A summer day pass on the tram is pricey, but gets you both up and down the mountain. The last tram takes people down just after 6 p.m., and the tram commonly closes when thunderstorms are in the area, so plan accordingly.

Finding the crags: To reach Corbet's Couloir, follow the obvious trail that parallels the tram line just to its south. The walk is about 500 feet to the lip of the couloir where you can pick your descent method.

To reach Rock Springs Buttress, follow the road off the summit to the south, switchbacking down Rendezvous Bowl. At the bottom of the bowl, you'll reach a meadow; take the trail that goes right, across the meadow and down the ridge for about a quarter mile. It is the less traveled path. When the ridge levels out, look for a cairn on the right that marks a climber's trail that descends into Rock Springs Bowl. This goes steeply down and then turns east toward the wall. The West Wall is the first clean, major buttress. It takes about 45 minutes to make the hike.

If you like hiking and have a few hours to use up, you can also walk up from Teton Village. Park in the upper parking lot and walk up the road through the private homes. You want to follow McCollister Drive, the second highest of the major roads in Teton Village, to its end. Here, between two driveways, you will meet up with a dirt path called the Union Pass Traverse, commonly used in the winter to get back to the lifts from the Hoback ski runs. Follow Union Pass for about half a mile, and then look for the trail that goes steeply up the hill. This will take you to Rock Springs Bowl below the buttress. From below the cliffs navigate through the talus to the base of the climbs. Our recommendation is you splurge on the tram ride. It saves about 2 hours and gives the climbing day more of a European alpine feel.

To leave Rock Springs Buttress, reverse the process. Remember that the last tram is usually around 6 p.m.

Heard in the Wind

John Colter

We climbers like to think of ourselves as a pretty tough and adventurous bunch, and those of us from the 307 probably more so, but we'd have to stand on our grand-mammies shoulders just to kiss the butt of a fur trapper of the early 1800s. In a nation of adventurers, the trappers stood above all others. And the grand Capitan of them all, the one who really initiated their treks to the West, was a man named John Colter.

Colter was born in Virginia a year before the outbreak of the American Revolution. His family survived, and in 1803 he joined Lewis and Clark for their three-year tramp across North America. Somehow the hardship of that adventure, complete with blizzards, Indian attacks, and bear maulings, was addictive to Colter. As the party of adventurers descended the Missouri, heading for St. Louis, in the spring of 1806, Colter asked to be released from his contract. He wanted to go back.

Colter teamed up with fellow hunter Manuel Lisa, and together they built a fort at the confluence of the Yellowstone and Bighorn Rivers. In late fall of 1807, Colter gathered his 30-plus pounds of winter clothing, his wood frame pack, wooden snow-shoes, a musket, and some ammo and set out southwest from the fort. He traversed the land of the Crow and skirted that of the Shoshone, moving up the Wind River drainage and crossing into what would later be called Jackson Hole. Historians have disputed his exact route for 200 years, but it is generally accepted that he crossed the northern end of the valley and exited to the west, near the southern end of Yellowstone.

The sense of loneliness on this trek must have been foreboding. There was Manuel Lisa and perhaps another trapper at the fort, but other than those two some 200 miles away, every face within a thousand miles was a threat. Wolves, lions, and the odd waking bear all needed him for winter protein. Temperatures were below zero almost every day, and as far as the eye could see, there was white. Colter turned north and east, and records show he was in Fort Raymond (in present-day southeast Montana) in the spring of 1808. He claimed seeing great vents of steam and boiling water pour from the ground and a wilderness full of furs that were ready for the taking.

The following year, 1809, Colter was captured and tortured by a band of Blackfeet. Stripped naked and forced to run from his attackers, Colter managed to evade all but one of the Indians. The last one he killed with the man's own spear. He managed to make it to the Jefferson River and float back to Fort Raymond, arriving naked and sunburned with cactus thorns through his feet. Another attack on Fort Raymond in 1810 convinced Colter it was time to return to civilization.

In 1810 John Colter married a woman named Sallie in St. Louis, then visited his old friend William Clark, who was working on a comprehensive map of the West for the US government. Colter provided details that would be noted on the map for the next seventy-five years. He died, probably of some sort of liver failure, in 1812 or 1813.

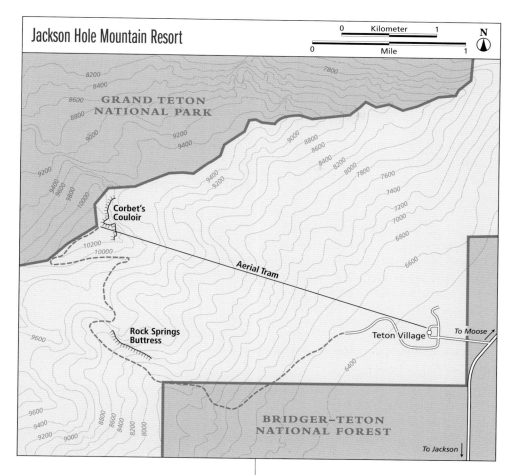

Jackson Hole Mountain Resort

GRAND TETON NATIONAL PARK

Corbet's Couloir

Aerial Tram

Rock Springs Buttress

Teton Village

To Moose

BRIDGER–TETON NATIONAL FOREST

To Jackson

The Classics

Corbet's Couloir

Dark Ages (5.12a)

Renaissance (5.13a)

Rock Springs Buttress

Exum Arête (5.10a)

Do It for Doug (5.10d)

Boxcar Arête (5.11a)

Waste Products (5.12c)

Grand Central (5.12c)

Corbet's Couloir

The walls that create the famed ski run are composed of Bighorn dolomite and offer some interesting climbing in an amazing setting. The tram hums by, paragliders soar overhead, and the Grand shows itself to the north along the spine of the Tetons. This area is at 10,000 feet above sea level, and though the radiant sun can take the hide right off you, it is rarely outright hot. The walls are the same rock as at Wild Iris, Sinks Canyon, and Ten Sleep, but the erosion has been different and thus it climbs different. Look for more technical edging routes than pocket pullfests.

Climbing down into Corbet's is not hard, but be careful. Helmets are recommended as you never know when some muggle-kid is gonna huck a rock into the ditch (despite the fact that there is a sign telling them not to). There can also be loose rock amid the scree where you belay. Most of the routes are sport climbs, so fourteen quickdraws will do unless otherwise stated. Some of the routes are old school in bolting, so be prepared for a runout here and there. Keep in mind they shut the tram down around six o'clock, and will shut it down if there are thunderstorms coming in. This area gets hit by lightning on a regular basis, so heed the warning of that distant rumble.

To get into the couloir, either rappel on anchors near the entrance or downclimb a chimney that is skiers-right of the drop-in point. For the Nature Hike area, either descend the couloir to the base of the routes or, from above the couloir, traverse up and around to the left and rappel in. Be careful at the lip. For the Renaissance area routes, it is much easier to locate the anchors of the climbs and rappel in to anchors on the ledge beneath the climbs. The anchor in the notch is best for this.

North-Facing Routes

You can rappel to the ledge where the climbs begin from the notch, or you can rappel via the Renaissance anchors, though they are a bit sketchy to reach.

1. Dark Ages★★ (5.12a) 70 feet. The best way to reach this splitter hand and finger crack is to rappel in via Renaissance (or the anchor in the notch) to the ledge, build

Corbet's Couloir North Face

Rappel to ledge

an anchor beneath the climb, and ascend. Bring pieces to 3.5 inches, mostly tighter hand sizes. **FA:** Sam Lightner Jr. and Mark Newcomb, 1991.

2. Renaissance✶✶ (5.13a) 85 feet. Taking twenty-three years for a second ascent, this is one of the hardest rock climbs in Jackson Hole. Below the roof block you can reach around to a good anchor—be careful. This allows you to rap the climb and hang the gear. A hand piece might make you happier at the start, though if you can climb at this grade you likely don't need it. **FA:** Sam Lightner Jr. and Mark Newcomb, 1991.

3. Right Wing Politics (5.11a) 40 feet. Climb up and right with some runouts on easier ground. **FA:** Bryan Silker.

4. Clash of Cultures (5.11b) 60 feet. Dirty and with questionable protection (old pins), this is not a classic. You need some large, offwidth-size pieces of gear for the start. **FA:** Paul Tureki.

Upper Ledge Routes

5. Turbulence✶ (5.11b) 60 feet. The easiest way to reach the base of this climb is to rappel off the ledge and then climb back up. **FA:** Greg Miles.

6. The Shining Path✶ (5.12b) 35 feet. This route is a bit committing; a stick clip helps, but a fall early on could be disastrous if the belayer isn't totally on it. Fun, powerful moves on a small but striking arête. **FA:** Sam Lightner Jr. and Mike Fisher, 1991.

7. La Chica Grande (5.10b) 35 feet. Up through a corner trending slightly right. **FA:** Greg Miles.

8. Escape Route (5.5) 25 feet. All chimney to get off the ledge. This is the easiest way up and down from the ledge below The Shining Path, but not the easiest way to Renaissance. **FA:** Sam Lightner Jr.

South-Facing Routes

9. Diffs and Diffs (5.10c) 60 feet. Trend up and left. Watch for loose stuff under the roof. **FA:** Andy Stewart.

10. Saxifrage★ (5.10a) 85 feet. Straight up and left to anchors at the lip. The crack to the right has been climbed at 5.10a, but there is no anchor on top, only scree, so it's a bit of a pain in the butt. **FA:** Richard and Catherine Collins.

11. ROUS's (5.10b) 85 feet. A fairly long route and requiring a baker's dozen quick-draws. Climbs up through the broken plates to reach the anchor. **FA:** Bryan Silker and Paul Babeneau.

12. Sky Pilot★ (5.11c) Thin at the beginning, then eases a bit as it trends up and right. The anchor is shared with Harebell and is over the lip, so take long slings to lower back into the couloir. **FA:** Richard and Catherine Collins.

13. Harebell★ (5.11b) Trend right at the start, then come back and reach the shared anchor over the lip. **FA:** Richard and Catherine Collins.

14. The Nature Hike★★ (5.11a) The first bolted line in the couloir, this route has a trait that was common with the first sport climbs: You have to climb between the bolts. Yelling "take" won't help much. Probably the best route on the wall. **FA:** Brents and Arcie Hawks.

15. Raven Roof Bypass (5.12a) Just right of Nature Hike and left of the nasty roof crack, this route gets a little contrived at the top . . . though that isn't anything new at Corbet's. If you traverse off before ascending the final boulder, it's mid-5.11. A dozen

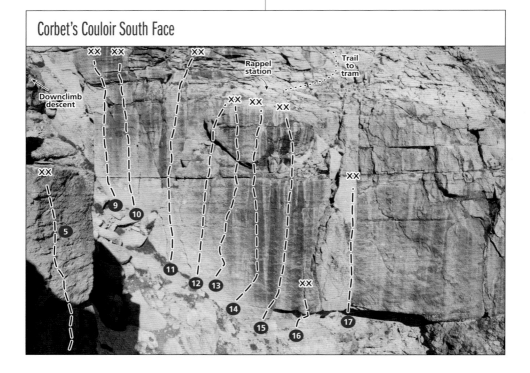

Corbet's Couloir South Face

quickdraws are needed. **FA:** Richard Collins and Mike Fischer.

16. Raven Roof (5.12a) A mix of gear, old bolts, and old pins are used to get up this overhanging coral reef. I suggest you give it a pass. **FA:** Richard Collins and Mike Fischer.

17. Whistlers Lid (5.12b) Out the roof to the right, then up the arête. A good climb. **FA:** Bryan Silker and Rachel Hartz.

Rock Springs Buttress

Rock Springs Buttress (RSB), composed of granitic gneiss, has become Jackson's premier cragging area. One often gets the sense of being at a remote crag in the Alps, and that is just as the original founders of the resort would have liked it. They envisioned the bowl below the cliff to someday hold a small alpine village, much like Kleine Scheideg below the Eiger. The cliff is fairly steep and well featured, with a mix of sport and traditional climbs.

It's possible to show up with just a rack of quickdraws, but bringing a light rack opens up more wall, as many of the climbs are mixed and can use a piece here and there. The wall has a lot of anchors, which can be confusing. Many of the routes have been rigged for descending with a single 60-meter rope, which can sometimes put an anchor in a seemingly odd place for a climber. If a pitch seems really short, you probably just found a rap anchor and not one intended for the climbing. Oh, and bring a helmet; this is the Tetons, not Red River Gorge.

The season can be pretty much all year if you catch the right winter day and are willing to ski to get there. However, most folks climb in spring, summer, and fall. The sun, which hits the wall around 1:30 p.m. in the summer, can be scorching at 8,600 feet, so wear sunscreen. And again, it's 8,600 feet, so bring a down coat and a shell as well. Anything is possible up here.

This wall has been climbed on for over fifty years; thus there are routes and combinations of pitches that have been linked together all over the place. There are some pure sport climbs and a lot of routes that mix bolts and gear. For the latter I recommend

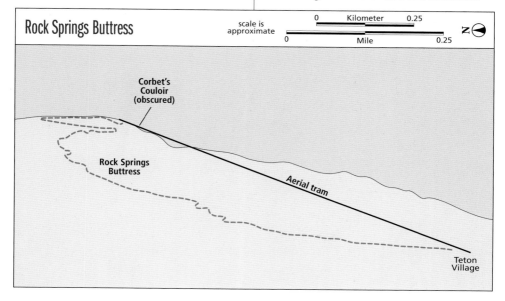

a set of nuts and a set of friends or cams to 3.5, including micro-cams, plus a handful of long slings. If you want to do the traditional lines, take two sets of cams. The routes are set up for 60-meter ropes, but only barely. Many of the anchors are stretching that 60 to its furthest, so you would be wise to bring a 70-meter rope. A tag line is not necessary if you rappel the correct route.

The topo is broken into two sections, one for the West Buttress, the first wall you meet when coming to the area from the top of the mountain, and the bigger Central Buttress. What you have here is a smattering of the best routes. For a more thorough topo of the crag, get a copy of Wesley Gooch's *Rock Climbing Jackson Hole and Pinedale*.

West Wall

1. Waste Products★★★ (5.12c) 90 feet. Fun, hard sport climbing. Take a dozen quick-draws. **FA:** Greg Collins.

2. Trash Culture★ (5.11c) An excellent sport climb, made mediocre by bad protection. Pitons have no place in sport climbing. This route connects to Coombs Crossover below its cruxes. **FA:** Paul Tureki and Phil Powers.

3. Coombs Crossover★★ (5.11b) Moving up and left, this is a great climb. A 60-meter rope barely reaches if the climber unties uphill. A 70-meter would be better. **FA:** Doug Coombs, Ty Vanderpool, and Paul Tureki.

4. Monkey Flower★★ (5.10a) Again move up and slightly left on a face reminiscent of the City of Rocks. Lots of bolts, but still spicy in places. Rappel down and left with a 60-meter rope, and you still only barely reach the ground. Be careful. **FA:** Tom Hargis and Bill Dyer.

5. Hargis-Dyer Arête★ (5.11b) From the anchor of Monkey Flower (stance), you can climb up and right on the obvious arête as

Rock Springs Buttress West Wall

Boxcar Wall

another sport pitch. With a full 60-meter rope, you can barely reach back to the Hargis-Dyer anchor and let the second toprope it. **FA:** Tom Hargis and Bill Dyer.

6. Triple Roofs★ (5.9) Two pitches of fun 5.9 climbing on gear with bolted anchors. Use the anchor on Monkey Flower for the end of the second pitch. Lots of finger and hand-size pieces. **FA:** Unknown.

7. Big Corner (5.10a) It looks worse than it is, as there is very little offwidthing to do here. Though it's a trad climb, bolts protect the widest sections, and there is a bolted anchor at the top of pitch 1 for the Old School 2000 route. Above that you have to build your own anchors. Rap a different line to get down. The anchor 30 feet up is to be used by climbers descending from the ledge above Boxcar Arête with a single 60-meter rope. **FA:** Unknown.

8. Sole Super Power★ (5.13c) Considered the hardest route in Jackson Hole, this is a clean, pumpy, technical face with some big moves. You need a 70-meter rope to toprope it. **FA:** Greg Collins.

9. Zion Storm Trooper★ (5.13a) A long, techy sport route that shares the anchor with Sole Super Power. **FA:** Greg Collins.

10. Hobo Rat Race (5.12c) Start with Zion Storm Trooper, then work right to Boxcar Arête. Pumpy. **FA:** Greg Collins and Ken Jern.

11. Boxcar Arête★★★ (5.11a, 5.10b obl.) 2 pitches: 5.11a, 5.10d. One of the first routes on the buttress, and a classic anywhere you place it. The first pitch takes eighteen quick-draws. Use long slings on the first half dozen or so to cut back on the drag, and then again on various bolts as the route works both sides of the arête. Bypass the first anchor,

which is for Ganger-Munger, and go to the big ledge to do the second pitch. This route is commonly climbed to access Old School 2000 and Generation Why. To get off all three routes, you either need two ropes or do a rappel from the anchor 10 meters up on Big Corner. Watch your ends. **FA:** Doug Coombs, Greg Collins, and Bill Dyer.

12. Old School 2000★★ (5.11d) Fun, pumpy, and technical climbing up and right across an exposed face. The best access route is Boxcar Arête. Take ten quickdraws. **FA:** Sam Lightner Jr. and Chip Brejc.

13. Generation Why★ (5.12c) A stout pitch of thin crimping into the Old School 2000 finish. All bolts. **FA:** Greg Collins and Jed Workman.

14. Ganger-Munger (5.10d, 5.10a obl.) 3 pitches: 5.6, 5.10d, 5.10d. Rarely climbed, but the second pitch is on pretty good rock and is a good way to push your trad skills if the grade fits. Belay the first pitch 30 feet off the ground at the obvious anchor—it's to limit rope drag. Second pitch is mixed bolts and gear, and the third pitch is all bolts. Use the anchor below the Boxcar Arête ledge to belay the third pitch. **FA:** Paul Ganger and Mike Munger.

15. Guides Route★ (5.8, 5.8 obl.) 3 pitches: 5.6, 5.8, 5.8. This is the obvious large corner right of Boxcar Arête. Anchors are bolted so guides could make five pitches from what should be three—perfect if you want the practice, but most people skip anchors on this one. A double set to #3 with a few slings is good for protection.

16. Blimpie★ (5.10a) A fun alternative finish to a few of the lines. From the third set of anchors on Guides Route and atop Gandhi and No Logo, step right into a large corner, then right again to a large flake and then up a gray wall to a bolted anchor about 65 feet up. Clip it and continue on to a ledge and anchor 50 feet higher. You can use the mid-anchor to get down with a single 60-meter rope. **FA:** Doug Coombs and Hans Johnstone.

17. Going Gandhi★ (5.11c) From that first set of rap anchors, about 40 feet off the ground, step out and right from the Guides Route and ascend through the roof to the third set of anchors on Guides Route. This pitch is bolted, but you will likely want a few pieces to reach that first anchor. **FA:** Greg Collins, Sue Miller, and Mark Postle.

18. No Logo★★ (5.12a) This pitch, which is generally liked by more folks than the previous, ascends to the third bolt of Going Gandhi and then goes farther right to the right side of the obvious arête before coming back left to the same anchor. It sounds weird, but it works. **FA:** Greg Collins.

19. Chocolate Corner★ (5.11b) A mix of bolts and gear take you up a polished brown corner and out an arête. This is a fairly short pitch with some powerful moves. **FA:** Paul Tureki and Scott Morely.

Central Buttress

20. Munger Crack★ (5.10b, 5.10a obl.) 5 pitches: 5.10a, 5.10b, 5.7, 5.10a, 5.9. The first two pitches and the top of the last have bolted anchors. The middle two are on natural gear. The route has few bolts and thus requires a more thorough rack than the other mixed routes on the wall. **FA:** Mike Munger.

21. Numerous mixed lines climbed in winter. Bolted anchors. **FA:** Hans Johnstone.

22. Clowns and Jokers★★ (5.11a, 5.10b obl.) 5 pitches: 5.6, 5.10b, 5.10b, 5.11b, 5.11a.

The first two are mixed, while the final three are all bolted. Find the start, shared by a number of routes, in a corner with a gnarled tree. Climb to a bolted rap anchor, then for pitch 2 go right and then up with mixed gear and bolts. Set up a belay at the top of the second pitch on the second set of anchors (10 feet higher). For pitch 4 skip the anchor below the roof and climb to the hanging stance 40 feet higher. After the access pitch (gnarled tree, then trending up and right with the gnarled tree corner), the route goes pretty much straight up to a spectacular finish. A more challenging start is to climb the Exum Arête Direct Start, all on bolts, to the first anchor. **FA:** Dave Ryan and friends.

23. Exum Arête★★★ (5.10a, 5.8 obl.) 6 pitches: 5.6, 5.7, 5.9, 5.9, 5.9, 5.10a. This is a mixed route that climbs cracks and an arête to the summit of the most conspicuous tower projecting away from the main wall. Great exposure. The route is divided into more pitches than it needs to be, so a smaller rack (single set to 2.5 Friend with Stoppers) will work if you break it up. If you are going to link things, you might want a few more midsize pieces. Find the start in the corner with the gnarled tree roots. Tip: There is a rappel anchor for the ugly chimney route that can pull you into said chimney on pitch two—don't go there. Go up and right to get to a large ledge out on the arête. Route 23A is a direct start to this climb that is all bolted and goes at 5.10d. You can use this start for Clowns and Jokers as well. **FA:** Tom Hargis and Bill Dyer.

24. Chucks Road to Thailand Named for climbing legend and Exum guide Chuck Pratt, this route climbs separate ground from Exum Arête but utilizes most of the same anchors. Most people only do the last two

pitches, which go out right from Exum Arête and are easier, but do require gear placements. Exum Arête is the better line. **FA:** Tom Hargis and Bill Dyer.

25. Do It For Doug★★★ (5.10d, 5.10b obl.) 5 pitches 5.9, 5.10b, 5.10d, 5.10c, 5.8. One

of the best routes in the valley, this climb uses all techniques, from working up corner systems to featured, exposed faces, in a spectacular setting. Find the start by looking left of a very large corner and high for that first bolt. Don't get pulled right to Grand

Nancy Johnstone and Liz Lightner on Exum Arête (5.10a), Rock Springs Buttress, Jackson Hole.

Central's first anchor. The first four pitches are bolted and can be rappelled on a single 60-meter rope (tie a knot in the ends). The last pitch needs traditional gear. **FA:** Greg Collins and Hans Johnstone.

26. Grand Central★★★ (5.12c, 5.12a obl.) 5 pitches: 5.10b, 5.12c, 5.11a, 5.11c, 5.9. An excellent rock climb up the middle of the wall. Great exposure, all bolt protected. Climb the approach pitch or, alternatively, climb most of the first pitch of Do It For Doug and then traverse to the anchor (5.9 move). This is the left-most anchor on the ramp. Pitch 2 ascends a series of bulges on small holds to a belay on the brown slab. Head straight on up from there to a hanging stance on a rust-brown face, and on from there to the anchor shared with Big Wally and Gray Wall. You can continue to the top on bolts, with a few pieces to help, or rap the route. By the way, partway up the second pitch you may see an anchor to the left—this is for an unfinished and closed project. **FA:** Greg Collins and Kent McBride.

27. Big Wally★★ (5.11c, 5.10d obl.) 5 pitches: 5.10b, 5.11c, 5.11a, 5.10a, 5.9. An excellent climb that is mostly protected with traditional gear. An approach pitch, used by Gray Wall and Grand Central, gets you to a 4th-class ramp. The left-most anchor set is for Grand Central, middle is Big Wally, and right is Gray Wall. A single bolt marks the lower moves of pitch 2, then it's gear the rest of the way (with bolted belays). Trend up and right then back left, following crack systems and corners. After the opening, steep corner on the 4th pitch, trend left to the Grand Central anchors. Take a double rack to 3.5 with some long slings. Rap either Grand Central or Gray Wall to get down. **FA:** Hans Johnstone and Greg Collins.

28. Gray Wall★ (5.11d. 5.11a obl.) 6 pitches: 5.10b, 5.11d, 5.10d, 5.11b, 5.10b, 5.9. A great route made "OK" by some less-than-perfect bolt and anchor placements. Ascend the approach pitch, then climb up and right on a seam through a series of bulges with some awkward and reachy clips. The anchor is slightly out of line with the obvious stance. Climb pitch 3 up and right, then follow a long crack and corner back left on this and the next pitch, taking you around the left side of the obvious giant roof. Look for the top of pitch 4 down and right of the Big Wally anchor. A couple of bolts help with the start of pitch 5, then follow a crack to broken ground, trending back left to the Grand Central anchor. You can continue up and right on gear to the top of the cliff or rap Grand Central to the base. Take a double set to 3.5 inches with long slings **FA:** Greg Collins and Hans Johnstone.

SWIFT CREEK SPIRE

■ OVERVIEW

Few climbers have climbed, seen, or even heard of Swift Creek Spire. Honestly, that's with good reason, as the tower is only about 100 feet tall and has less than ten climbs on its north and south faces. However, Swift Creek Spire is made up of fairly solid Madison limestone, like Blacktail Butte in Jackson, but it is overhanging on all sides and more featured. The climbs that have been established are a lot of fun, the canyon is a beautiful place, and Swift Creek Spire is an easy stop when driving along the very western edge of Wyoming.

Swift Creek flows west from the Salt River Range into Star Valley, Wyoming. Star Valley was comfortably inside the territory of the Shoshone when Lewis and Clark first explored western North America, and the surface salt deposits found in the area are thought to have been important to the tribe. In the 1870s Mormon pioneers, including Brigham Young Jr., made their way north from the Salt Lake Valley and managed to find ways to survive the valley's harsh winters. For some reason the Edmunds-Tucker anti-polygamy act of 1882 made this distant, self-regulated community even more popular with Mormon pioneers, and the population boomed (more women than men). Interestingly, the Snake River, flowing south out of Jackson through Snake River Canyon and into the northern reaches of Star Valley, was so difficult and dangerous to traverse that no one ever made their way from the settlement into Jackson Hole. Instead, the Mormons found plenty of wild game and good soil for farming along the Salt River and Swift Creek, and Star Valley became a satellite ward of the Salt Lake City–based LDS Church.

Afton, near the mouth of Swift Creek Canyon near the south end of the valley, is a sleepy little town of less than 2,000. There is a grocery store, a few restaurants, and perhaps a bar tucked away somewhere. It is not a destination climbing town, but if you are driving up the west border of Wyoming, Swift Creek Spire is worth a stop.

Trip Planning Information

General description: A small, quiet canyon with a handful of routes on one picturesque limestone spire

Location: 3 miles east of Afton, Wyoming

Land manager: Bridger-Teton National Forest

Fees: None

Climbing seasons: Spring, summer, fall

Camping and hotels: Afton is on one of the main routes to Jackson and the national parks, and it is a destination for anglers, so there are plenty of hotels in the area. For a small fee there is a small, shady, seldom-used Forest Service campground, with water and toilets, near the mouth of Swift Creek Canyon.

Food: You will not find a culinary windfall in Afton, but there are a couple of diner-type restaurants along Main Street. There is also a grocery store on the east side of Main as you go north out of town.

Guidebooks and other resources: Wesley Gooch's *Rock Climbing Jackson Hole and Pinedale* also covers Swift Creek Spire. However, you will have to order it online or purchase it in Jackson, as there are no climbing shops in Afton. There is information on Mountain Project as well.

Nearby shops and guide services: The closest climbing shop is Teton Mountaineering in Jackson. Mountain guides are also going to have to come from Jackson, either Exum or Jackson Hole Mountain Guides.

Emergency services: For most emergencies you should just call the Lincoln County Sheriff's Department in Afton at (307) 885-5231. The phone number for the Forest Service office in Afton is (307) 886-5339. Keep in mind any search-and-rescue personnel in this part of the state will very rarely, if ever, perform high-angle rescues. In other words, you might be better off on your own. The Star Valley Medical Center in Afton can be reached at (307) 885-5800.

Restrictions and access issues: Swift Creek Spire is in the Bridger-Teton National Forest and has no restrictions on climbing.

Finding the spire: (See the Wyoming overview map in the table of contents.) To find the spire, turn east onto 2nd Avenue in Afton. Follow 2nd Avenue as it becomes Swift Creek Canyon Road, continuing on for about 4 miles into the canyon. The spire will be quite obvious on the left side of the road. Find a trail just west of the spire that circles up and around its north side. The walk from car to rock is 4 minutes.

The Climbing and Gear

The climbing is on Madison limestone with edges and a few pockets, most routes being gently overhanging. The North Face routes end just below a ledge, but can be linked to the summit. The South Face route goes almost all the way, but you will want a 70-meter rope to get down on this side. All routes are bolted with lowering anchors.

The first ascent of the tower was made by the Idaho Falls Mountaineering Club in the 1960s or 1970s. For some reason they left a register on top but then chopped their bolt ladder on the way down. I call that "bad style." One thing you will notice in Swift Creek Canyon is the abundance of rock that has not been developed. It is off the beaten path, so all things in their time. Some of the fins of rock are pretty chossy and would take a fair bit of cleaning, but no more than you see in Rifle, American Fork, or Logan.

The Classics

Pull the Plug, 5.11b
Hustler, 5.12a

North Face

This wall is in the shade all day. Most routes start off a ledge that you would not want to fall from. Be careful.

1. Mental Hopscotch★★ (5.10d) 50 feet. Begin low on the far left arête. Belay from an anchor at the end of the airy ledge. **FA:** Sam Lightner Jr. and Sandy Boling.

2. Walking in L.A.★ (5.12a) 50 feet. Steep, technical crimping. **FA:** Sam Lightner Jr. and Kyle Mills, 2006.

3. Destination Unknown★★ (5.11c) 55 feet. Pumpy and sustained, unless you wallow your way into a hueco. **FA:** Sam Lightner Jr. and Kim Mills.

4. Hustler★★★ (5.12a) 75 feet. Right-most route. A pumpy and fun route that would be well recommended anywhere. Start with the arête and work back left up high. **FA:** Sam Lightner Jr. and Kyle Mills, 2006.

5. Idaho Falls Route (5.8) This is the continuation to the summit. The Idaho Falls Mountaineering Club appears to have aid climbed Mental Hopscotch and then chopped their ascent bolts. They must have freed this section. Getting off the top with two rappels is best. **FA:** Idaho Falls Mountaineering Club.

Swift Creek Spire South Face

South Face

6. Pull The Plug★★ (5.11b) This long climb is incredibly fun. Take a dozen quickdraws and don't stop at the anchor in the middle—it's there to come down with a shorter rope. Do not lower without at least a 70-meter rope, and then watch the ends. Best is to do it in two lowers, the second being from the middle anchor that was established just for this purpose. **FA:** Sam Lightner Jr. and Kim Mills, 2006.

7. Open project, bolted by Sam Lightner Jr. and Kim Mills. It needs some cleaning.

CODY AREA (THE ISLAND)

■ OVERVIEW

While other communities in the West grew because people had a need for a town near their ranches, mines, or forts, the town of Cody was a planned community. The founders of Cody, a group of Sheridan, Wyoming, businessmen and the legendary Buffalo Bill Cody, recognized there was a future in western tourism. They saw the Bighorn Basin, which lies in the shadow of the Owl Creek Mountains, the Bighorn Range, and the Absaroka Range and newly formed Yellowstone National Park, as a great place for hunting and the new industry of "dude" ranching. Until 1868 the Bighorn Basin had been off-limits to white settlers, but ten years after the Fort Bridger Treaty of 1868, the region opened to immigration, and by 1897 the foundations of Cody, Wyoming, were being laid.

The Bighorn Basin was very dry, but Bill Cody had a plan for that. The Shoshone River, what the Crow called the "Stinking Water" for the Thermopolis and nearby DeMaris Hot Springs, had the potential to thoroughly irrigate the region. Cody and his investors created an irrigation company that took ownership of the land around the town site and drew in the federal government's new Bureau of Reclamation to assist in making the land arable. The company then sold certain key plots of land to the B and Q Railroad so they were invested, and the Bureau of Reclamation went about damming the Shoshone and creating an irrigation system. Soon a rail link was established, and water was flowing to the town that took the name of its biggest investor.

Cody could be called the quieter entrance to Yellowstone when compared to Jackson, but the two towns have a lot in common. Both were ranching communities, but derive their existence principally off tourism today. Cody lies just 25 miles east of Yellowstone and is well known as a hunting destination. The Buffalo Bill Center of the West, created in 1917, is actually a collection of museums that could be called the Smithsonian of the American West. Over a million people a year pass through the town for the museums, art galleries, and the world-famous Cody Stampede Rodeo.

Climbers, who tend to lean toward masochistic pursuits, know the area more for the ice climbing along the South Fork of the Shoshone River than for the abundant rock that lies just outside of town. If you want to ice climb, Joe Josephson's *Winter Dance* thoroughly covers the South Fork drainage, but Cody is also a great place for rock climbers. There are half a dozen climbing venues, on both Bighorn dolomite and granite, within 10 miles of town. Also, the north slope of Cedar Mountain is home to one of the better bouldering areas in the state. We will cover the roadside crags known as The Island and Riverside Granite, both areas being primarily sport crags on well-featured, 2.5-billion-year-old granite.

As you will see with a visit, Cody has an enormous amount of rock. With all that rock comes a rich history of climbing. Curt and Todd Cousins were early influences of the scene, and they were followed by Bobby Model and Pat Mees. However, one man stands out over the years as the biggest influence of what we climb in Cody today, and that is Mike Snyder. Mike has put up 90 percent of the routes featured in this chapter. When he isn't climbing, he is often working on climbing-related causes, like rebolting the classics and serving on the board of directors

The beautiful Lower Granite Walls and the Shoshone River in Shoshone Canyon.

for the Bighorn Climbers Coalition. Mike works tirelessly to help climbers in northern Wyoming, so if you see him give him a pat on the back and maybe buy the man a beer.

Trip Planning Information

General description: Vertical and overhanging sport climbs on granite

Location: 5 miles west of Cody, Wyoming

Land managers: Buffalo Bill State Park, Bureau of Reclamation, and Bureau of Land Management's Bighorn Basin District

Fees: None

Climbing seasons: Spring, summer, fall

Camping and hotels: There are a number of campgrounds around Cody. The Ponderosa has all the amenities you could ask for and it's right in town. Three miles east of Cody is a KOA with the same level of comfort and cabins for rent. Just past the climbing areas, in Buffalo Bill State Park, there is a campground on the north shore of Buffalo Bill Reservoir with basic services.

Cody has a host of hotels to stay in if you want to get out of the elements. Best Western, Super 8, Holiday Inn, and all the other chains are here, as are locally run motels that are nice, clean, and have the same level of service for often less money than the chains. I stay in the Moose Creek Lodge, as it is in the middle of downtown and has easy access to restaurants and such. Keep in mind that these places fill up in the summer, and there are in- and off-season prices that may make a spring or fall trip more affordable than Fourth of July weekend.

Food: For breakfast the standard is Our Place, on the left as you head west out of town. It's your classic, small-town greasy spoon, and has become a "must" for climbers. Another excellent option is The Beta Coffeehouse on 10th, just off Sheridan Avenue and across the street from the giant rifle. It's a cafe with good coffee and a number of breakfast choices. For lunch or dinner you cannot beat Local. It's reasonably priced and one of the best restaurants in the state. You are in cattle country, so the majority of dinner places are steak houses. The Proud Cut Saloon, on Sheridan in the middle of town, is a good place for some dead cow.

There is a Smiths, an Albertsons, and a Safeway, as well as a Walmart Supercenter in Cody. The Hole Foods Trading Company, which is connected to Local, is a good place for vegi, vegan, and organic stuff.

Guidebooks and other resources: You are holding it. There is no local guidebook to the hundreds of climbs in the Cody area, so this is it. The local climbers have done a pretty good job maintaining the pages on Mountainproject.com.

Nearby shops and guide services: The local climbing shop is Sunlight Sports, located on the north side of Sheridan Avenue (1131 Sheridan Ave.) about halfway through town. They are also an excellent source of information on The Island and other crags in the area, as well as Ten Sleep Canyon if you happen to be heading that way.

As for climbing guides, the best guide for Wyoming cragging is Micah Rush. He works for Exum Mountain Guides, is fully certified and an EMT, and is based out of Casper. However, he knows all the cragging areas of the state like the back of his hand. Micah can be reached at (307) 267-4815 or wyoboulder@hotmail.com.

Emergency services: Of course, any emergency can be handled by dialing 911, but the Park County Sheriff's Department can be reached at (307) 527-8710 if you need them specifically. West Park Hospital is across the street from the Buffalo Bill Center of the West and can be reached at (307) 527-7501. For very serious injuries you will likely be flown to Billings, Montana. Keep in mind that cell service is spotty at best in the canyon.

Restrictions and access issues: There are no restrictions on the established climbs, but establishing any new routes above the highway tunnels is an absolute no-no. Also, don't climb on the tunnels themselves, and walk single file through them when getting to the crag. Our access is based on the good relationship we have with the highway department, so be as considerate of the motorists as possible. Finally, do not attempt to park any closer to the crag than is listed below. Just pulling off the highway between the tunnels is dangerous and illegal.

Getting there: Cody's airport is served by SkyWest from both Denver and Salt Lake City, and there are plans to have direct flights from Chicago in the future. The airport in Billings, Montana, just 2 hours away by car, is served by numerous airlines from all over the country.

Of course, from both airports you will need a car. There are the usual rental agencies, but as with all areas in this book, it's probably best if you drive your own vehicle to Wyoming for your climbing trip. Cody is in north-central Wyoming at the crossing of a few major highways. Cody is about 2 hours from Ten Sleep, 3 hours from Lander, 6 hours from Devils Tower, and anywhere from 5 to 10 hours from Jackson because of the traffic in Yellowstone National Park.

Finding the crags: To reach the parking for the crags, go west on the North Fork Highway, which is US 14/16/20, toward Yellowstone National Park. Just over 5

miles out of town, slow down and park at a pullout just before the first tunnel. There is more detailed info on the approaches in each section. Make sure you leave space for other vehicles in the pullout.

The Climbing and Gear

There are enough crags in the Cody area to make a book in their own right, and eventually there will no doubt be such a tome. For now, we are just covering a couple of the better and easier-accessed granite crags. Most of the routes are sport climbs, with only a few requiring a mixed rack or complete traditional rack. However, if you want all your options open, bring a light rack.

The majority of the climbs at The Island face northeast, making it a great crag for the summer months. The Single Malt Wall is lower in the canyon and thus gets its share of shade, but it also faces southeast, so when the sun is high in the sky it cooks. Climbing here is best in the afternoon hours in summer, or in spring and fall when you are looking for those warm rays.

The Classics

Bruce's Crack (5.7)

Feelin' All Right (5.8)

Pea Green Limousine (5.10c)

Turbo Charger (5.10c)

Wild Thing (5.10d)

Big Ben (5.10d)

Illegal Dihedral (5.11a)

"Ah . . . Me Wrikey" (5.11b)

Light Tension (5.11b)

Last Freedom (5.11d)

Spider Pig (5.12b)

Stranahans (5.12c)

McClelland Strong (5.13b)

Heard in the Wind

Washakie

Over the last 500 years, there have been many impressive leaders of the Native American tribes, but none stand out more than Chief Washakie. Washakie was born a member of the eastern Shoshone sometime around 1808. The Shoshone, also referred to as "the Snakes," were a dominant tribe in western Wyoming and eastern Idaho. They were known to have begun using horses sooner than most of the other tribes in the region, and held alliances with some of the more powerful tribes that traded for guns with Mexico. For those reasons, and despite being outnumbered by other tribes of the region, they were able to hold sway over western Wyoming.

Washakie became chief of the eastern Shoshone around 1840. He took his name, like most Shoshone, as a young brave. Washakie translates to either "shoots on the run" or "the rattler," both fitting for the man who was known as a good shot with a rifle or bow and for carrying a large rattle into battle to unnerve an opponent's horse.

The eastern Shoshone controlled the Wind River Valley, an area renowned for its wild game and mild winters. The area was so coveted that the Shoshone constantly found themselves at war with one tribe or another in defense of their land. When Washakie was a teenager, his father was killed by a party of Blackfeet.

War with the Sioux, who killed Washakie's eldest son, was also common, but the most famous battle took place between the Shoshone and the Crow. As the oral tradition has it, Washakie and his warriors met the Crow about 35 miles north of Lander. The combat raged for five days, at which time Washakie convinced the Crow chief, known as Big Robber, that the two of them should fight in a winner-takes-all match for the area. That brawl ended with Washakie and the Shoshone retaining the area and the Crow chief's heart on the end of a lance. (This was actually a sign of respect, rather than the disrespectful scalping. It is also common to hear that Washakie took a bite of the heart, an even more respectful action.) The metropolis of Crowheart and the nearby butte take their names from this event.

Washakie was wise enough to see how the western migration of the new white tribe would affect his tribe. Understanding the new tribe would come by the millions, he negotiated and signed the 1868 Treaty of Fort Bridger. It made the Shoshone and white Americans allies who would help each other against common foes, and gave the Shoshone the heart of the land they had fought other tribes so hard to keep. This land would become the Wind River Indian Reservation with Fort Auger (today's Lander) its seat. Washakie and his warriors then served as scouts in battles against the Sioux, Cheyenne, Arapaho, and Blackfeet. ®

Through his life Washakie was an animist, a Mormon, and eventually an Episcopalian, all at times that served his tribe best. He claimed Osborne Russell, Kit Carson, and Brigham Young (whom he called "Big 'Um") as friends, and had Jim Bridger for a son-in-law. He was on excellent terms with Presidents Ulysses Grant, Andrew Johnson, and Chester Arthur, the latter of which visited him at Fort Washakie in 1883. His name has carried on in many ways, including the town of Fort Washakie, a county, a national forest, schools, lakes, at least one mountain, and an untold number of buildings. He died in 1900 having secured one of the largest parcels of land, and still the most coveted land, for his tribe through his wisdom and skillful negotiating. He was buried in the town that still bears his name with full US military honors.

The Island

The Island is an amphitheater of granite that was seemingly designed for climbers. It is perhaps the most "roadside" crag in the state. This unique setting is a giant alcove of granite between highway tunnels, with a plug (The Island) in the middle—almost how you would design a gym. The area was once a paved parking lot created for the construction of the tunnels, and its manicured past has made for a great base to start all the routes. The routes range from 5.7 to 5.13a, and there are a few traditional and mixed lines amid the sport climbs.

Finding the crag: The Island is between tunnels two and three about 5 miles west of Cody. To reach it, take the North Fork Highway, which is US 14/16/20, west from town toward Yellowstone National Park. Setting your odometer at the Buffalo Bill Center of the West (BBCW), drive 5.3 miles west, passing a large paved pullout (used for

Riverside Granite). Continue on 0.2 mile farther to a pullout just before the first tunnel. Park far off the road, leaving space for other vehicles. Walk through the first and second tunnels, reaching a large amphitheater before the third tunnel. The far wall is Tunnel Wall and Egyptian Wall, the plug of rock in the middle is the original "Island," and the wall on the right is The Arrowhead.

Walk quickly and single file when in the tunnels, and remember there is no reason to slow down motorists trying to get to Yellowstone. For what it's worth, this is a kid-friendly crag once you get past the tunnels, but you have to walk that gauntlet first. Keep pooches on a tight leash, as a couple have been hit in the tunnel and when wandering about at the crag.

The topos begin on the far wall, Tunnel Wall, on the left side, then pass around the alcove going to the right. As a final note, if you can figure out why people need to honk their horns in tunnels, let us know.

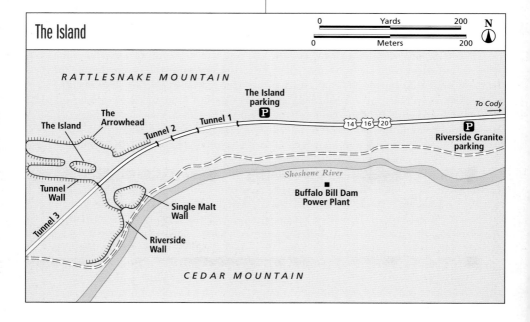

The Island

Zayne Hebbler on Bitch with a Broomstick (5.8), The Island, Cody.

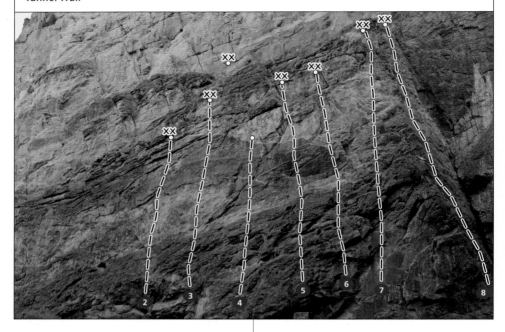

Tunnel Wall

1. Dried Fish (5.9) Climb broken ground to the tree using gear, then rap from the tree. Do not climb any closer to the tunnel than here.

2. Squintch (5.12b) 40 feet. Bouldery route following five bolts up vertical wall. **FA:** Mike Snyder.

3. Spring Cleaning★★ (5.10c) 40 feet. Just right of Squintch is a far more fun undertaking. Five bolts. **FA:** Pat Meese.

4. Rub the Nub★ (5.9) 35 feet. Rub the Nub climbs to an anchor that is slightly lower than the others on the wall. **FA:** Mike Snyder.

5. Wild Thing★★★ (5.10d) 40 feet. A classic left to us by the late, great Bobby Model. Find the start behind the stone and concrete pillar. Five bolts lead to an old-school finish. **FA:** Bobby Model.

6. Mild Thing★ (5.9) 40 feet. The line of bolts just right of Wild Thing. Much easier finish. **FA:** Mike Snyder.

7. Community Service★ (5.10b) 45 feet. Climbs the blunt arête on the right side of the wall. **FA:** Mike Snyder.

8. Bitch with a Broomstick★★ (5.8) 50 feet. Another good one from Bobby that climbs somewhat differently than many of the other routes. Slightly sporty between the five bolts. **FA:** Bobby Model.

Egyptian Wall Left

Just right of Bitch with a Broomstick is the Egyptian Wall.

9. "Aah . . . Me Wrikey"★★★ (5.11b) 80 feet. Consistent good climbing with nine or ten bolts for protection. **FA:** Dan Miller and Mike Snyder.

10. Balls★★★ (5.11a) 80 feet. Climb to a large ledge then out a bulge and up excellent rock. Take ten or eleven quickdraws. **FA:** Mike Snyder.

11. Light Tension★★★ (5.11b) 80 feet. Many people's favorite in the area. Up a corner then an arête on slightly overhanging ground. **FA:** Richard Plumber.

12. Silent Spaz★ (5.10a) 60 feet. Climb in a small corner then on broken ground with six bolts for gear.

13. Crank Like an Egyptian★ (5.10a) 70 feet. Climb in the dark streaks on technical ground. There might be a sequence in that name. **FA:** Kurt Cousins.

Egyptian Wall Right

14. Value Jet★★ (5.10c) 65 feet. Just right of Egyptian. Protect with half a dozen quick-draws to an anchor just below a small bush. **FA:** Mike Snyder.

15. Last Freedom★★ (5.11d) 60 feet. Steep line of five bolts. **FA:** Todd Cousins and Pat Mees.

16. Certain Damage★ (5.12b) 70 feet. The routes get close together here, all beginning in the darker rock. Ascend straight up with nine bolts for pro. **FA:** Dylan Etscorn and Mike Snyder.

17. Digital Jedi★★ (5.11d) 80 feet. Climb steep ground with nine bolts for gear to a small ledge with an anchor. **FA:** Mike Snyder.

18. Spider Pig★★★ (5.12b, 5.11d obl.) 3 pitches: 5.11d, 5.8, 5.12b. Highly recommended by those who have done it. Pitch 1 is generally done as Digital Jedi. Pitch 2 is on easier ground, 5.8, with about nine bolts to a large ledge. The final crux pitch (5.12b) climbs up and right from the anchor. (The third pitch continues out of the photo topo.) You can get down in three rappels with a single 60-meter rope. **FA:** Mike Snyder.

19. Illegal Dihedral★★★ (5.11a) 85 feet. One of the best routes in the area. Same start in the black rock as Digital Jedi, then climb up and right, trending into a steeply overhanging dihedral. Follow this crack line to an anchor at the lip, and save a little energy for the ending. **FA:** Mike Snyder.

20. Free Time★★ (5.11d) 60 feet. Begin in the scree just a little way up the hill. Climb to a steep, blunt arête with seven bolts. **FA:** Mike Snyder.

Egyptian Wall Right

The Island Left Side

21. Hole-a-Day★ (5.11a) 60 feet. Found on the far left of the formation, near the cleft and about 60 feet left of Bruce's Crack. Follow the arête up and over a roof with eight bolts. Tricky crux right where you think it would be. **FA:** Troy Meredith and Mike Snyder.

22. Changing Dihedral (5.10c) 70 feet. A trad climb with some loose rock. Not recommended.

23. Bruce's Crack★★★ (5.7) 50 feet. The obvious hand crack up the slab and over the roof. A very good first traditional lead and our vote for best in the state at the grade. Bring extra 3- to 4.5-inch cams. **FA:** Bruce.

24. Welcome to Billings★ (5.9) 90 feet. A hard slab start (crux) takes you up the left side of the arête then over a roof and onto broken and easier ground. Some loose rock up high. **FA:** "Some Montana guys."

25. Horn O'Plenty★★ (5.12a) 40 feet. Starting with a seam, this V4 boulder problem doesn't relent until the anchor at the end of the steepness. **FA:** Mike Snyder.

26. Feelin' All Right★★★ (5.8) 75 feet. A strong contender for best 5.8 in the state, this route seems way too steep to be 5.8, but it is. Trend left up high into the dihedral and crack. Protected by nine bolts. **FA:** Mike Snyder.

27. Search★★ (5.8) 65 feet. Climb the slab, passing left of the roof to an anchor under the bigger roof, using six bolts for pro. **FA:** Mike Snyder.

28. Search Continued★ (5.11a) 80 feet. Continue on over the big roof to a bolted anchor or onto easier ground and the summit. **FA:** Mike Snyder.

The Island Right Side

29. Rescue★ (5.8) Beginning 8 feet right of Search, follow seven bolts up the slab to an anchor just under the arête. **FA:** Mike Snyder.

30. Nose★ (5.4) 80 feet. A mixed rack of varying pieces and one bolt protect this low-angle line. There is a bolted anchor high on the formation.

The Island Right Side

31. Jesus Loves You★ (5.8) 75 feet. A steepish start leads to lower-angle ground with roughly eight bolts for protection. **FA:** Paul Dinking.

32. Bobby and a Bosch★ (5.10a) 80 feet. Going farther up the face, this is a popular route. **FA:** Rick Aune.

33. Pea Green Limousine★★★ (5.10c) 75 feet. Just right of the blunt arête is this excellent climb with technical moves while still being pumpy. **FA:** Scott Born and Leslie Paul.

34. Blackwall★★★ (5.11d) 65 feet. One of the better routes of the grade in the area. Seven bolts and the anchor. Easily toproped from Pea Green Limousine. **FA:** Pat Mees.

35. Big Ben (5.10d) 100 feet. Taking advantage of the basalt that is stuck to the granite wall, this line has some loose rock. **FA:** Mike Snyder.

The Arrowhead

This impressive wall has perhaps not seen as much love as it deserves. The next three routes all begin with the obvious corner.

36. Red Head★★★ (5.13a) 90 feet. The most difficult line at The Island, usually climbed in winter. Ten bolts for gear. **FA:** Dan Miller, Richard Plummer, Mike Snyder, and Pat Meese.

37. Arrowhead★★ (5.11c) 90 feet. This route ascends the large crack then the face and crack system that splits the center of the formation. There are five bolts, but a rack of pieces up to hand size is needed. **FA:** Rick Aune.

38. Easy Ramp (5.6) 95 feet. A long pitch on gear from tiny to large cams. Some loose rock up high.

39. Unknown 5.7 (5.7) 75 feet. Climbs the obvious crack after moving over a broken corner system. Some loose rock. **FA:** Unknown.

40. Sleeping Puma (5.9) 70 feet. Out of the frame of the topo, the right side of the lower wall has a seldom-climbed offwidth crack. Some loose stuff getting there and a funky anchor at the time of this writing. **FA:** Jordan Jolly and Christian Baumeister.

Riverside Granite

These crags are the lower flanks of what you climb on at The Island. The walls are along the old highway to Yellowstone, and what a spectacular drive it would have been. Deep in Shoshone Canyon, with the river flowing by and the various colors of rock rising for thousands of feet, this is definitely one of the most beautiful crags in the state.

To reach it, drive out of Cody the same as for going to The Island, but at 5.3 miles park in a large, paved pullout. Step over the guardrail and find a trail behind the interpretive sign that descends steeply to the obvious paved road below. Follow that road up canyon for 0.5 mile to the big granite buttress below The Island. There are a few climbs along the walk that were left out of this book, but the most concentrated stuff is included here.

The road is maintained for use by the Bureau of Reclamation to service the dam and the hydroelectric facilities. To be sure, they have a big say in your access, so even though there are few cars traveling the road, you should make sure you do not block it with gear. Besides the Bureau of Reclamation vehicles, there are also anglers, hikers, bikers, and others taking advantage of the canyon, so be a good ambassador. Also, if you accidentally knock a rock into the road, move it ASAP. Make sure the Bureau of Reclamation vehicles are not blocked in any way.

It is possible to reach the Lower Canyon directly from The Island, but you have to descend a steep and very loose scree slope to do so. We recommend you follow the main trail and road.

The Arrowhead

Single Malt Wall

The climbing is characterized by slopers and small, square-cut crimps. It is a little steeper than The Island, and the routes tend to be more sustained. There is one traditionally protected climb down here, but all the others are bolted. The routes are listed from upper right to lower left. Find the trail to the upper portion of the wall 100 feet downstream from where Single Malt Wall meets the road.

1. The Desert Jew★★ (5.11b) 50 feet. Climbs the upper-most side of the beautiful brown face. **FA:** Jason Litton.

2. Cock the Hammer★★ (5.11c) 60 feet. Technical and thin, this route runs up the middle of the face. **FA:** Jason Litton.

3. Cool Hand Luke★★★ (5.11b) 70 feet. The other one; there is a Cool Hand Luke in Vedauwoo too. This one climbs the face just right of Chill Arête. **FA:** Jason Litton.

4. The Chill Arête★★★ (5.11c) 70 feet. A popular and sustained climb. Don't do it in the sun.

5. Turbo Charger★★★ (5.10c) 60 feet. Many consider this the best route on the Riverside Granite. Climb the obvious corner with great traditional gear of varying size. Lots of good nut placements. This is the only traditionally protected route down here. **FA:** Rick Aune.

6. Cragganmore★★ (5.12c) 60 feet. Start this one at the base of the wall on the ramp. There is a single bolt to clip into. Climb, switch walls, then follow bolts using a flared crack and edges to a chain anchor. **FA:** Mike Snyder and Winter Ramos.

7. The Industrial Chiller (5.11a) Same start as Cragganmore, then traverse left 15 feet and follow four bolts to the anchor. A bit of drag if you don't bring the belayer up to the lower wall.

8. McClelland Strong★★★ (5.13b) 65 feet. An interesting workout, even for the grade. Begin from the road using every trick in the book. Stick clipping the first bolt is wise. **FA:** Mike Snyder.

Upper Single Malt Wall

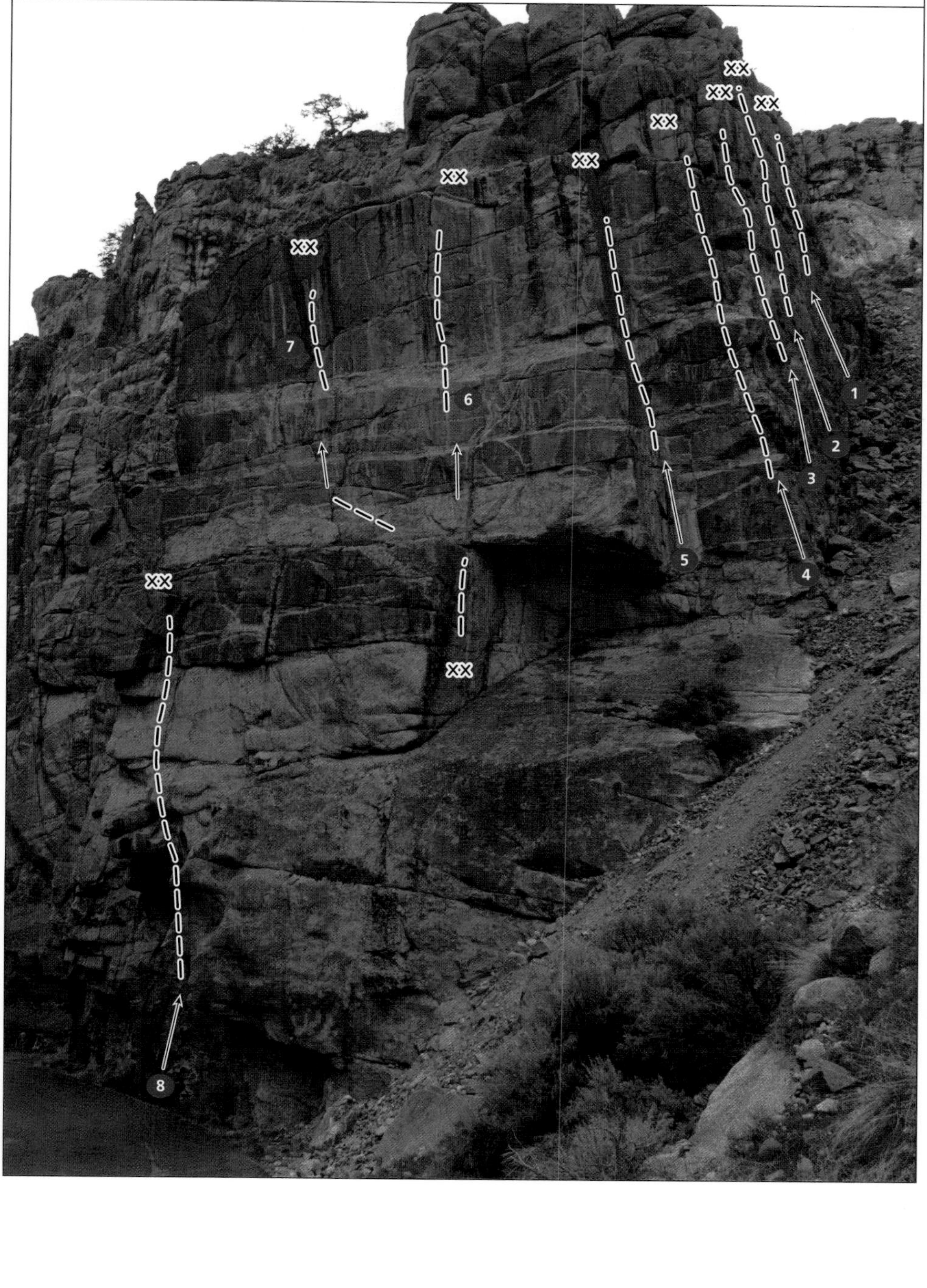

9. Bowmore★★★ (5.11a) 100 feet. A long and involved climb with good protection. Begin in the broken crack above the 1920s initials of "O.B.N." About 35 feet up traverse right and over a small roof to an anchor high on the face. You need like fifteen quickdraws. Watch the end of the rope when lowering. **FA:** Mike Snyder.

10. The Bowbeg★★ (5.10c) 100 feet. A combination of Bowmore and Ardberg. Again, bring at least a dozen draws. **FA:** Mike Snyder.

11. Ardberg (5.10c) 50 feet. This is essentially a second pitch to Glen Morangie, and it is generally done as one big 100-foot pitch. Watch the ends of the rope. Take sixteen quickdraws.

12. Oban★★ (5.12b) 50 feet. Three boulder problems in a row. Climb the start of Glen Morangie, then step left onto the face and begin pulling hard. Can't be seen on the topo, but it's there. Protected by seven or eight bolts. **FA:** Mike Snyder.

13. Glen Morangie★★ (5.10b) 55 feet. Look for two large lag bolts placed by the Bureau of Reclamation or highway department when the road was being put in. The first protection bolt is near these relics. Climb the crack with your feet out right. This is the start for Ardberg and Angels Share. **FA:** Mike Snyder.

14. The Angels Share (5.12d) 100 feet. Actually a pitch above Glen Morangie. Linking the two often creates drag. Hard moves getting to and in the roof. It's fifteen bolts long if done from the ground rather than from the ledge. **FA:** Mike Snyder.

15. Stranahans★★ (5.12c) 50 feet. Beginning 8 feet left of Glen Morangie, climb broken then steep ground to the obvious shield of rock. Get ready to channel your inner Michael Jordan. Protected by nine bolts. **FA:** Mike Snyder.

16. La Phroaig★★★ (5.11a) The most fun you can have and still be sober or upright. Climb easy ground until the wall steepens, then work a boulder problem out a bulge. A bit of a rest, then get the pump on and save some energy for the end. Clip seven bolts; the anchor is above the obvious ledge. **FA:** Mike Snyder.

17. Single Track★★ (5.11a) Good pump. A popular route just left of La Phroaig with nine bolts. Pumpy for the whole body up high with plenty of oppositional climbing. To the left of this climb is a cleft with lots of loose rock. **FA:** Mike Snyder.

18. Balvenie★ (5.11c) Oddness. Climb into the chimney 20 feet left of Single Track and then take a seat. Force yourself out of the chair and go right and up the face with nine bolts for protection. **FA:** Mike Snyder.

Lower Single Malt Wall

Riverside Wall

Fifty yards past a large gully and upstream of Balvenie is the Riverside Wall.

19. Mind Punch★ (5.11b) 40 feet. It is hard to look up the gully and not be drawn to the giant chockstone wedged in the canyon. This is the Dragons Lair, where numerous hard projects are being put together. On the left wall, under the giant Indiana Jones–chasing boulder, is Mind Punch, protected by seven bolts. **FA:** Jason Litton.

20. Slappin' the Fridge★ (5.12a) 80 feet. Just out of the picture and slightly uphill, find a dark gray, blocky arête feature with a line of a dozen bolts leading up and right through an overhanging crack system. **FA:** Mike Snyder.

21. Marty's Coffin★ (5.11c) 90 feet. A clean line of a dozen bolts goes up through the dark band of stone then onto the slab and out the bulge.

22. Phoenix★ (5.12a) 90 feet. An excellent rock climb currently marred by a bad bolt placement. Watch your head. It follows the impeccable brown varnish up steep ground to a broken crack system. **FA:** Jason Litton.

23. The Art of War★★ (5.12c) 60 feet. This follows the dark gray and light banded arête just left of Phoenix with eight bolts for protection. Weird moves in the chimney up high. **FA:** Mike Snyder.

24. The Dog Soldier★★ (5.13a) 50 feet. It's steeper than it looks, and the holds bring out a hellacious pump. Starts on the red slab, up the white bands, and then out the bulge to chains. **FA:** Mike Snyder.

25. Crime of the Century★★ (5.12d) 70 feet. Beginning right off the pavement about 75 feet left of The Dog Soldier, look for some black diorite blobs in a slab of pretty brown stone. Goes up and left using nine bolts. **FA:** Mike Snyder.

26. In Stitches★★ (5.11a) 75 feet. A little farther down the road, about 100 feet before the old-school tunnel, is a dark chimney that is the start of In Stitches. Ascend the chimney and odd features to reach a great lieback, then move out left on steep ground for a good pump. Popular. **FA:** Mike Snyder.

Riverside Wall

TEN SLEEP CANYON

■ OVERVIEW

Slicing its way deep into the Bighorn Range, Ten Sleep Canyon is a geologic wonder. US 16, otherwise known as the Cloud Peak Skyway Scenic Byway, allows one to drive through layer after layer of earth's history. All told, the total displacement of earth, from the base layer under the Powder River Basin to the top of Cloud Peak (high point in the range at 13,167 feet) is nearly 30,000 feet. Over 500 million years of time is exposed as history in the walls of Ten Sleep Canyon.

As you begin the drive from the sleepy town of Ten Sleep, you are in the heart of land once contested in the Johnson County Range War. Fought between wealthy cattle ranchers and small-time farmers, this lore of the West conjures such names as the Wyoming Stock Growers Association and Tom Horn. Rustling, lynchings, and even the intervention of the US Cavalry to end the bloodshed have inspired numerous movies on the subject.

The first modern climbers in the Bighorns naturally focused on the distant big peaks. When US Army engineer W. S. Stanton first ascended Cloud Peak in 1887, he found the remains of an Indian enclosure, likely built and maintained for ritualistic purposes. The first climbs on the dolomite were actually put up in the 1970s on gear. A few sport climbs were established in the late 1980s, but development of Ten Sleep Canyon began in earnest in the mid- and late 1990s. There is a lifetime of rock in the Bighorns, but only so many route developers in Ten Sleep, Cody, and Buffalo. The focus of those locals has yielded hundreds of routes and one of America's greatest sport climbing areas.

Trip Planning Information

General description: Steep, endurance-oriented sport climbs on Bighorn dolomite

Location: The west slope of the southern Bighorn Range in north-central Wyoming

Land manager: Powder River District of the Bighorn National Forest

Fees: None

Climbing seasons: Spring, summer, fall

Camping and hotels: Most people camp when they come to Ten Sleep Canyon. There are numerous Forest Service roads branching off the highway, and you can find your own personal campsite on that public land for up to two weeks. The old highway, running along the southeast side of the canyon, has a lot of popular sites. From June to September the Forest Service keeps the Leigh Creek Campground open. The campground is about 8 miles east of the town of Ten Sleep on a road that branches off to the south. Bears are common, so take all the precautions, and bring plenty of bug spray after June. The Sitting Bull and Boulder Park Campgrounds are located above the canyon and are open in the summer months. There is potable water and bathrooms at all three fee campgrounds.

If you want to be near a restaurant, a flushing toilet, and a bar or two, then you need to stay in the town of Ten Sleep. The Ten Broek RV Park has showers and Wi-Fi, and is walking distance to all you might want in Ten Sleep. It is pricey for a couple tents, though, and I don't recommend it if you are visiting when the Sturgis biker thing is about to happen. Perhaps a step up from the campground is the Log Cabin Motel or the Carter Inn.

Liz Lightner on Women vs. the Eternal Masculine (5.10c), The Ark, Ten Sleep Canyon.

Ten Sleep Canyon

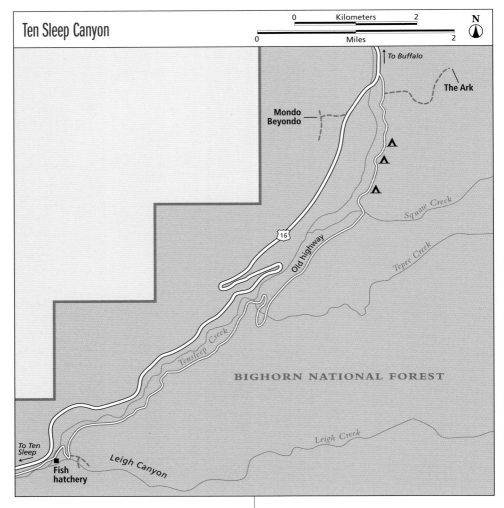

Food: The first thing you need to know is that there is no grocery store. Stock up on what you want in Worland or Buffalo. There are, however, a few meal choices. For breakfast go to the Crazy Woman Cafe, located just down the block from the RV park. Sackets Pizza makes whatever pizza you want, and there is often live music next door to enjoy while you eat. The Ten Sleep Saloon and Steakhouse offers the obvious and pizza, and the Ten Sleep Brewing Company has great beer and occasional meals, but it's about a mile west of town.

Guidebooks and other resources: Aaron Huey's *The Ten Sleep Bible* thoroughly covers the climbing in the canyon. It currently retails for $100. Although expensive, I advise you to pick it up if you are there for an extended amount of time. Various places in Ten Sleep sell it. Mountain Project has pretty thorough coverage routes and opinions, but not that many topos.

Nearby shops and guide services: There are no climbing shops anywhere near Ten Sleep, so make sure you have everything you need. The closest would be Back Country Bikes &

Mountain Works in Sheridan, Sunlight Sports in Cody, or Wild Iris in Lander.

Mr. Micah Rush from Exum Mountain Guides is again your guide of choice. Contact him at (307) 267-4815 or wyoboulder@hotmail.com.

Emergency services: There aren't any. Once you leave the town of Ten Sleep, there isn't even cell service. If you get hurt in a not-so-bad way, the fastest fix is via a drive to Worland and the Banner Health Washakie Medical Center (307) 347-3221. If you get hurt bad, someone needs to go to town and call 911. They may advise a heli-evac from Billings, Montana, or Casper. If you need a cop, the Washakie County Sheriff's office can be reached at (307) 347-2242.

Restrictions and access issues: There are currently no restrictions on climbing in Ten Sleep Canyon. However, the roads and crags are crowded with climbers at times, which puts some stress on our friends from the US Forest Service. Please be on your best behavior here, by parking in a way that allows as many other cars as possible in the lot, carrying out all waste, and generally following the Leave No Trace ethics. If the parking area you want is full, move on to the next one—it is not far. Do not park along the highway except at obvious pullouts that are designed for parking.

Finding the cliffs: By most people's standards, Ten Sleep Canyon is not near anything. OK, it's near the town of Ten Sleep, Wyoming, population 257 ("saaaluude!"), but it's not near any large cities. US 16 runs through the canyon and the southern Bighorns. From mid-canyon to Buffalo, Wyoming, where you can meet I-25, it's about 45 miles, or just under an hour. From Worland, Wyoming, to mid-canyon is about 35 miles due east, or 40 minutes in a car.

The nearest airport with regular commercial service is Sheridan at 85 miles and about 1.5 hours. It's 3 hours by car to Lander, and 3 hours the opposite direction to Devils Tower. Denver and Boulder are 6.5 hours away, but you can probably find someone who claims he does it in his Jetta in half that.

The Climbing and Gear

Bighorn dolomite, the stuff you climb on around Lander and atop the tram in Jackson, takes its name from the dolomite found in Ten Sleep Canyon. The routes at Ten Sleep tend to be longer and more endurance oriented than those of Wild Iris, but still with pockets and juggy edges. Most are slightly overhanging, and you will find the occasional sandy hold. This is a sport climbing crag, and though a few routes were established on gear in the 1970s, the norm is plenty of well-placed (though aging) bolts. Leave the rack in the car, but bump your quickdraw count to sixteen or more. The routes here can be long. Oh, to that effect, a 70-meter rope with a knot in the end is wise.

The Classics

Schools Out (5.10d)

Number One Enemy (5.11a)

The Wagon Wheel of Death (5.11b)

Bobby's Got a Dirty Mouth (5.11c)

Weight of the World (5.12a)

Crematorium/Burning Grandma's Bones (5.12a)

Happiness in Slavery (5.12b)

Exo-atmospheric Kill Vehicle "EKV" (5.12c)

Crux Luthor/Luthor (5.12c)

Crown Prince Abdullah (5.12d) 80

Super Love Bliss Machine (5.12d)

Gold Member (5.13d)

Heard in the Wind

Red Cloud's Warriors

Knowing the outcome of an event often skews our perspective. Despite our perception, the "Native" Americans put up a pretty good fight and won a number of major battles against the US Cavalry troops. The slopes of the Bighorn Range, and the Powderhorn Basin to their east, were the site of some of the harshest of the Indian battles. The most famous was Custer's defeat along the Little Bighorn in Montana, some 50 miles north of the Bighorn Range. A number of less known battles took place on the eastern foothills of the mountains, a mere 30 miles or so from Ten Sleep Canyon.

Fort Phil Kearny, north of the modern town of Buffalo, was established to support travelers on the Bozeman Trail. Jim Bridger had warned against sending wagons trains through this area, knowing the Lakota, Cheyenne, and Arapaho would likely go to battle. Still, the army thought it knew best, and Manifest Destiny was going to be met somehow. On December 21, 1866, a group of some thirty woodcutters from the fort were attacked by a band of Chief Red Cloud's warriors. A few were killed, but the Lakota warriors pulled back, with one feigning an injury. Word was sent back to the fort that the lumberjacks needed help.

Captain William Fetterman had risen quickly through the military during the Civil War, and it showed in his attitude. When assigned to the Bozeman Trail, he had purportedly told his superior he could "ride straight through the Sioux Nation with 100 men." Such arrogance probably would have made Jim Bridger snicker, and any Crow scouts quiver with the thought of the attempt. On this day Fetterman rode out of Fort Phil Kearny with seventy-nine men and orders to bring back the woodcutters but not go over Lodge Trail Ridge some five miles north of the fort.

When Fetterman reached the lumberjacks, he was briefed on the Indian attack. With word that at least one warrior was injured and riding slow, Fetterman decided to give chase. His unit rode over Lodge Trail Ridge, disobeying his orders and blundering into a classic trap. Within a few minutes the Fetterman cavalry unit was surrounded by over 1,000 Lakota and Cheyenne warriors under the direction of Red Cloud. In only half an hour, all eighty men were dead; their bodies were then stripped and mutilated and left randomly on the prairie.

This would be the second-worst defeat the US Army would suffer during the Indian Wars. The worst would come at Little Bighorn, and the ties between the two are interesting. Custer was also an arrogant officer, having risen fast in rank through the Civil War, who believed he could defeat any Indian force with his men. He was told by his scouts, just as Fetterman was, to not go into a particular area. Perhaps most interesting was the role played by the young warrior who had feigned injury and drawn Fetterman into the fight. His name was Crazy Horse, and he would go down in history not only as one of America's most innovative generals, but also as the war chief who defeated Custer.

Mondo Beyondo

Mondo Beyondo is one of the best crags in the United States. With routes ranging from 5.7 to 5.13, sun in the morning and shade in the afternoon, and great views of the plains and Bighorns, this area should not be missed. We have broken it down into sectors that roughly equate to the names of the most popular routes.

Many people come to Ten Sleep from Buffalo to the east. The distance from here to the exact parking location for this crag lacks a good reference, so we do it from the west. The pullout you want is on the northwest side of the canyon (left when coming from the town of Ten Sleep). If you are in town, you can set your odometer at the Ten Sleep Saloon. Drive northeast reaching the first switchback at 11.7 miles. Pass a second hairpin turn at 12.4 miles and then proceed for another 2.1 miles to the dirt pullout on the left—a total of 14.5 miles from the saloon. Coming from the east, there are no really good markers to set an odometer from. The best reccomendation is to pull off the

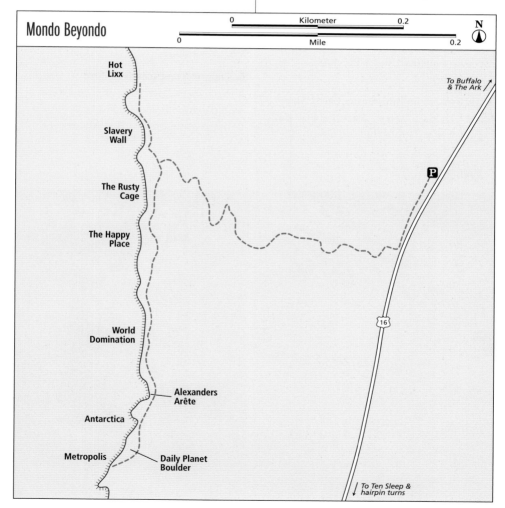

Mondo Beyondo

0 — Kilometer — 0.2
0 — Mile — 0.2

N

Hot Lixx

Slavery Wall

The Rusty Cage

The Happy Place

World Domination

Alexanders Arête

Antarctica

Metropolis

Daily Planet Boulder

To Buffalo & The Ark

P

16

To Ten Sleep & hairpin turns

road at the first big hairpin turn (there is a pullout) and go back 2.1 miles to find the pullout. It sounds odd, but it will assure you find the correct parking space.

Metropolis

1. Crux Luthor/Luthor★★★ (5.12c) 120 feet. Get ready to get your pump on. Climb the lieback crack to the anchor then on up the dark streak. Luthor is the 5.10a to the first anchor. You need like seventeen quickdraws. Use a 70-meter rope and watch the ends. **FA:** Aaron Huey.

2. Black Narcissist★★★ (5.12b) 70 feet. Climb the dark, thin seam to the break in the wall. Bouldery. Ten bolts. **FA:** Aaron Huey.

3. Fortress of Solitude/Jesus Christ Super Man★★ (5.13a) 110 feet. A less popular starting crack than Luthor, but still fine for the grade, leads into the fifteen-bolt endurance monster. Fifteen quickdraws and watch the ends of your rope. **FA:** Mike Snyder.

4. Gettin' Rich/Mining Space Rocks★★ (5.12b) 110 feet. Climb the lower crack, known as Gettin' Rich (5.10c), then go up Mining Space Rocks for another 60 feet and eight bolts. That's a total of fifteen quickdraws. **FA:** Mike Snyder.

5. Jesus Christ Super Jew★★★ (5.11b) 110 feet. Perhaps the best sport climb of its grade in Wyoming. The 50-foot hand crack to the first anchor is perhaps 5.10a, then it's perfect pockets for another 60 feet or so. Take sixteen quickdraws plus stuff for the anchor. **FA:** Aaron Huey.

6. Captain Tombstoner★★ (5.8) 50 feet. Lieback up the right side of a large flake with good footholds (behind Daily Planet Boulder on topo). **FA:** Aaron Huey.

Metropolis

Just below and up canyon of Metropolis is the Daily Planet Boulder. The routes on it are shorter and require power rather than endurance.

Daily Planet Boulder

7. Solid Gold Secret Sauce★ (5.12a) 30 feet. Steep left side of the boulder. **FA:** Aaron Huey and Willem Becker.

8. I Got Sweeded★ (5.12a) 30 feet. Pockets and edges just right of Sold Gold. **FA:** Willem Becker.

9. Smoking Lois★ (5.11c) 35 feet. Up the middle, passing a small roof. **FA:** Aaron Huey.

10. Choking Lois★ (5.11c) 30 feet. Climbs good pockets and edges to an anchor in the dark bulge. **FA:** Aaron Huey.

11. Poking Lois (5.11d) 30 feet. These tiny holds are kind of sharp. **FA:** Jim Hausman.

12. Moon Unit's Secret Shinto Ride★★ (5.10a) 50 feet. The cleft above the Daily Planet Boulder and at the right end of Metropolis is known as Zappa's Corner. This juggy, fun route is one of the better 5.10a's on the wall. Takes six or seven quickdraws. **FA:** Aaron Huey.

13. The Fabulous Gordini (5.10b) 50 feet. Well, at least it's a 5.10b near a good 5.10a, right?

Antarctica Sector

Varied cragging area that will someday have twice as many routes as it does now.

14. Man-Bear-Pig★★ (5.11a) 70 feet. For your first 5.11a you could not go wrong here. Lots of bolts (like a dozen) for its length. A fun climb the whole way. **FA:** Aaron Huey.

15. Crematorium/Burning Grandma's Bones★★★ (5.12a) 100 feet. Rare to have an arête into a roof. An outstanding climb with a bouldery start and pumper finish. Sixteen quickdraws to the anchor. **FA:** Aaron Huey.

16. Wild Turkeys★ (5.10a) 80 feet. Climb a chimney then onto the arête on the right. Twelve bolts. **FA:** Charlie Kardaleff.

17. Just Like Diocletians Blues★★ (5.10d) 75 feet. Starts a few feet right of Wild Turkeys on excellent rock. Twelve bolts. **FA:** Charlie Kardaleff.

18. Elvis Shades Rule★★ (5.10c) 80 feet. Thin holds lead to easier ground. Again twelve bolts. **FA:** Charlie Kardaleff.

19. Vikings and Ghetto Blasters★★ (5.11a) 80 feet. Thin and technical at the start. A dozen bolts. **FA:** Charlie Kardaleff.

20. Killer Frat Cat★★ (5.10d) 80 feet. Climb the slab and then gently overhanging rock on the center of the buttress (known as Alexanders Arête). Twelve bolts. **FA:** Stan Price.

21. Big Man on Campus★ (5.11b) 75 feet. Ascend the right arête to a ledge then over the bulge and up the steeper rock. **FA:** Aaron Huey.

22. Blutarski's Delta House Roof★ (5.10d)
65 feet. Climb from the small cleft up a corner and left onto the face.

23. Frat Boys with Razor Blades★★ (5.10b)
75 feet. Do a bouldery start and then pull on
great holds with eight bolts for protection.
A newish 5.11a (not numbered on topo)
goes up just right of this line to an anchor at
the very right side of the flake. **FA:** Charlie
Kardaleff.

24. Giddyup Grasshopper★ (5.10c) 75 feet.
A thin seam on a slab to steeper holds with
ten bolts. **FA:** Charlie Kardaleff.

25. Dust, Wind, Dude★ (5.11a) 75 feet.
Climb a crack to a ledge then over a tricky
bulge. **FA:** Charlie Kardaleff.

26. Lizard in a Bottle★ (5.11b) 75 feet. Thin
face climbing along a seam then pockets over
a bulge. Ten bolts. **FA:** Charlie Kardaleff.

27. Sorority Girl Blues★★ (5.12a) 75 feet.
Climb a techy lower section, then powerful
moves through the roof and above. Pumpy.
Ten bolts. **FA:** Aaron Huey.

28. Meat Head★★★ (5.12b) 75 feet. Fun
climbing to a very reachy roof and then
more fun moves protected by ten bolts. **FA:**
Aaron Huey.

29. Keg Stand★ (5.11c) 75 feet. Start the
same as Theta Dorka and traverse farther left
to a line of ten bolts. **FA:** Aaron Huey.

30. Theta Dorka Tool Shed★★ (5.11b) 75
feet. Traverse slightly left and then straight
up to a bouldery crux. **FA:** Aaron Huey.

Jesse Jakomait feeling the pump on Captain Insane-O (5.12a), Mondo Beyondo, Ten Sleep Canyon.

World Domination

The routes below fall on what is known as the World Domination Wall. It could have been called "super-cluster," considering the number of stars it holds.

31. Mike's Got a Dirty Diaper★★★ (5.11d) 85 feet. Just right of a hanging slab of stone, climb on great pockets with a dozen bolts. **FA:** Bobby Model.

32. Bobby's Got a Dirty Mouth★★★ (5.11c) 85 feet. Considered one of the best routes at the grade in Ten Sleep. Ten bolts. **FA:** Mike Snyder.

33. World Leader Pretend★★★ (5.12b) 80 feet. Climbs the brown rock to the distinct black streak. Loved by all. **FA:** Aaron Huey.

34. Captain Insane-O★★ (5.12a) 85 feet. Starts with a dihedral then goes steep on interesting holds to a tragically placed anchor. Fourteen bolts. **FA:** Mike Snyder and Dan Miller.

35. Pocket Seeking Drone★★★ (5.12c) 95 feet. Starts just right of Insane-O and trends up and right on a slab and then the steep headwall for sixteen bolts. **FA:** Gordon and Todd Anderson.

36. Berserk Osama★★★ (5.12a) 95 feet. Begins in a faint corner just left of Weight of the World. Protected by a mere fourteen bolts. **FA:** Gordon and Todd Anderson.

37. Weight of the World★★★ (5.12a) 90 feet. Thin and tricky on the slab, the perfect two du-doirs to the anchor. Very popular. **FA:** Aaron Huey.

38. Napoleon's Highchair★★★ (5.12a) 95 feet. Stick clip the thin start and work upward on holds that get bigger. Look for stacked rocks at the start right off the trail. **FA:** Aaron Huey.

World Domination

39. Sofa King★★ (5.12a) 95 feet. Climb a dihedral for four bolts, then trend left and up with eight more bolts. Pumpy and tricky finish. **FA:** Mike Snyder.

40. Came as a Rat★★ (5.12b) 95 feet. Same start as Sofa King but straight up. Twelve bolts. **FA:** Mike Snyder.

41. Moltar!★★ (5.12a) 75 feet. Thin start. Shares the finish with Thor. **FA:** Aaron Huey.

42. Thor★★★ (5.10b) 75 feet. Trying for best sport route of its grade in the state, Thor follows two parallel cracks up and left to an anchor shared with Moltar! **FA:** Charlie Kardaleff.

43. Bare Back Knuckle Bunnies (5.11b) 70 feet. With sharp holds and plenty of dirt, this is not a popular climb. **FA:** Bobby Model.

44. Cowgirls Smuggling Yo Yo's (5.11b) 70 feet. In the dark water streak . . . and that's all one can say. **FA:** Charlie Kardaleff.

45. Redneck Bungee Jumping★★ (5.12a) 70 feet. Fun climbing to a rest and then a sporty finish. **FA:** Aaron Huey.

46. Boubonic Rodeo Queen★ (5.12a) 70 feet. Sequential finish to fun climbing. **FA:** Aaron Huey.

47. A Few Degrees of Freedom★ (5.10a) 100 feet. This is a long, good 5.10a, though the holds are a bit sharp. Climb it more and they won't be. **FA:** Jim Hausman.

48. Sensory Stream★★★ (5.8) 100 feet. Maybe the best beginner route in the canyon. Ten bolts to the anchors. **FA:** Charlie Kardaleff.

The Happy Place

This little wall, locally known as The Happy Place, is about 200 feet left (down canyon) of Slavery Wall.

49. Chillin' Like Bob Dylan★★ (5.10c) 60 feet. Thin and technical into a faint corner. Seven bolts. **FA:** Charlie Kardaleff.

50. Praise Be to Dwight★★ (5.11d) 60 feet. Running up the dark streak just right of a blunt arête, with hard climbing right off the deck. Technical. **FA:** Charlie Kardaleff.

51. Nickel Bag of Funk★ (5.11c) 60 feet. The bottom is out of the topo just left of the obvious corner. Pull over the bulge to find the rap-hanger anchor. Seven bolts. **FA:** Aaron Huey.

52. Super Love Bliss Machine★★★ (5.12d) 65 feet. Up the pillar right of the corner and out the dark headwall. Loved by all who can make it to the anchor. **FA:** Aaron Huey.

The Rusty Cage

Find this steep, heavily pocketed crag, The Rusty Cage, about 100 feet left (down canyon) of the Slavery Wall.

53. Loki★ (5.11c) 50 feet. The pocketed wall just right of the fat, loose crack. **FA:** Charlie Kardaleff.

54. Great White Buffalo★★ (5.11b) 50 feet. Five bolts to the anchors. Pumpy for the length. **FA:** Charlie Kardaleff.

55. Blackalicious★★ (5.12a) 50 feet. Half a dozen bolts up the black streak with lots of two-fer's. **FA:** Mike Snyder.

56. Meet Me in Heaven★ (5.12a) 50 feet. Big moves on a smallish, for Ten Sleep, climb. **FA:** Aaron Huey.

57. Urine Luck★ (5.12b) 50 feet. Hard moves open the orange streak. **FA:** Matt Wendling.

58. Raining Ice Picks (5.12b) 50 feet. Super bouldery start. **FA:** Aaron Huey.

59. Micro Epic (5.10d) 50 feet. Just left of the small roof. **FA:** J. B. Haab.

60. Burwin Dinosaur Bones (5.10c) 50 feet. Right of the small roof on somewhat sharp stone. One difficult clip up high. **FA:** Charlie Kardaleff.

Slavery Wall

One of the premier sectors of climbing in Wyoming, the Slavery Wall has something for everyone. It is best known for its climbs that are 5.12a and harder, but there is something here for everyone.

61. The Wagon Wheel of Death★★★ (5.11b) 95 feet. Start on the left side of the flake and ascend the crack, trending left, on terrain that is steeper than it looks. Uses fourteen bolts for protection. Going to the first anchor below and right of the bulge is Alto Antes La Merda (5.6). **FA:** Mike Snyder and Kristine Hoffman.

62. Ka-blamo★ (5.12b) Trend right for a harder finish to Wagon Wheel. **FA:** Kevin Wilkinson.

63. Gold Member★★★ (5.13d) 95 feet. Begin on a large detached flake to a slab. Follow the beautiful gold streak out the bulge of the Slavery Wall. Our vote for best route of its grade in Wyoming. **FA:** Kevin Wilkinson.

64. Burden of Immortality★★★ (5.12d) 100 feet. Shares the start with Gold Member. A few bolts worth of bouldery moves make a crux in an otherwise enduro masterpiece. Loved by all. Linking this back to Gold Member (after the bulge) creates Burden of my Member (5.13c). Sixteen bolts. **FA:** Aaron Huey.

65. Heart, Balls, Swagger★★ (5.13b) 100 feet. Begin on the Schools Out flake, then trend left through the longest part of the bulge, crossing multiple other lines. The anchor is at the far left end of the great roof. Needs eighteen quickdraws. **FA:** Kevin Wilkinson.

66. Aunt Jemima's Bisquick Thunderdome★★★ (5.12d) 90 feet. Another rope-stretching pumper that has a hard boulder problem. **FA:** Aaron Huey.

67. Screaming Night Hog★★ (5.12c) 90 feet. Hard slab moves just left of the obvious crack, then a rest, then pumpy dynamic moves that get smaller the higher you go. Go fast. **FA:** Aaron Huey.

68. Jackabite★★ (5.12a) 60 feet. Follow a crack in a faint dihedral, then trend left over bulging rock. Traversing to Screaming Night Hog in the bulge makes the Jack a Hog linkup at 5.12c. **FA:** Jim Hausman.

Slavery Wall

69. Schools Out★★★ (5.10d) 75 feet. El Matador at Devils Tower has this grade tied up for best in the state, but if we were to give it to a sport climb, it would likely be right here. Again start in the crack and trend right in the bulge for nine bolts of fun. There are pitches above it as well (5.9, 5.10c), though no one has much good to say about them. The rappels are tricky, and there is loose rock. **FA:** Charlie Kardaleff.

70. Colors of Heaven★ (5.10d/5.9/5.10c) 150 feet. This three-pitch breakup of the wall only sees a few ascents because climbers show up here wanting to sport climb near the ground. Also, the rappels are difficult due to the overhanging nature. Climb Schools Out, then continue on. Back clip for the raps. **FA:** Aaron Huey.

71. Momma's Mental Medication★★ (5.12a) 35 feet. A short 5.12a for those who like their sport routes bouldery. **FA:** Mike Snyder.

72. Papa Knows Best★★ (5.12d) 80 feet. Just right of Momma's. Up a corner and on jugs that shrink the higher you get. Eleven bolts. **FA:** Mike Snyder.

73. Exo-atmospheric Kill Vehicle "EKV"★★★ (5.12c) 85 feet. Best 5.12c in Wyoming? Many think so. Ascend the left of the corner on consistently positive and steep climbing with eleven bolts for protection. **FA:** Mike Snyder.

74. Calm Like a Bomb★★★ (5.12d) 85 feet. From the back of the corner, follow a crack and jugs out the steep. Trend right and finish bouldery. **FA:** Mike Snyder and Dan Miller.

75. Crown Prince Abdullah★★★ (5.12d) 80 feet. Bouldery. Pumpy. Bouldery. Only Osama Bin Laden would dislike this route, and then only for the name. Stiff for the grade here. A dozen clips. **FA:** Aaron Huey.

76. Happiness in Slavery★★★ (5.12b) 80 feet. Half a dozen 5.11 cruxes on a consistently overhanging wall for 80 feet add up to the best 5.12b in Wyoming. Endurance is a must. **FA:** Aaron Huey.

77. Head Like a Hole★★ (5.12a) 70 feet. A little more bouldery up high than Slavery. **FA:** Aaron Huey.

78. Number One Enemy★★★ (5.11a) 65 feet. Climb up and left following intermittent thin cracks and pockets. Easiest stance for belaying is at the base of Head Like a Hole. Eight bolts.

79. Superfly★★ (5.12c) 90 feet. Found on the more northeast face of the wall and thus hard to show on the topo, this is a crimpy pumpfest that gets sun only early in the day. **FA:** Jim Hausman.

80. Strut Your Funky Stuff★★ (5.12a) 55 feet. Between Superfly and the corner, this route gets thinner and harder as you go higher. **FA:** Jim Hausman.

81. Shake Your Money Maker★★ (5.7) 65 feet. This is the obvious giant corner and crack. Protected by seven bolts, it's a fun stem corner with a crack that opens higher. The second pitch, rarely done, is 5.11c. **FA:** Charlie Kardaleff.

82. Fake Snake★ (5.7) 40 feet. Well-pocketed, low-angle climbing. Good fun for the grade. Four bolts. **FA:** Charlie Kardaleff.

83. Dougie and Jimmy's Excellent Adventure★ (5.8) 35 feet. Harder but shorter than its pal to the left. **FA:** Charlie Kardaleff.

Hot Lixx

Follow the trail up and right of Slavery Wall for this sector.

84. Asleep at the Wheel★ (5.12a) 65 feet. Thin, technical cruxes with good rests. **FA:** Charlie Kardaleff.

85. Wired Me Awake★ (5.11a) 75 feet. Also thinner, but a fair bit easier than its neighbor. **FA:** Charlie Kardaleff.

86. Beer Bong★★★ (5.10b) 80 feet. Almost unique. If you have ever done Groove Tube or Flushed in Thailand, you will feel some déjà vu here. Protected by nine bolts.

87. Hooray For Boobies★★ (5.10b) 65 feet. Just right of Beer Bong is this fun route. **FA:** Mike Snyder.

88. Itty Bitty Titty Committee (5.10d) 65 feet. A bit weird. **FA:** Mark Devries.

"X" marks the spot with these last four.

89. Neon Forest★ (5.10d) 65 feet. Go on big pockets to a slab, traverse right, then take a hard left back up using the crack and pockets. One long quickdraw will help with this.

90. Wild Dog Attack★ (5.11a) 65 feet. This is the linkup of Neon Forest and Brooklyn that allows you to skip the opening crack of the latter.

91. No Sleep Til Brooklyn★★ (5.11b) 65 feet. Start on a steep crack, then through a bulge and up the face to an anchor at the horizontal.

92. B-52 Deja Vu★ (5.11) 65 feet. Start with Brooklyn and follow the upper crack to the Neon Forest anchor.

Hot Lixx

The next eleven routes are all high quality, and all take such advantage of the stone that they essentially make a grid of bolts to follow. This makes it difficult to fit each on the topo, but the descriptions will get you there.

93. Shafts Big Score★★★ (5.11c) 65 feet.
Starts just right of the Brooklyn crack. Dynamic moves—hit them correctly. Stick clip that first bolt if you can. **FA:** Aaron Huey.

94. Turbotronic Dyno-master★
(5.12b/5.13a) 65 feet. Originally intended to go straight up and require a dyno, people now climb around said move for the easier grade. Seven bolts. **FA:** Aaron Huey.

95. Resurrection of a Solid Gold Rock Star★★ (5.11d) 65 feet. A well-liked line of pockets just left of the crack. Seven bolts. **FA:** Aaron Huey.

96. Stereosonic Keyboard of Death★
(5.10d) 65 feet. A thin start leads to big holds in the bulge. This climb is just right of the crack. **FA:** Aaron Huey.

97. I Was a Teenage Ronald MacDonald★★
(5.10d) 65 feet. Following the line of pockets in slightly darker rock, this is a fun climb. **FA:** Aaron Huey.

98. Air Guitar★★ (5.11c) 75 feet. A bit steeper than the routes to the left, this has a hard start and distinct crux. **FA:** Aaron Huey.

99. 1815 Squeezenstein★★ (5.11b) 65 feet.
Find the start at a blotch of orange lichen. Big reaches on good holds. Nine bolts. **FA:** Charlie Kardaleff.

100. Tear the Roof Off the Sucka★ (5.11c)
65 feet. This route is characterized by a clean white panel after passing the right side of a roof. Seven bolts. **FA:** Aaron Huey.

101. Egg McMuffin God★★ (5.11b) 55 feet.
The light gray streak at the left side of the wall. Well protected with eight bolts. **FA:** Charlie Kardaleff.

102. Orange Likin' Delight★★ (5.10a) 75 feet. Great 5.10a on the far right side of the wall. Long, with nine bolts over its 75 feet. **FA:** Unknown.

103. Lil Smokey Goes to the Mondo (5.10a)
30 feet. You're in the neighborhood so might as well. Small holds at the start of this three-bolt route. **FA:** Charlie Kardaleff.

The Ark

A little more difficult to reach, and nearly impossible to spot from the road, this crag is very much worth the effort. It is a unique, freestanding erratic wall that stays cool on the hottest summer afternoons.

Reaching it takes about 30 minutes, 20 if you find the right trail from the start. There is a myriad of cow trails through here, and the climber's trail sort of takes the best line. Know that if you get off-trail, this is not a difficult bushwhacking area, even in the forest. Just point yourself uphill and east from the car, and eventually you will pass over the long north-trending section of the trail up high. This will then lead you to the boulder field and behind The Ark.

Turn off US 16 onto the old highway about half a mile up canyon from the Mondo Beyondo parking area. The best possible hiking route starts on a fairly sharp curve about 400 yards down this dirt road. There is a pullout for three cars just before the curve, but if it is full, find another pullout, as blocking the road is not an option.

Follow a climber's trail up from the curve in the road, then turn directly up the hill (east) for about 200 feet to a solid cow

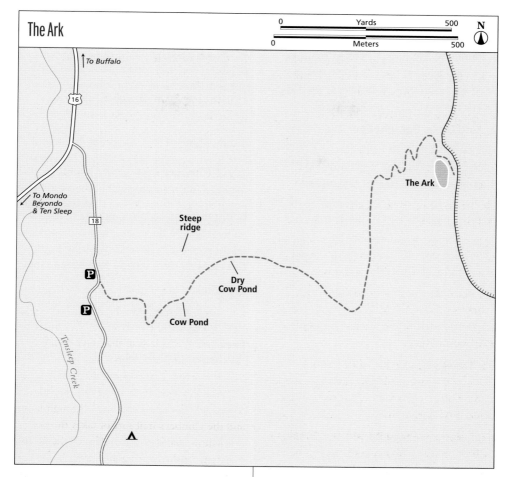

The Ark

0 Yards 500
0 Meters 500

N

To Buffalo

16

To Mondo
Beyondo
& Ten Sleep

18

P

P

Steep
ridge

Dry
Cow Pond

Cow Pond

The Ark

Tensleep Creek

trail that runs across the slope. Go right on the cow trail a short distance, maybe 50 yards, then turn uphill on a climber's trail that becomes a cow trail and leads you to Cow Pond. You will not be tempted to fill your water bottle here. Continue on up the slope to the right of the steep section of ridge. A few hundred more yards will bring you to Dry Cow Pond. It's filled with grass now. Go straight uphill on the back side of this, then trend right into the trees and then through a meadow beyond that first tree line. Eventually you'll pick up a more solid trail that runs north, up canyon,

gently gaining altitude. The trail turns to switchbacks that lead into a small boulder field. Traverse the boulders, going behind the walls. After about 100 yards of moving through the boulders along the walls, you'll reach the Radhakrishna Pillar and then The Ark.

Through all of this, keep in mind you are trying to go up the faint gully just down canyon of that steep section of ridge that you know you don't want to walk over. Also, there are cairns marking the way, but cows like to knock them down.

Radhakrishna Pillar

1. People of the Book★ (5.6) 45 feet. Just out of the topo on the low-angle side of the pillar is this six-bolt beginner line. **FA:** Mikey McGee.

2. Auto Erotic Decapitation★ (5.10b) 45 feet. A fun way to start the day. Five or six bolts. **FA:** Kristin Moore and Aaron Huey.

3. Women vs. the Eternal Masculine★★ (5.10c) 45 feet. Good fun and slightly steeper than its neighbor. **FA:** Aaron Huey.

The Ark Right Side

4. The Last Starfighter★★ (5.12a) 85 feet. Begin on the crack down in the cool dark slot and work your way out steeper ground, roofs, and then to the striking arête. **FA:** Aaron Huey.

5. July Jihad★★★ (5.12b) 85 feet. One of the best 5.12b's at Ten Sleep. Go up the crack and then slightly right and straight up the headwall. **FA:** Aaron Huey.

6. Unsubstantiated Propaganda★★ (5.12a) 85 feet. Follow the crack, then climb straight up through the bulge on interesting features and seriously steep terrain. **FA:** Aaron Huey.

7. Bazooka Face★★ (5.12a) 85 feet. Begin just left of the crack and climb steepening terrain, then through the roof and up the headwall to an anchor just left of Propaganda. **FA:** Aaron Huey.

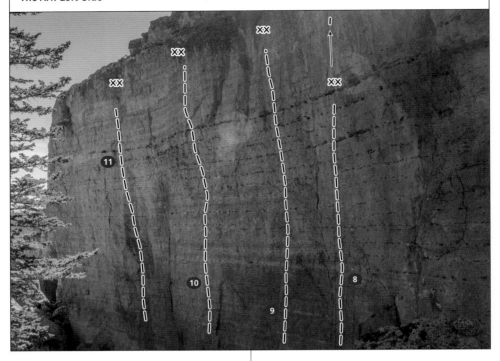

The Ark Left Side

8. Atheist Childhood/Born Again★★★
(5.11a/5.11c) 95 feet. Incredibly fun climbing. From a cool cave below a boulder, follow a crack and then move onto a steepening face. From the anchor 75 feet up, you can keep going for a real pumpy finish as Born Again. Takes about fifteen quickdraws for the full monte. **FA:** Aaron Huey.

9. Ocean of Terror★★ (5.12b) 85 feet. Just left of Atheist Childhood is a steep line of thin but positive holds. This evolves into good holds, but then steepens substantially. **FA:** Aaron Huey.

10. The Joy of Heresy★★★ (5.11d) 95 feet.
It is rare you get three good monos in a technical crux but still have a route that is all about the pump, and for that we give this the award as Best in State. Step across a deep chasm to technical terrain that quickly steepens and keeps on your arms all the way. Takes thirteen or fourteen quickdraws. **FA:** Aaron Huey.

11. Sh(Aar)ed★★★ (5.11c) 100 feet. A great climb however you say its name. Takes like a dozen quickdraws.

Leigh Creek

Leigh Creek takes its name from a cow-boy/hunter who rode his horse off one of our beloved cliffs in a blizzard. The crags of Leigh Creek Canyon can be seen to the right as you drive up the canyon from Ten Sleep. To reach them, drive 7.5 miles from the Ten Sleep Saloon and turn onto the old highway. It is marked as the access road to the Ten Sleep Fish Hatchery. Drive another 1.2 miles, passing the Leigh Creek Campground and then the fish hatchery, and pass through a gate that blocks the road in winter. This may be closed, in which case park on the side of the road and hike the next 200 yards. Assuming the gate is open, drive on for 200 yards to a hairpin turn. Just around it find a large pullout on the left; park there. Walk down to a large boulder that lies two-thirds of the way through the turn and find the trail on the rock's uphill side. The trail immediately forks, with the upper trail going to the Side Walk Buttress and the lower trail leading to a stream cross-ing and then the Psychoactive Walls and Godfather Boulder. Total hike time to either crag is about 10 minutes.

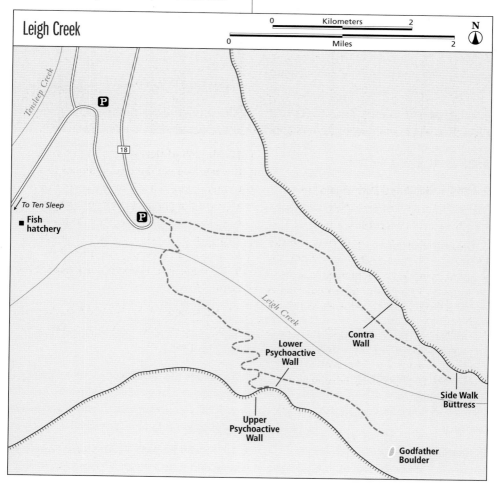

Leigh Creek

Kilometers

Miles

To Ten Sleep

Fish hatchery

Tensleep Creek

18

Leigh Creek

Contra Wall

Lower Psychoactive Wall

Upper Psychoactive Wall

Side Walk Buttress

Godfather Boulder

Lower Psychoactive Wall

The route topo for these blocks, which obviously detached from the upper wall eons ago, is obscured in the trees. The trees help to maintain shade most of the day, though the sun does poke through in the early morning hours of summer. The descriptions should help you sort it out.

1. Lil Smokie Does Super Mamma (5.11b) 25 feet. A very short boulder problem of a route on a large chockstone up and left of Short 5.6.

2. Short 5.6★ Left of Short 5.7 and out of the topo, this three-bolt route is a good first lead. **FA:** Mike Decker.

3. Short 5.7★ Another short route that makes a good introduction to leading sport climbs. **FA:** Mike Decker.

4. Tumbleweed★ (5.9) 50 feet. Climb over some large blocks and then over the left side of a small roof to an anchor in the gray rock. **FA:** Charlie Kardaleff.

5. Drama Queen (5.11a) 50 feet. A hard starting move to a thin slab. **FA:** Mike Decker and Alli Rainey.

6. Greenie Invasion★ (5.10c) 60 feet. Thin holds lead to good pockets. The start is in a shallow corner. **FA:** Charlie Kardaleff.

7. Star Fucker★★ (5.11a) 50 feet. A very high first bolt (stick clip) is the first of six on the left side of the arête. **FA:** Mike Decker and Alli Rainey.

8. Strangely Compelled★★ (5.12a) 50 feet. The very steep right side of the arête, inside the cleft, is powerful but fun. **FA:** Charlie Kardaleff.

9. Heathen (5.11a) 40 feet. Right of Compelled, this steep route is not pictured on the topo and not nearly as good as its neighbor. **FA:** Mike Decker.

10. Decades of Dung (5.12b) 50 feet. From the back of the cave, on the opposite sides as Heathen, this route climbs up and right to a shared anchor. **FA:** Matt Wendling.

11. Left Arête (5.12c) 50 feet. Very powerful. Thin crux and thin pockets lead to an anchor shared with Dung. **FA:** Matt Wendling.

12. Right Face★ (5.12a) 55 feet. This has a tram start (stick clip and pull yourself to the first bolt), or it might get more love. **FA:** Mike Decker.

13. Psych 535★ (5.11a) 35 feet. Climb up and left to an anchor below the gray rock. **FA:** Mike Decker.

Upper Psychoactive Wall

The upper wall is a great place on a hot day, as it sees very little sunshine after about 10 a.m. This is a wall for technicians and those who can recover from a pump while still on route. In other words, the cruxes tend to be high. Due to some unorthodox and socially distorted thinking, many of these bolts have been chopped and replaced, and you will note some extra studs and junk up high.

The next three routes begin in the chasm between the boulders and the main wall.

14. Baby Model (5.10c) This is the short and steep line down in the gully left of Under the Influence. Not a popular route. **FA:** Matt Wendling.

15. Under the Influence★ (5.12b) 95 feet. Big holds get you thinking it will be easy— wait till you get up high. Takes like a dozen quickdraws. **FA:** Matt Wendling.

16. Psychodrama★ (5.12d) 95 feet. Another long one. The bolts are well spaced enough

Psychoactive Walls

To Godfather Boulder

To parking

up high to perhaps get an R rating. **FA:** Matt Wendling.

17. Alien Semen Rash/Mirth★★ (5.10b/5.12b) 40/90 feet. Find the start of this route at the high point of the boulder ledge. The 40 feet of 5.10b to the first anchor gets the first name. Very popular and worth both stars. The second half, where it bumps up to 5.12b, is a bit like a Devils Tower corner if they were bolted. Not as much fun and a very hard crux. **FA:** Mike Decker.

18. Fangs (5.13d) 90 feet. The line just right of Rash/Mirth to a shared anchor. Thin.

19. Psychoactive (5.13b) 95 feet. Jugs take you up and just left of the small roof. Thin at the top. Most people do the next route by linking the start of Psychoactive with the finish of Shut the Fuck Up.

20. Link That Shit★★ (5.12c) 100 feet. Climb the first half of Psychoactive, then traverse right to the upper half of the wall's classic line. **FA:** Alli Rainy.

21. Shut the Fuck Up★★★ (5.13a) 100 feet. With this variety of holds, it is perhaps the best 5.13a sport climb in the state. Climbs the center of the face just left of Suck the Nipple to a high anchor shared with the extension of that route. **FA:** Alli Rainy.

22. Suck the Nipple★★★ (5.11c) 75 feet. Super cool endurance climbing with progressively smaller holds to the anchor. You can keep going to do a 5.13a, though most focus on the better route of that grade to the left (Shut the Fuck Up). **FA:** Alli Rainy.

23. Go Back to Colorado★★★ (5.12b) 80 feet. Pass a roof on its left side and climb a flake then a juggy face to a very hard finish. **FA:** Matt Wendling.

24. Gloom★★★ (5.11b) 75 feet. Farthest route on the right, this goes over a small roof.

Takes like a dozen quickdraws. Save something for the end. **FA:** Luke Decker.

Godfather Boulder

A couple hundred yards farther into the canyon is this steep boulder with some very cool climbs. This is actually an erratic boulder of Madison limestone, while the main climbing walls in the canyon are Bighorn dolomite. The climbing tends to be steep and juggy, and all routes take about half a dozen quickdraws. We did not include a topo, but you should be able to figure out the lines. The routes are listed from left to right.

25. Umpahlumpa Humpachu★★ (5.10a) 50 feet. On the far left end of the overhanging face is this juggy, fun line. **FA:** Charlie Kardaleff.

26. Godfather 1★★ (5.10c) 55 feet. Just right of Umpahlumpa is this slightly longer line of jugs. **FA:** Stan Price.

27. Godfather 2★★★ (5.11a) 60 feet. To get harder you have to throw a smaller hold or two in with the jugs. **FA:** Stan Price.

28. As Wicked as It Seems★★★ (5.12a) 60 feet. Very interesting climbing on the second route from the right. **FA:** Charlie Kardaleff.

29. The Ol' Roer 714 (5.10d) 55 feet. A distinct crux gives way to easy climbing on less than clean stone. **FA:** Charlie Kardaleff.

Contra Wall, Side Walk Wall, and Side Walk Buttress

This is the sunny side of the canyon and a pretty good place to go if it's late in the season and cold. The Buttress, inherently a bit crumbly (helmet?), has some of the longest sport climbs in the state. There is room for plenty more routes over here too.

Becca Roseberry sorting out Suck the Nipple (5.11c), Leigh Creek, Ten Sleep Canyon.

Contra Wall

This sector has excellent rock and goes into the sun around 11:30 in the morning.

1. Swisher Sweet★ (5.9) 100 feet. The easiest line on the wall, but you need a rack to do it. Mostly hand and finger pieces to a hand-drilled anchor. **FA:** Aaron Huey.

2. Indigenous★★ (5.11d) 45 feet. Fun moves on good pockets. Seven bolts and anchors. **FA:** Terry Twomey.

3. Alien Terra (open project)

4. Psuedo (open project) Very thin.

5. Endemic Biology★ (5.11b) 45 feet. Follow a seam to a good stance. Five bolts. **FA:** Terry Twomey.

Side Walk Wall

6. Side Walk Left★ (5.11d) 45 feet. Thin and technical to a bulge. **FA:** Eric Decker.

7. Side Walk Center★★★ (5.10c) 45 feet. Super cool moves on amazing stone. Harder than it looks and well worth the trip up despite its short length. Seven bolts, I think. **FA:** Eric Decker.

8. Side Walk Right★★ (5.12a) 55 feet. Another great route. Technical and pumpy. **FA:** Eric Decker.

9. Side Walk Tweek (5.12c) 35 feet. Bends your fingers over backwards. **FA:** Eric Decker.

10. Side Walk Crack★ (5.8) 35 feet. Follow the lieback crack right of the main wall. Four bolts. **FA:** Eric Decker.

Just out of the picture is another line that you might want to ignore. Ignore that anchor between Crack and Sharp as well.

11. Side Walk Sharp (5.11b) 40 feet. Icky. **FA:** Eric Decker.

Side Walk Buttress

Crumbly rock is often very fun to climb, and that is the case here. You will need to pool together quickdraws, as the two longest climbs have something on the order of twenty-four bolts.

12. Where the Sidewalk Ends★★★ (5.11a) 130 feet. Take everything you could possibly clip, and that includes a spare rope, as you cannot lower off this thing with a 70-meter cord. You need two ropes. Like twenty quickdraws. **FA:** Stan Price.

13. "If Dreams Were Thunder . . ."★★★ (5.12b) 90 feet. ". . . and lightning were desire." It looks short on the topo, but you need about fourteen quickdraws for this fun line. **FA:** Stan Price.

14. Sheep Reaction★★★ (5.12a) 125 feet. This sharply angled arête goes way high on the buttress. You need two ropes to get down. **FA:** Todd Anderson.

15. Sshhhhh Eeeep★★ (5.10b) 85 feet. Just around the arête from the other three lines is this fun ten. Lots of old bolts. **FA:** Stan Price.

SOUTH PINEY CREEK CANYON

■ **OVERVIEW**

The sun can be ferocious on the east slope of the Bighorns, but the shade granted by pine and spruce trees lining the South Piney Creek crag make for a pleasant climbing environment. Climbing from the cool canyon, with the babble of the stream dulling all sounds but perhaps those of a raven or hawk, it is hard to imagine the horrors that took place so recently here during the American conquest of the West.

Being amid the territory of the feared Blackfeet, Sioux, and Crow, the Bighorns were well north of the common immigration corridor across the United States. The Bighorn Basin and grassy plains to the east of the range were thus some of the last territory in the United States to be settled. Keep in mind that 1876, the year Custer was crushed at the Battle of the Little Bighorn, was the same year that New York and San Francisco had powered commuter trains, Thomas Edison was getting a patent on what was essentially the first office copy machine, and professional baseball was forming its National League. It just wasn't that long ago that the Wagon Box Fight was fought a mere quarter mile from South Piney Creek's cragging.

We cover South Piney Creek as much for what it will be, as for what it already is. There are some good moderate climbs here, and some excellent harder routes up at the Bermuda Triangle, but there is room for far more development. Someday South Piney may have over 200 routes, many of them well beyond the 5.13 grade. There are a few locals establishing new lines, and they have developed a curriculum for putting up new routes. Everything needs to be in stainless steel and of a size that works for sport climbing falls (⅜ inch or larger). You need to paint all the hardware to match the tan rock so non-climbers are less offended. Finally, you need to clean your routes and de-burr the pockets. If these rules are followed, South Piney Creek will be a great climbing area in the future.

The climbing is on that same Bighorn dolomite for which climbers have come to love Wyoming. Located just outside the tiny town of Story, the crags of South Piney Creek see both sun and shade on any given day. One nice trait of the area is that even though you may climb into the sunshine, the base of the wall is shaded by trees, making for a comfortable hang and belay. The area is new to climbers, but has been a popular hiking and party zone for years to the Story locals. Try not to block trails with rope bags, as you will likely see people walking the dog or just getting some exercise.

Trip Planning Information

General description: Mostly moderate sport climbs on Bighorn dolomite in a pretty canyon

Location: East slope of the Bighorn Range near Buffalo and Sheridan, Wyoming

Land manager: Tongue River District of the Bighorn National Forest. The parking and part of the trail are on private land.

Fees: None

Climbing seasons: Spring, summer, fall

Camping and hotels: There are no campgrounds in Story, and you cannot camp at the trailhead. Sheridan is the third-largest city in Wyoming, so it has all the chain hotels. The best campground in the area is Indian Campground in Buffalo. It has Wi-Fi, a pool, showers, and lots of trees for shade; you

Braden Herbst high above South Piney Creek on The Paintbrush Arête (5.10b), The Bermuda Triangle, South Piney Creek Canyon.

on your budget. If you want to stay in Story, the Story Pines Inn has rooms through the summer months. They can be reached at (307) 683-2120.

Food: All the food options are available in Sheridan, with the Cowboy Cafe being a great homestyle breakfast place and Java Moon being the modern coffeehouse. Frackelton's is the best restaurant in town, and the Blacktooth Brewery is one of the best breweries in the region. Dash Inn is a well-liked American-style cafe in Buffalo that is conveniently close to the Indian Campground. Winchester Steakhouse does exactly what the name implies very well. The food and entertainment (Thursday night bluegrass) at the Occidental is great.

Guidebooks and other resources: Trevor Bowman's *Rock Climbs of the Eastern Big Horns* thoroughly covers South Piney Creek. Some updated information can be found on Mountain Project as well.

Nearby shops and guide services: The Sports Lure in Buffalo caries some climbing gear and plenty of camping supplies. They can be found on the west side of Main Street near the post office and Clear Creek Brewery. There is also Back Country Bikes & Mountain Works on Main Street in Sheridan.

If you want a mountain guide, contact Micah Rush at (307) 267-4815 or wyoboulder @hotmail.com. Micah is a certified guide who works throughout the state.

can even rent cabins if the weather is really bad. Reservations are wise. The website is at Indiancampground.com, or you can call (307) 684-9601. Buffalo also has a host of chain hotels to choose from. The Occidental Hotel in Buffalo is an amazing combination of Old West and modern convenience, while the Bighorn Motel is comfortable and easier

South Piney Creek Canyon Area

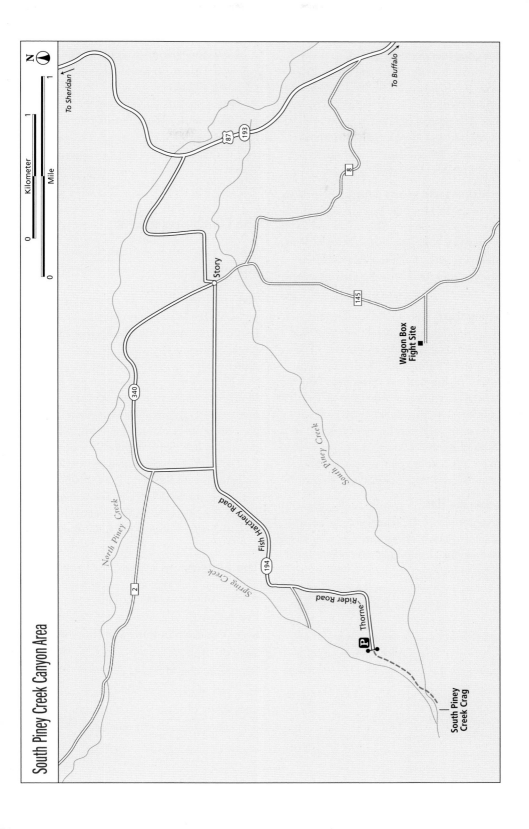

To Sheridan

To Buffalo

0 1 Kilometer

0 1 Mile

N

87 193

8

340

2

145

Story

North Piney Creek

Spring Creek

Fish Hatchery Road

194

Rider Road

Thorne

South Piney Creek

P

South Piney Creek Crag

Wagon Box Fight Site

Emergency services: As always, 911 gets you to the dispatch. Story and South Piney Creek are in Sheridan County. The Sheridan County sheriff can be reached at (307) 672-3455. The nearest emergency room is at the Johnson County Health Center in Buffalo. They are at 497 W. Lott St. and can be reached at (307) 684-5521.

Restrictions and access issues: The parking area and a fair bit of the trail are on private property. Please keep that in mind and be on your best behavior, as the owners are not required to give climbers access to the crag. Camping is prohibited at the parking area—do not camp there!

Getting there: The nearest commercial airport is in Sheridan, Wyoming. You will need a car to actually get to the crag. The crag is about 24 miles or 35 minutes from Buffalo, or 20 miles and 25 minutes from Sheridan. Driving here from Ten Sleep is just under 2 hours, while Devils Tower is 2.5 hours away. From Fremont Canyon it is 3 hours to South Piney Creek, and from Lander it is 5 hours. Jackson is a 7.5-hour, 350-mile drive from South Piney Creek.

Finding the cliffs: If you are coming from Buffalo or one of the other climbing areas in this book, follow I-25 as it merges with I-90. Continue for 11 miles and take exit 44 to US 87, going north for about 5.5 miles. After you enter a forested part of the plains, take a left onto Fish Hatchery Road. Fish Hatchery Road makes a hard left, then a hard right and another hard left as it winds its way through the hamlet of Story. After 2.6 miles of driving through the Story suburbs, Fish Hatchery Road banks to the right, but you take Thorne-Rider Road (well-maintained dirt), which continues straight. Follow Thorne-Rider for just over half a mile and park at the green gate with the No Parking and

Authorized Vehicles Only signs. Make sure you do not block the gate, and leave room for others to park.

From the parking area, walk through the gate for about half a mile, passing the Forest Service boundary. The first routes are just after the Forest Service sign on Cottonwood Wall behind an obvious cottonwood tree. Trailside Wall is about 100 yards past the sign.

The Climbing and Gear

For the most part, South Piney Creek is bolt protected, but there are some traditional leads to do as well. A rack of one set of nuts and cams, plus some larger cams, should get you up the cracks. For the sport climbs, the harder lines can take many quickdraws—one line needs eighteen. Obviously a 70- or 80-meter rope would be useful for lines that long.

The cliff faces south and thus gets lots of summer sun, but the shade offered by the trees make for a comfortable hang between goes. There are bears and mountain lions in the area, so don't let your pooch wander too far. The most common complaint here has more to do with flora than fauna; South Piney Creek Canyon has a lot of poison ivy, so be careful what plants you touch, and even watch where your rope lands when you pull it.

The Classics

Addled Ambitions (5.8)
Pug Addicts (5.9)
Super Dihedral (5.10b)
Take the Ride (5.11b)
Manicuring the Millennia (5.11b)
Prospects of Paid Time Off (5.11d)
Over Forty (5.12c)
The entire Bermuda Triangle Wall

Heard in the Wind

Wagon Box

After the routing of Fetterman in December 1866 (see sidebar in chapter 9, Ten Sleep Canyon), Red Cloud and his Sioux warriors must have felt giddy with success. Not only had they managed to inflict a sting to the arrogant US Cavalry, but the terror instilled in wagon trains and miners had also slowed the flow of immigrants to a trickle. Despite the confidence and brazen attacks of Red Cloud's men, however, the United States had not given up on Manifest Destiny. Instead, they dug in and allowed innovation to lend a helping hand.

The digging-in was done by fortifying the walls of the three forts along the Bozeman Trail. For Fort Phil Kearny, much of the wood for those walls would come from South Piney Creek. Civilians were hired by the military to do the cutting, with cavalry and scouts standing by in case of an attack. Innovation came from the Springfield Arms company late in 1866. In the previous Fetterman fight, the Indians had been primarily armed with bows and the cavalry with muskets. This sounds lopsided, but perhaps not how one would think. A musket could fire two to three shots a minute, while a talented warrior might get a dozen accurate shots with the bow. The new Springfield cartridge rifles accurately fired up to twenty rounds a minute.

In midsummer of 1867, Red Cloud gathered approximately 900 warriors in the Powder River Basin. Early on the morning of August 2, a group of lumberjacks and soldiers began cutting trees along Piney Creek. Knowing trouble could come at any moment, they arranged the wagons in a large oval on the open plain above the drainage. The wagons were essentially large wooden boxes on wheels. By arranging them in a semicircle, the army created a fortified area that men could lie in and fire from during an attack.

That attack came midmorning, when the Lakota warriors and their Cheyenne and Arapaho allies simultaneously began firing on the wagons and the woodcutters. Many of the cutters hid in the forest, while others made their way back to the wagons. All able-bodied men began firing at the attacking force through holes in the sides of the wagon boxes. Meanwhile, the Indians attacked in multiple surges both on foot and mounted. The battle went on for much of the day, with thirty-two soldiers and civilians holding off around 900 natives. In late afternoon the Lakota broke off the fight after a large contingent of cavalry attacked from Fort Phil Kearney with a wagon-mounted cannon. ®

Reported losses have varied according to who told the story. It seems likely that 100 or so Lakota and allies died, with only seven of the soldiers and civilians killed. Though lopsided in numbers, this battle only intensified the resolve of both sides. The US Cavalry went away thinking their new weapons and tactics could easily defeat the enemy, while Crazy Horse, Red Cloud's best tactician, understood the best way to fight this enemy was through a protracted guerilla campaign, not by directly attacking defensive positions. The next decisive battle would be 60 miles north and nine years later at the Little Bighorn, with the US Cavalry suffering a major defeat. But as Crazy Horse would later discover, you can win the battles and still lose the war.

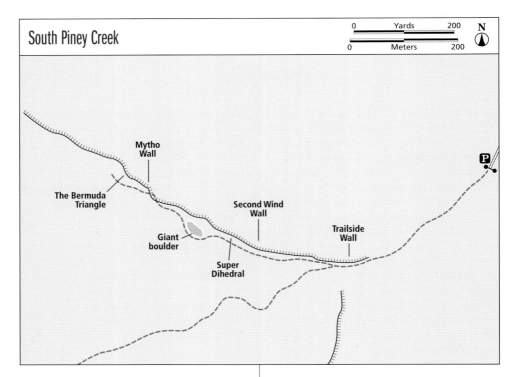

0   Yards   200   **N**

0   Meters   200

Mytho Wall

The Bermuda Triangle

Second Wind Wall

Trailside Wall

Giant boulder

Super Dihedral

P

Trailside Wall

The first few routes of the Trailside Wall are good for true beginners. They are right above the trail where South Piney Creek constricts in the canyon. Because a lot of people use the canyon for hiking and fishing, try to keep the base tidy so everyone can get by on the trail. Continuing on another 100 feet, you reach the main buttress of Trailside Wall.

1. AARP (5.4) 30 feet. Directly behind the tree, past three bolts to a shared anchor. **FA:** Rick Dare.

2. Fourth of July (5.3) 30 feet. Low-angle arête with three bolts to a shared anchor. **FA:** Rick Dare.

3. Cottonwood Corner (5.3) 30 feet. The obvious crack in a corner. A few small cams and nuts can be worked in, though the gear is not good.

4. Addled Ambitions★ (5.8) 45 feet. Six bolts of fun climbing to an anchor just over the roof. **FA:** Trevor Bowman.

5. Chemical Endeavors★ (5.10b) 45 feet. The middle of three lines up the face, over the roof, and up the slab to an anchor.

6. Pug Addicts★★ (5.9) 45 feet. Just right of the cave on the blunt arête using five bolts for pro. **FA:** Trevor Bowman.

7. Cave Crack (5.9) 45 feet. You can find routes that are more fun than this.

8. Gardener's Delight (5.9) The crack a few feet left of the cave. Protectable with micro-cams up to 1.5 and small nuts until the last 15 feet, which have no gear. The name says a lot.

9. Munge-kin★ (5.10a) 45 feet. A fun sport climb just left of the cave. **FA:** Trevor and Eddie Bowman.

10. Landscape Architect★ (5.9) 55 feet. Another fun sport route just left of Munge-kin. Look for a large section of light-colored, spalled rock just above the start. **FA:** Trevor Bowman.

11. Cleans Up Well★ (5.10d) 55 feet. A line of pockets and edges next to the obvious cottonwood tree. Very thin midway. Six bolts and shares an anchor with Facelift. **FA:** Trevor and Eddie Bowman.

12. Facelift★★ (5.10c) 55 feet. Just left of Cleans Up Well. Fun climb with a definite crux. **FA:** Trevor and Eddie Bowman.

13. Buy a Ticket★★ (5.11a) 55 feet. Gently overhanging face with flakes in lighter rock. Fun, techy climbing with six bolts for pro. **FA:** Trevor Bowman.

14. Take the Ride★★ (5.11b) 55 feet. Seven clips get you up this pumpy, fun route. Look for the start above a large bush. **FA:** Trevor Bowman.

15. Manicuring the Millennia★★ (5.11b) 55 feet. More sustained. Seven bolts to the anchor. **FA:** Trevor Bowman.

16. Wanderlust★ (5.10b) 55 feet. This and the next two routes share a start. Climb the dihedral to the slab trending right, then over the tricky bulge to an anchor. Seven bolts and the anchor. **FA:** Trevor Bowman.

Just out of the topo are two trad leads to bolted anchors.

17. Right Flake (5.9) 60 feet. Same start as Wanderlust to the right crack. Not recommended. There are two bolts and then it's an assortment of gear.

18. Left Flake★ (5.7) 60 feet. Better than its neighbor to the right, this is a decent trad line with a couple bolts and a general assortment of gear up to hand size. Shares a cold shut anchor with Right Flake.

The following two routes are on the wall just left of Left Flake.

19. Chosspectors Choice Nugs★★ (5.10b) 95 feet. A fun line on large holds 20 feet left of Left Flake. Ten bolts to the anchor. Take a dozen quickdraws, and watch the end of the rope when lowering. **FA:** Trevor Bowman.

20. Thundercling City★★ (5.12c) 45 feet. Just left of Chosspectors, this route has a powerful start. **FA:** Clay Stoner.

About 50 yards up the trail that runs along the base of the wall are the following three routes. They all have characteristics strong enough to not warrant a topo.

21. Tight Dihedral★ 55 feet. A steep dihedral with features on either side eventually widens to offwidth. A host of gear from finger to offwidth pieces. You can bypass the obvious shrub by climbing out left to Hands Off/Pants Off.

22. Hands Off/Pants Off★ (5.10a) 55 feet. This bolted line follows the wide, diagonalling crack just left of the dihedral. It's better than it looks. **FA:** Clay Stoner.

23. Prospects of Paid Time Off★★ (5.11d) 90 feet. To date, this is the only line up the obvious face just left of Hands Off. The start is about 8 feet left. Take fourteen quickdraws. **FA:** Clay Stoner.

Trailside Wall Left Side

Second Wind Wall

Another 100 yards up the trail is a promising cliff known as Second Wind Wall.

24. A bolt or two on the face right of Over Forty mark this project.

25. Over Forty★★★ (5.12c) 55 feet. A beautiful arête with a bouldery crux and pumpy finish. Shares a start with One for the Doctor. Eight bolts. **FA:** Trevor Bowman and Yale Preston.

26. One for the Doctor★★ (5.11d) 65 feet. Shares the first three bolts with Over Forty then goes left on the featured wall. Nine bolts. **FA:** Trevor Bowman.

27. Refrigerator Chimney (5.10a) 120 feet. Named for the blast of natural cold air that flows from its depths, this route is at the very back of the cleft of Second Wind Wall. Most people do two raps on a single rope to get down from anchors to the left (on Second Wind).

28. Second Wind★ (5.12a) 65 feet. On the bulging wall just left of the chimney, this technical climb is no giveaway for the grade. The second pitch is not popular. **FA:** Trevor Bowman.

29. Deer in the Headlights★★ (5.10d) 70 feet. Found by locating the large spall of rock leaving a white scar on an otherwise gray wall. Long pulls on good pockets in the bulge, then the slab. Take eight quickdraws. It has been extended another six bolts to a second anchor, but it's a rope stretcher if you do this second section. **FA:** Trevor Bowman.

30. When the Levee Breaks . . .★ (5.10c) 45 feet. ". . . there will be no place to stay." Just left of Deer in the Headlights, this route climbs the lower-angle rock to a low anchor. **FA:** Trevor Bowman.

Second Wind Wall

31. Vice Gripped★ (5.10d) 50 feet. This is the leaning, bolted dihedral left of Levee. Harder than it looks. **FA:** Trevor Bowman.

32. Shorty★ (5.9) 25 feet. Not the longest route in the book, but if you like the grade, it has some fun moves. It's just out of the topo about 10 feet left of Vice Gripped. **FA:** Trevor Bowman.

About 150 feet farther up the hill is a tall, yellow wall with a lot of potential. The obvious landmark is the dihedral capped by a large roof. These routes require a 70-meter rope and lots of quickdraws.

33. Super Streak★★ (5.12d) 130 feet. Eighteen bolts of steady endurance on thin holds. This is just right of Weekend Warrior. Thin. **FA:** Chris Hirsch.

34. Weekend Warrior★★ (5.12c) 110 feet. You will need over a dozen quickdraws for the face and arête just right of the dihedral. **FA:** Trevor Bowman.

35. Super Dihedral★★ (5.10b) 110 feet. A beautiful crack in a small corner, this is currently done on gear, though there are plans to equip it with fixed protection. A full assortment of gear, with lots of medium nuts and cams to 3.5 inches (#3 Friend) is advised. There has been loose rock from inside the crack, so it would be wise for the belayer to have a helmet. Also note the length—your 60-meter rope may not reach, so tie a knot in the end. **FA:** Trevor Bowman.

Braden Herbst shakes out for the final crux on Cyclops (5.12b), The Bermuda Triangle, South Piney Creek Canyon.

The Bermuda Triangle and Mytho Wall

Continuing up the trail perhaps 750 feet, passing a very large boulder that is detached from the main wall and at least a half-dozen unbolted lines that will make 5.15 climbers drool, brings you to the premier walls of the area. At the time of this writing, there were just a handful of routes completed, but many more are in the works. You may find stone plaques at the base of the wall that tell you of more than is listed here. The Mytho Wall, 150 feet of steep dolomite, had bolted projects but no completed routes when we went to print. The Bermuda Triangle, named for the first route bolted here, is juggy and steep. It stays in the shade until around 1 p.m. on summer days.

The Bermuda Triangle

XX
Unused
anchor

XX

XX

XX

XX

Some loose rock

XX

XX

38

37

41

40

39

36

36. Cyclops★★★ (5.12b) 80 feet. About a dozen quickdraws are needed. Save something for the end. **FA:** Braden Herbst and Terry Twomey.

37. Star Tiger★★★ (5.12d) 80 feet. Addiction in Sinks Canyon got our vote for best 5.12d in the state, but if we'd left that climb at the local grade (5.12c), Star Tiger would be the best 5.12d. Thirteen quickdraws. **FA:** Braden Herbst and Terry Twomey.

38. Sulfur Queen★★★ (5.12a) 70 feet. Incredibly fun jug pulling to a high crux.

Shares a start in a fracture with Star Tiger. **FA:** Braden Herbst and Terry Twomey.

39. The Bermuda Triangle★★★ (5.12c) 85 feet. Jugs the whole way as you pass just under the rim of the wall. **FA:** Braden Herbst and Terry Twomey.

40. Lost at Sea★★ (5.11a) 40 feet. Same as the others, but loses a star for being short. **FA:** Sam Lightner Jr., Terry Twomey, and Braden Herbst.

The Bermuda Triangle

(20/51 meters)

(31 meters)

Some loose rock

41

39   36

41. The Paintbrush Arête* (5.10b, 5.9 obl.) 2 pitches: 5.8, 5.10b, PG13, 170 feet. A two-pitch climb straight out of the Alps, this has incredible exposure. The foliage on this line is so beautiful, with blooming Indian paintbrush and mat rock spiraea, that we had to make it a climb. It is bolted like one of the big classics of the Italian Dolomites or Switzerland's Bernese Oberland; the cruxes are well protected, but it can be 15 feet from bolt to bolt on the easier ground. It's hard to spot some of the glue-in bolts. There are loose rocks in the large pockets along the lip of the overhang, so pick your holds wisely, and use the jugs that don't support flowers. The crux comes in the bulge above the first anchor. A 60-meter rope barely reaches from the first anchor. From the second anchor you have to do a 20-meter rap to reach the top of the slab. It can be climbed in one giant pitch with eighteen quickdraws and a 70-meter rope. Do not lower your partner. **FA:** Sam Lightner Jr., Braden Herbst, and Terry Twomey.

DEVILS TOWER

■ OVERVIEW

According to the Crow, who have made northeast Wyoming their home for the last 300-plus years, there is a legend that explains the size and wild appearance of Devils Tower. The Arapaho, Cheyenne, Lakota-Sioux, Kiowa, and Shoshone all have legends about the monolith, a few of them very similar to the Crow legend. While on a climbing trip to the tower, I was told the legend and will attempt to explain it as best I can in climber parlance:

A band of Crow were bivied between the Bears Lodge Mountains, the hills in the northeastern-most corner of Wyoming, and a large erratic rock on the prairie. While the men were hunting, a few young girls went to check out the boulder. With all the giggling and discussion of beta, the girls were noticed by the Great Bear, who thought, "Those little things look tender and delicious." The girls saw the bear charging them, but being strong climbers they managed to boulder to the top of the rock. Unfortunately, bears can climb too, and the big grizzly began trying to unlock the sequence that would give him a fine meal. The Great Spirit, who kind of had a thing for these girls, saw the giant bear working the moves at the base of the boulder. He threw some sort of elevator-hex on the rock, and it began to grow with the girls safely standing on top. The giant bear apparently lacked slab technique and thus clawed at the sides of the rock, scraping away cracks and giant chan-

nels of stone. The grizzly circled the rock trying to find a problem he could manage, but it had grown too big. What had been a boulder minutes before was now a great tower rising above the plains. The bear realized he had no chance to climb it without a belayer or a really, really big crash pad, so he bailed. The girls, however, were ropeless and stuck on the summit. They remain there in spirit today.

At least that's how I remember it.

Rising 1,267 feet from the Great Plains, Devils Tower is a complete geologic anomaly, so it only makes sense the locals would come up with interesting explanations for its existence. Its otherworldly appearance was strong enough for Stephen Spielberg to use it as an icon in *Close Encounters of the Third Kind*, and even modern geologists cannot completely agree on how it formed, though a few have expressed doubts about the giant bear. The modern name seems to have come from a misinterpretation of "Bad God's Tower" (the Great Bear being the bad god), thus the "Devils Tower" in western European parlance.

For us, the tower is a crack climber's and stem master's heaven. That giant bear scraped hundreds of cracks and corner systems out of the igneous rock. The first people known to stand on its 5,114-foot summit were local ranchers William Rogers and Willard Ripley in 1893. Lacking climbing skills, but with an abundance of construction knowledge and guts, they actually nailed wood pegs into a crack (near the Bon Homme route) and climbed the pegs like a ladder. Though ropeless, this was still an aid climb, so Fritz Wiessner, William House, and Lawrence Coveney upped the ante in the summer

The imposing West Face of Devils Tower between two July thunderstorms.

The Great Bear making great climbs on the east face of Devils Tower. PAINTING BY HERBERT A. COLLINS, PROVIDED BY DEVILS TOWER NATIONAL MONUMENT

of 1937 with a free ascent. Climbers today make about 4,000 ascents of Devils Tower a year, with the fastest known ascent being 18 minutes by Todd Skinner in 1983. Todd's Hollow Men, on the north face of the tower, has gone over thirty years without a repeat. Tell yourself "it's only 5.12c" when you place fourteen #2 RPs in a row.

As mentioned, geologists still argue a bit about how the tower came to exist. Most agree that the rock, a rare igneous formation known as phonolite porphyry, formed as an intrusion of magma between other solid surfaces. It appears this took place roughly 40 million years ago. Some believe it formed as a hard volcanic plug, flowing as magma into a semi-cylindrical tube of material that rose above the surface of the earth. That surrounding material then eroded away, and the solid plug was left behind as a tower, much like a giant Jello mold might do. Others claim it formed underground in a similar

mold, but was then pushed through the surface of the earth with the mold, thus allowing the material to erode away. In any event it is igneous rock, like granite and basalt, and was thus once at an extreme temperature of at least a few thousand degrees. When it cooled, the variations in temperature from outside to inside made for variations in contraction. This split the tower into the cracks and columns we stem our way up today.

Devils Tower, like most other geologic anomalies climbers want to explore, is considered sacred to a number of the local tribes, so there is a voluntary closure to climbing in June (see Restrictions and access issues). However, that leaves about seven other weather-friendly months of the year for climbers to do their thing. Enjoy yourself on Devils Tower, and keep your eyes out for the Great Bear when hiking up through the boulder field.

Trip Planning Information

General description: Long, traditionally protected cracks and stemming corners on one of the world's most iconic mountains

Location: Northeast Wyoming, near Gillette, off WY 24

Land manager: National Park Service

Fees: A fee for a seven-day pass is charged; check the monument's website at www.nps .gov/deto for current fee information

Climbing seasons: Spring, summer, fall

Camping and hotels: Without question, the best place to stay is the Devils Tower Lodge, which is owned by the wonderful character Frank Sanders. This place was at one time the home of the superintendent of the monument, and it has now become a Shangri-la for climbers. Frank has made climbing on Devils Tower the focus of his life, so lots of great stories and beta can be found here. Tent sites come with access to a bathroom and shower, and you can buy into a daily meal plan. Frank asks climbers to make a donation to the operation of the place for camping here. The Devils Tower Lodge also has rooms; find the lodge by going into the monument and taking a left turn onto a dirt road 2.2 miles after passing through the kiosk. Take your first right, and it will lead you to the place. Frank takes reservations over the phone at (307) 467-5267.

The Devils Tower KOA, just outside the park entrance, has shaded campsites, showers, and a heated pool. If the weather is particularly Wyoming-esque, there are one-room cabins as well. In the summer months they also have a small restaurant to give you a break from cooking. Devils Tower KOA can be reached at (307) 467-5395 or at devilstowerkoa.com.

The Belle Fourche Campground, operated by the Park Service has restrooms and water; it's first-come, first-served. The campground usually closes for the season in late October and reopens in April.

Food: Fortunately, the KOA also has a small general store where the basics can be purchased. For a real grocery store, you need to go to Hulett. Just down the road a spell is the Crook County Saloon, also with a limited menu. A couple other restaurants can be found in Hulett, but for the most part you should plan on cooking your own meals.

Guidebooks and other resources: There are a couple of guidebooks that do a pretty thorough job of covering Devils Tower, with Steve Gardiner and Dick Guilmette's *Devils Tower National Monument: A Climbers Guide* probably being the easiest to read. Some good route descriptions can be found on devils towerclimbing.com, as well as tips for having a good stay in the area. Of course, Mountain Project covers the tower fairly well too.

Nearby shops and guide services: Above All Climbing is the best local guiding outfit for the tower. You can reach them via devils towerclimbing.com or at (888) 314-5267. Exum Mountain Guides' Micah Rush has also guided at the tower for years. You can reach him at (307) 267-4815 or wyoboulder @hotmail.com.

Emergency services: The Park Service runs a search-and-rescue program on the tower. They use the local dispatcher, so the recommendation is to simply dial 911 for assistance and explain the situation. Cell phones work better the higher you are on the tower, and better on the north side than the south and west sides. If you need it, the number for the Crook County Sheriff's Department is (307) 283-1225.

Restrictions and access issues: Devils Tower is the focus of Devils Tower National Monument, the first national monument in the United States. As part of the National Park System, it falls under the same rules as the national parks, including no dogs and no use of power drills.

Climbers are required to register with the monument before an ascent. This is easily done at the obvious kiosk in the middle of the parking lot.

There can be seasonal closures of certain routes due to resting raptors, so if you come in the spring, be prepared to have to change your climbing objective.

Devils Tower is also the focus of certain religious festivals held by local and semi-local Indian tribes, most notably the Lakota-Sioux. In the 1990s a push to make climbing on the tower illegal was made by the Lakota, with a group of climbers arguing that such a ban was illegal on federal land under the separation of church and state. The Park Service, seeking to find some middle ground between the two groups, asked for a "voluntary closure" of the tower for the month of June. Most climbers adhere to this closure. I also endorse it if for no other reason than to keep all things copacetic with the powers that be. If you absolutely must climb on Devils Tower in June, you will get the evil eye, as you will be upsetting a few people who claim you are desecrating one of their churches. It is simply best to avoid the tower in June.

Getting there: Devils Tower National Monument is just off WY 24 in the very northeast corner of the state. That means it's pretty far from anything you have ever heard of. However, as you will see, if you can find WY 24, you can spot the tower. The nearest commercial airports are in Gillette, 65 miles to the west, and Rapid City, South Dakota, 110 miles southeast.

Finding the tower: Most approaches use I-90. Branch off I-90 at either Moorcroft or Sundance onto US 14. Eighteen miles from Sundance and 25 miles from Moorcroft, WY 24 goes north. Follow it for 9 miles to Devils Tower National Monument.

The Climbing and Gear

Devils Tower can be climbed in any month of the year, but winter is pretty dicey. Spring and fall are best, and summer works but you will be chasing shade. In the summer months you can expect afternoon thundershowers, and the tower is not a good place to be when lightning is striking. Be prepared to bug out. Snowstorms are common in spring and fall, and just as common is a warm day right after the snow where you have perfect temperatures. In the summer months most climbers go to the shady West Face in the morning and then leave for the South East Face about 1 p.m. when the sun begins to heat up the wall. The South East Face begins to go into the shade about 2 p.m.

Most of the climbing involves thin footwork, stemming, and crack technique. A good background in Yosemite will help, while an entire life of European sport climbing will only make for frustration. Calf exercises before a trip are more important than any number of one-finger chin-ups. For most parties a route up the tower is a Grade III, meaning it will eat up most of your day. We recommend a couple of headlamps, food, extra clothes, and water in the second's pack. The length of the pitches, and the size of the racks needed, make for hard ratings. If you look at the grade of the route and say, "Well, I climb 5.12; I'm not sure a 5.10 is even worth going," you may be sharply rebuked. Devils Tower can be humbling to anyone.

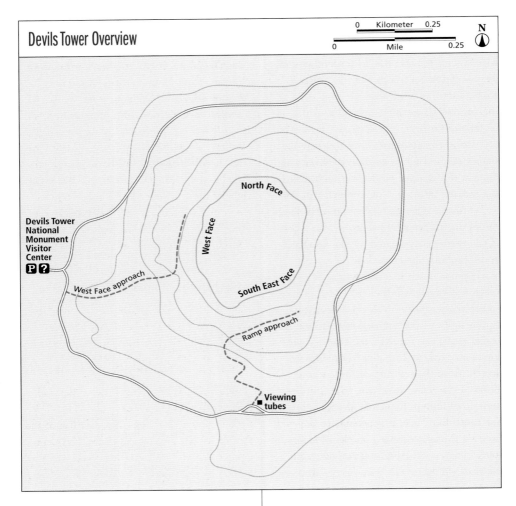

Devils Tower Overview

0   Kilometer   0.25

0   Mile   0.25

N

North Face

West Face

Devils Tower
National
Monument
Visitor
Center

P ?

West Face approach

South East Face

Ramp approach

Viewing
tubes

The standard Devils Tower rack begins with a full set of cams and a full set of nuts, plus the extra pieces associated with the particular size of crack you will be climbing. For most climbs you will want plenty of extra finger-size pieces, as even the hand and fist cracks tend to tighten down and take nuts well. You can expect to lug along a pretty large rack of gear for protection, plus quickdraws and slings to minimize drag.

Many of the anchors on Devils Tower are not bolted, so you will need to factor those extra pieces into the top after that 165-

foot pitch. A 60-meter rope is considered standard length for some of these very long pitches, and a 70-meter is optimum. And with that, remember that almost all of these routes are made up of very long pitches. You will carry a big rack and use lots of rope on each segment.

Finally, note that most of the corners on Devils Tower, and many of the arêtes, have been climbed; this book is only intended to give you the highlights. A comprehensive book of every single climb on Devils Tower has yet to be written. Because most of the routes were aid climbed long before they were free climbed, we often list the FFA, as in "first free ascent."

As always, treat all fixed protection with some suspicion. If it looks old and rusty, you might want to back it up with a piece of your own. An interesting point about the geology of Devils Tower illustrates how questionable fixed gear can be. The tower is like a giant wad of matchsticks all leaning together. As such it flexes and contracts a bit with temperature changes. Not so much that you would notice as a passing geologist, but if you are a climber who banged a whole line of pins into a crack on a cold day, you might find them all lying at the base of the crack when it warms up. In other words, don't put a lot of faith in fixed gear.

Descent

There are anchors that allow a double-rope descent from the summit on some of the West Face routes, like El Matador, but the most commonly followed descents are on the South East Face. It is possible to descend from the Meadows with a single 60-meter rope, but it is real tight, and rappelling off the ends will kill you. Again, that is from the Meadows, not from the summit. If you go to the summit and refuse to carry two ropes, you will need to either downclimb the Meadows Finish (5.4) or build your own anchor in one of the many cracks near the main rappel points. This is possible, but we recommend that if you go to the summit you take two ropes.

The Durrance rappels, aka the Bowling Alley rappels (read what you want into that name), require two 60-meter ropes and pass over and to climbers-right of The Durrance Route. The top anchor can be found about 130 feet climbers-left of where the Meadows Finish reaches the summit. The second of these rappels is very long, like nearly 60 meters, so pay close attention to your knots.

The Meadows Rappel can be found about 75 feet climbers-left of where the Meadows Finish reaches the summit, and it requires a slightly committing move to reach. If you have any question about your downclimbing abilities, belay that move. Below the Meadows Rappel you can walk down to the Bon Homme Rappels, which run climbers-right of the Bowling Alley. A single 60 can get you down through these stations, but it is very close, so tie knots in your ends and be careful. A couple of the stations are hanging.

Farther right, following El Cracko Diablo and Exit US, is another series of anchors that allow you to use a single 60-meter rope, but again, some downclimbing is required and rappelling off the ends will be fatal. Take two ropes if you are not sure of your downclimbing abilities.

For the West Face most people end up climbing only the first couple of pitches, and many of those anchors were replaced in 2015 by the Central Wyoming Climbers Alliance and the Black Hills Climbers Coalition. If you are going to the top, most people actually come down via the Meadows Rappel on the other side. Coming down the West Face from the summit is possible, and there are anchors, but the upper reaches of the wall have loose rock and a decent potential for snagging your rope.

The Classics

The Durrance Route (5.8)

Soler (5.9)

Walt Bailey Memorial (5.10a)

Tulgey Wood (5.10c)

McCarthy West Face (5.10c)

El Matador (5.10d)

Mr. Clean (5.11a)

Heard in the Wind

What's for Dinner?

Climbers like to talk about eating roadkill, but when you put a bottle in front of them and push for the real truth, usually the opossum turns out to be some sort of strangely marinated chicken from the grocery store bargain bin. However, there was one group of climbers who I believe were honest in their car-meets-culinary adventures.

One afternoon I was riding with Todd Skinner through Custer, South Dakota, as he prattled on about his greatest summer at Devils Tower. It seems he, Beth Wald, and Bill Hatcher had arrived at the tower in the summer of 1984 "with nothing but a teepee and $63 between us," Todd said through a smile. "We decided the best allocation of funds was to spend $60 on gas and $3 on a big bag of beans." It seems the group pitched the teepee on a nearby ranch and earned their keep by herding goats and sheep on their rest days. A few times a week, they drove the highway, late in the evening, to look for dead deer, noting each carcass on a map, then woke early and drove the same road again. "If there was a deer lying dead that hadn't been there the night before, we knew it was fresh and took it," Todd explained. "Yep, you just had to feel around in the shoulders to figure out which side got the bumper, and which the pavement. Pavement side was always less bruised." ®

Now Todd's tales could go into great detail, but my B.S. detector was starting to go off as he explained the dangers of getting past one of the larger billy goats with a mule deer over your shoulder. Todd didn't focus much on driving if Amy wasn't there to remind him about the road. He was animated, using both hands and staring me in the eye as the maroon Honda crept through downtown Custer. Suddenly there was a bump, and the Honda screeched to a stop. We both looked forward as a small doe stood up in front of the car. She shook off the hit and staggered into someone's yard, limping badly. Without taking the car out of gear, Todd grabbed a throwing knife from the tray between the seats and jumped out the door, yelling "Take the wheel" as he charged after the wounded beast. The car staggered a bit, then stalled when I yanked the emergency brake. Meanwhile, Todd jumped a hedge and gave chase as the wounded deer ran behind a garage. He came out a minute later, knife in hand and sans deer. "It was just stunned," he said, sadly shaking his head from side to side. I knew right then that the tales of cheap venison were not a farce; Todd Skinner really enjoyed roadkill.

South East Face

The South East Face sees most of the daily traffic on the tower, with The Durrance Route seeing most of that. This area has the easiest routes to the summit and also catches the first rays of the morning sun.

Reach these routes by following a climber's trail up from the Ladder Route viewing tubes. The Durrance Route (as it is climbed now) begins in the obvious bowl of the Bowling Alley. The other routes are found by following 3rd-class terrain, sometimes very exposed, up and right from the bowl. There are a number of routes reaching the summit from the Meadows, but most aren't very good, and all of them, save one, have a lot of loose rock. Most parties finish via the Meadows Finish, a 5.4 chimney and corner system on the far right end of the Meadows. We recommend that, and thus all routes listed after The Durrance Route should have that finish added if you intend to summit.

1. The Durrance Route★★★ (5.8, 5.7 obl.) 8 pitches: 5.6, 5.6, 5.8, 5.8, 5.6, Jump, 3rd class, 5.2. This is one of America's classics, with variations in climbing techniques, lots of exposure, and plenty of history. Take a standard rack plus a few wider pieces up to a #5. If you really fear wide cracks, take two. With longer ropes and slings, a few of the pitches can be combined to shorten the day. Most parties take 5 to 6 hours. As alluded to above, the first ascensionists originally came up to the left of the Bowling Alley on some very exposed and often loose terrain, while the modern variation of the line avoids that area with extra walking.

South East Face

Pitch 1 climbs a corner from the bottom of the bowl in the Bowling Alley to a set of anchors, then traverses 50 feet left to an obvious tree on easy climbing. Pitch 2 ascends the left side of the leaning column at 5.6 to a fixed anchor. Pitch 3 goes up a stem box to another ledge and anchor. Pitch 4 goes up a short chimney using wide crack technique (back cleaning can help with rope drag) and traverses right, then passes a belay ledge (and old anchor) to another ledge. Pitch 5, the chockstone pitch, is short and traverses around the chockstone to a ledge and anchor. Pitch 6 is the "Jump" pitch . . . hard to rate—it's a jump. Can be climbed at 5.8. The leader makes the leap; the follower can be protected with a micro-cam. Pitch 7, which hardly needs a belay, traverses across the Meadows on the obvious trail. Pitch 8 climbs the broken chimneys and ledges at 5.2 or so. Find the rappel station about 75 feet left of the finish pitch. Reaching it requires an exposed 4th-class move. **FFA:** Jack Durrance and Harrison Butterworth, 1938.

2. Bon Homme Variation★★ (5.8, 5.7 obl.) 2 pitches: 5.8, 5.7. Approximately 150 up and right from the Bowling Alley, you can work up to this fun corner system. Find it by looking for a corner three columns right of the obvious big roof and three columns left of the Ladder Route. About 50 feet up, below a couple of small roofs, traverse out of the wide crack and into a more pleasant size. This is the crux and protects fairly well with small gear. The second crack then becomes a double crack with very interesting climbing. The first pitch is long but ends with a ledge (bolts). The second pitch is not quite as long and is mostly a 5.7 hand crack. **FFA:** Dennis Horning and Howard Hauck.

3. Ladder Route Because of the historical significance of the wood ladder that can still be seen in portions of the climb, this crack is closed to climbing. It was the original ascent route, actually climbed by hammering logs into the crack to make ladder rungs. The two ranchers hung from their belts when they needed both hands. Bold! Can you imagine starting back down the "ladder" after getting to the summit? **FA:** William Rogers and Willard Ripley, 1893.

4. Walt Bailey Memorial★★★ (5.10a, 5.7 obl.) 2 pitches: 5.4, 5.10a. Take a standard rack plus many extra finger to thin hands pieces. It is tradition, it would seem, to rate this climb 5.9. I'm breaking tradition and calling it 5.10a . . . kind of a stiff 10a at that. The route was first ascended on aid by the Casper College Mountaineering Club in 1959. They had recently lost a member, Walt Bailey, in an accident in Alaska.

Traversing along the ramp you eventually reach a few wind-hardened pine trees. Look up and you can see the very long (170-foot) pitch of Walt Bailey. Find a level spot to rack up, and then climb exposed 4th-class terrain to a ledge. Staying slightly right of the upper crack, in a couple of broken dihedrals, is easiest. From the obvious large ledge, where an anchor can be built, ascend the long crack. Despite being slightly under vertical, the route is quite sustained. There are two bolts at the end, but they are in a bad place for an anchor. Best to build your own with finger-size gear or by throwing a cordelette over a block. You can continue up on 3rd-class terrain, then to the Meadows Finish trail. **FFA:** Jeff Overton and Scott Woodruff.

Mike Lilygren and Becca Skinner on the second pitch of Soler (5.9), Devils Tower.

Soler Staging Area

Continue past a couple more tough trees on the exposed ledges of the ramp to reach a shaded ledge that is the Soler Staging Area.

5. Hollywood and Vine (5.10c, 5.10a obl.) 2 pitches: 5.6, 5.10c. The standard rack to hand size, plus plenty of small nuts and tiny cams, will protect this climb. For years, if you wanted to climb Devils Tower, the Park Service made you prove yourself first by aid climbing this line. That was in the piton years, so it became a line of pin scars. Scott Woodruff and Jeff Overton freed the route in 1974. From the Soler Staging Area, climb up and left into a bush-choked corner (5.6) to a comfy ledge. Build an anchor and then ascend the second pitch at 5.10c, using plenty of small nuts. When balancing on the tiny foot- and handholds, try to imagine being Henry Barber and soloing the route without sticky rubber. **FFA:** Scott Woodruff and Jeff Overton.

Hollywood and Vine

6. Soler Eclipse★★ (5.11c. 5.11b obl.) 2 pitches: 5.11c, 5.10d. Eleven quickdraws plus a small rack of Friends if you continue to the top. This is the closest thing to a sport climb that ascends Devils Tower. If you hate crack climbing, you can do this, plus some 4th class to the Meadows Finish, and reach the summit. Pitch 1 is interesting climbing on the arête through the obvious roof to a small stance. Tricky, reachy, and about 150 feet long. Pitch 2 has fewer bolts but is a little easier. From the bolted anchor atop pitch 2, you can get to the Meadows and on up the Meadows Finish with a single set of Friends and some slings. **FFA:** Eric Fazio Ricard, Dennis Horning, and Brent Kertzman.

7. Soler★★★ (5.9, 5.7 obl.) 2 pitches: 5.9, 5.8. Take a standard rack plus a few extra hand and finger pieces. This is the obvious 90-degree dihedral rising above the staging area. It gets lots of sun in the morning and lots of shade in the afternoon, so you can tick it in most months of the year if you time the ascent right. The sustained first pitch becomes a double crack after about 50 feet, giving you multiple climbing and protecting options. Find two aging bolts (easily backed up with a small cam) about 130 feet up for the hanging belay. The second belay is on any one of a number of comfy ledges another 110 feet higher. Third classing leads to the Meadows Finish. **FA:** Tony Soler, Herb Conn, Art Lembeck, Ray Moore, and Chris Scordus. **FFA:** Layton Kor and Raymond Jaquot.

8. Tad (5.8, 5.7 obl.) 2 pitches: 5.8, 5.7. The standard rack plus some extra nuts for the belay and some larger pieces for pitch 2. Very few people would call this their favorite. Hand jams aplenty on the first pitch, but it widens out, has some loose rock, and is generally not enjoyable on the second pitch. **FFA:** Dan Burgette and Charles Bare.

9. El Cracko Diablo★★ (5.8, 5.7 obl.) 2 pitches: 5.8, 5.8. A standard rack plus some extra big hands to larger Friends. If you don't like offwidth, drag a #5 along. This is the third crack over from Soler. Yeah, I said bring offwidth gear, but it's well featured and actually pretty fun with plenty of hand jams and face holds. You can rappel the route to get back down on the bolted anchors. **FFA:** Rod Johnson and Pat Padden.

Ramp
traverse

Soler Staging
Area

5

5   6

7

8   9

Curtis Allred leading Juliusz Brewczyk up the second pitch of McCarthy West Face (5.10c), Devils Tower.

West Face

You gaze up at the West Face from the main parking area. This is the face that gets the most action by the hard men, and the one that gets the most action from tourist cameras. You won't be alone on the wall as there could be thousands watching at any one time. Go potty before you launch upward, and remember your voice carries in the right conditions.

From the split in the paved trail just above the parking area, take the right fork. After about 50 yards of winding through the talus, you reach a grove of trees. Start up and eventually wander through the most stable bits of talus (there are many routes) to a couple of signs that dissuade non-climbers from going farther. The easiest line takes you to a landing at the highest trees just below El Matador. To reach the base of Mr. Clean and Tulgey Wood, go up a little and to the left, then descend the 3rd class 40 feet or so to the left and traverse to another tree beneath that section of the face. It is exposed, but not too difficult.

If you like beginning your pitches from a comfortable stance, a 60-meter rope is a must and a 70-meter is useful. The higher you go, the steeper the tower gets until you are in 5th-class terrain. The original ascents were done with a 3rd-class approach pitch to the point where each corner system really steepens, but the longer lines allow you to start down in the highest trees.

Keep in mind that all the descents on the West Face require two 60-meter ropes.

1. Mr. Clean★★★ (5.11a, 5.10b obl.) 4 pitches: 5.7, 5.11a, 5.10a, 5.9, 400 feet. Gunning for best 5.11a in the state, and certainly the best finger crack, this is a Devils Tower classic. Find it about 20 feet left of the first pitch of Tulgey Wood as a short pitch of 5.7 that ends at a stance just below the yellow-lichen-covered roof. For pitch 2, pass the roof with a thin, powerful move, then plug and go for 160 feet. The pitch is fingers to thin hands, so a huge rack of midsize nuts and 0.75-inch to 2-inch cams is called for, with a couple of hand-size pieces up high. It ends with a hanging belay on a bolted anchor. Pitch 3 widens to hands and then fists (with that size gear) for 160 feet. Pitch 4, rarely done, ascends the broken ground up high via a 5.9 chimney to the summit. **FFA:** Henry Barber and Chip Lee.

2. Dead Point (5.11b) 90 feet. A thin, then flared crack between Tulgey Wood and Mr. Clean, this is not a classic and is rarely ascended. Take lots of thin cams and nuts. **FFA:** Jay Smith and Jo Bentley.

3. A Bridge Too Far★★ (5.11d) 120 feet. A unique climb that works your deltoids as much as your quadriceps. Climbs the open corner just left of Tulgey Wood on mostly small cams and nuts. There is one bolt about a third of the way up the pitch. This route shares an anchor with the first pitch

of Tulgey Wood. **FA:** Todd Skinner, Mark Sonnenfeld, and Steve Hong.

4. Tulgey Wood★★★ (5.10c, 5.10a obl.) 5 pitches: 5.10b, 5.10c, 5.10a, 5.8, 5.4, 400 feet. This route is identifiable by the fact that it climbs the crack on the right side of a column that is broken into numerous angles. Pitch 1 is 120 feet long and begins with hands, then pinches down to fingers and stemming with a very thin crux. Belay from the ledge atop A Bridge Too Far so you can correctly protect pitch 2. This is also thin and with a lot of rope stretch— like from the ground with a 70-meter rope, you might hit the ledge—so belay at the first anchor. After 45 feet you are on a nice ledge that shares an anchor with Mystery Express and Way Layed. The 130-foot pitch 3 looms above as a gaping fist crack. Use many (at least ten) 3- to 4-inch cams for this, though there are spots where hand-size gear can be placed deeper in the crack. Belay on a ledge at the start of the broken, loose headwall. This can be ascended by two short chimney pitches, the first trending right onto the spacious West Ledge and the second being only 5.4 to the summit. Most people forgo the last two pitches, which were originally part of McCarthy West Face, to avoid the less than perfect rock. **FFA:** Mark Heese and Dan McClure.

5. Mystery Express★ (5.13a) 165 feet. A sport route that takes a bit of gear to reach the first of sixteen bolts. Thin, balancy, crimpy. Best accessed from the base of Tulgey Wood. **FA:** Andy Petefish.

6. Way Layed★★ (5.11a) 165 feet. This ascends the brown corner that is the right side of the Tulgey Wood column, or one crack left of McCarthy West Face. It gobbles

West Face

up thin to midsize nuts, but the varied nature of the crack makes small cams less useful. Take lots of nuts. Rappel from the Tulgey pitch 2 anchors. **FFA:** Eric Richard and Mark Smedley.

7. McCarthy West Face★★★ (5.10c, 5.10a obl.) 5 pitches: 5.10a, 5.10c, 5.8, 5.8, 5.4, 400 feet. A brilliant free climb identified by a large brown roof on the right and then a smaller brown roof on the left side of the first pitch. The crack goes around a third, larger brown roof on the second pitch. For pitch 1, start at the tree below El Matador and work up and left with face holds and the finger-size crack in the corner. Above the second roof, find a thin ledge with a good anchor. Pitch 2 ascends the finger crack going up from the left side of the ledge. This goes up to the roof and then passes it on the right with a committing move. Fingers, then thin hands, then hands, then wide hands to the top of the column between this line and El Matador. It is 150-plus feet long, so you need a lot of hand and thin hands pieces for this pitch. A single fist-size cam and perhaps a #4 will help up high, and there is a bolt (quickdraw) to keep the rope out of the cams at the lip of the roof. Pitch 3 goes up the left crack from the anchor, moving left onto the West Ledge. From here, pitch 4 climbs the right-most wide crack, using offwidth-size pieces and slinging chockstones where possible. The short, final chimney pitch goes at 5.4 from here. **FA:** Chris Ballinger, Dennis Horning, and Steve Gardiner freed the line originally aided by Jim McCarthy and James Rupley in 1955.

8. McCarthy West Face Hong Variation★★ (5.11c, 5.10b obl.) 2 pitches: 5.11b, 5.11c, 250 feet. For pitch 1, climb the thinner crack on the right side of the McCarthy column. This requires tiny nuts and small cams. It ends at the same ledge as the regular route. Three cracks go up from this ledge: The left crack is the regular free route, the middle crack is still an aid line, and the right line is the Hong Variation at 5.11c. This is thin hands and fingers for 90 feet to the ledge atop the business pitch of El Matador. Take plenty of finger- and thin hands-size gear. Rappel from El Matador's anchor. **FA:** Steve Hong and Karen Budding.

9. El Matador★★★ (5.10d, 5.9 obl.) 5 pitches: 5.8, 5.10d, 5.8, 5.10a, 5.4, 400 feet. A world classic and perhaps one of a kind. If you train your calves and feet like you do your hands, the 50-plus moves of 5.9 feels like 5.10d. If you train by sport climbing, you will think that grade is off by a lot. Pitch 1 goes straight up from the shade tree on easy ground, then steepens to a few moves of thin 5.8 in the last 15 feet before the "box." The ledge is comfortable. Pitch 2 is the monster you have seen pictures of all your life. Take as many midsize pieces of gear as you can carry; this pitch gobbles up finger- to thin hands-size gear. The unstable nature of the wide, pumpy stemming might make you place more than you think you need. After 130 feet, crawl onto the spacious ledge and clip into the anchor shared with the Hong Variation. Pitch 3 climbs the hand crack from the right side of the ledge and then shares an anchor on a ledge where pitch 2 of McCarthy West comes in. From here, pitch 4 climbs up and passes the gray roofs on the right with a 5.10a move. The crack widens, then take the finger crack. A full mix of gear for 160 feet; bring plenty of slings. There is plenty of loose rock up here, and lots of people below, so be careful. The final chimney pitch at 5.4 is shared by McCarthy West Face and Tulgey Wood. **FA:** Fred Becky and Eric Bjornstad aided the line in the late 1960s, but it was Bob Yoho and Chick Holtcamp who freed it in 1978.

10. Digital Extraction★★ (5.11d, 5.11c obl.) 4 pitches: 5.11d, 5.11d, 5.10b 5.8, 400 feet. This climb ascends the clean crack system just right of El Matador on very small cams and wired nuts. Pitch 1 is balancy and technical and has one old, ugly bolt to back up your tiny brass nuts. Belay 110 feet up at a bolt and pin (back it up). Pitch 2 gets wide enough to get fingers (most of them) into the crack. Take plenty of tiny gear and finger stuff for the second pitch. The anchor is again a pin and a bolt. The upper two pitches require much larger gear, lots of slings, and travel over plenty of loose rock that could kill those below. We thus recommend you rappel after the first 250 feet and summit some other way.

BIBLIOGRAPHY

Bouldering in the Wind River Range, David Lloyd and Ben Sears, 2013

Climbers Guide to Fremont Canyon and Dome Rock, Micah Rush, 2013

Climbers Guide to Sweetwater Rocks, Greg Collins, 1997

Cracks Unlimited: A Climbing Guide to Vedauwoo, Layne Kopischka, 1987

Devils Tower Climbing, Zach Orenczak and Rachael Lynn, Extreme Angles Publishing, 2006

Devils Tower National Monument: A Climbers Guide, Steve Gardiner and Dick Guilmette, The Mountaineers, 1986

Fremont Canyon and Dome Rock, Steve Petro, Chockstone Press, 1997

Guide to the Wyoming Mountains and Wilderness Areas, 3rd ed., Orrin H. and Lorraine G. Bonney, Sage Books, 1960

History of Wyoming, 2nd ed., T. A. Larson, University of Nebraska Press, 1978

The Island Pamphlet, Mike Snyder, Sunlight Sports, 2014

Lander Rock: Rock Climbs of Central Wyoming, Greg Collins and Vance White, 2003

Lander Sport Climbs, Steve Bechtel, First Ascent Press, 2011

Lies and Propaganda from Ten Sleep Canyon, Aaron Huey, Extreme Angles Publishing, 2011

Rising from the Plains, John McPhee, Farrar-Straus-Giroux, 1986

Roads Through Time: A Roadside History of Jackson Hole, Sam Lightner Jr., Exotic Rock Publishing, 2009

Rock Climbing Jackson Hole and Pinedale, Wyoming: The Authoritative Day Climbing-Guide, Wesley Gooch, Climbing Wyoming, 2011

Rock Climbs of the Eastern Big Horns, Trevor Bowman, 2009

South Pass City and the Sweetwater Mines, Jon Lane and Susan Layman, Arcadia Publishing, 2012

The Voo: Rock Climbing in Vedauwoo, Zach Orenczak and Rachael Lynn, Extreme Angles Publishing, 2011

More than relying on any book, I called on my friends and peers for the information they had about each of these areas. On the route descriptions and ratings, I often took into account the views expressed on Mountain Project. I also called on WyoHistory.org for the particulars in some of the Heard in the Wind sections.

ROUTE NAME INDEX

RATED ROUTE INDEX

ABOUT THE AUTHOR

Sam Lightner Jr. grew up in Jackson, Wyoming, cutting his teeth on the gneiss faces of the Tetons. He attended the University of Wyoming, but spent most of his time in the wide cracks of Vedauwoo. Sam has since chased climbing all over the world, including living in

Thailand for sport climbing, Banff for ice, and Moab for the cracks and towers. Sam's passion for climbing has led him to Borneo, Patagonia, the Alps, and Alaska. He is the author of eight books and dozens of articles focusing on climbing, its history, or both. Sam has served on the board of directors of the Access Fund, was president of the Friends of Indian Creek, and currently serves on the board of the Central Wyoming Climbers Alliance and is the Access Fund's Wyoming Regional Representative. He lives in Lander, Wyoming, with his wife, Liz, and their three dogs, Moki, Zoe, and Lexi.

PHOTO BY SHEP VAIL

PROTECTING CLIMBING **ACCESS** SINCE 1991

Jonathan Siegrist, Third Millenium (14a), the Monastery, CO. Photo by: Keith Ladzinski